My Body Was Left on the Street

Innovations and Controversies: Interrogating Educational Change

The titles published in this series are listed at *brill.com/icie*

My Body Was Left on the Street

Music Education and Displacement

Edited by

Kính T. Vũ and André de Quadros

BRILL

SENSE

LEIDEN | BOSTON

Cover illustration: Image by Anissa Martínez Lozano (2020)

All chapters in this book have undergone peer review.

Library of Congress Cataloging-in-Publication Data

Names: Vũ, Kính T., editor. | De Quadros, André, editor.
Title: My body was left on the street : music education and displacement /
    edited by Kính T. Vũ and André de Quadros.
Description: Leiden ; Boston : Brill | Sense, 2020. | Series: Innovations
    and controversies: interrogating educational change, 25429302 ; volume
    10 | Includes bibliographical references and index.
Identifiers: LCCN 2020012746 (print) | LCCN 2020012747 (ebook) | ISBN
    9789004430457 (Paperback) | ISBN 9789004415898 (Hardback) | ISBN
    9789004430464 (eBook)
Subjects: LCSH: Music--Social aspects. | Music--Instruction and
    study--Social aspects. | Displacement (Psychology) | Internally
    displaced persons. | Refugees.
Classification: LCC ML3916 .M999 2020 (print) | LCC ML3916 (ebook) | DDC
    780.86/914--dc23
LC record available at https://lccn.loc.gov/2020012746
LC ebook record available at https://lccn.loc.gov/2020012747

Typeface for the Latin, Greek, and Cyrillic scripts: "Brill". See and download: brill.com/brill-typeface.

ISSN 2542-9302
ISBN 978-90-04-43045-7 (paperback)
ISBN 978-90-04-41589-8 (hardback)
ISBN 978-90-04-43046-4 (e-book)

Contents

PART 1
The Setting

PART 2
Process/Pedagogy

PART 3
Belonging

Foreword: Slippers and a Broken Guitar [in English and in Persian]

On a hot day on Manus Island, Australian guards entered the refugee prison-camp and snatched a young man's broken guitar from his hands. As they left with triumphant looks on their faces, the young man followed them as far as he could inside the prison, beseeching them to return his guitar to him. He was repeatedly told in no uncertain terms that he should forget about it. When asked why, they said that it was forbidden to keep musical instruments in prison, as he might hang himself with the strings of the guitar. This surreal scene depicts the life of a musician in a far-away prison on a distant island, a man whose only possessions were a pair of slippers and a broken guitar.

The system that administers the camp and is the source of all the psychological and physical violence prevailing in it, reveals its terrifying face when confronted with music and musical instruments, the most beautiful things in the world.

Music and art are defined and condemned as instruments of violence: music, which by nature is liberating and life-giving, is represented as something that can destroy life. Looked at from another angle, this scene shows how today's international order justifies violence and ignores all that has to do with life and freedom, silencing within the confines of an ostensibly rational order all those who dare protest. In this prison, a young refugee uses music to redefine himself as a human being vis-à-vis a system that denies him his individuality and tries to control him.

In later years, when the situation evolved in the island camp, music created a space in which prisoners could survive under violent and inhuman conditions. When the Papua New Guinea Supreme Court declared that it was illegal to confine refugees to the camp, the doors between the four prisons within the camp were opened, and instrumentalists and singers were allowed to form an ensemble. This was a major improvement for the young musicians, who could now sing and play music together. On that isolated island this was an amazing change, as from then on these musicians would every now and then stroll through the camp like street musicians, playing for the other refugees.

In an environment such as the refugee camp, music not only allows the internees to have a life and an identity, it also allows them to remain connected to their past and their homeland. Their imagination and creativity acquire meaning, and this is the most fortunate gift for refugees who feel that they are lost in time.

I am very happy that this book brings together different perspectives on the lives of displaced musicians.

Acknowledgement

The Persian to English translation of Behrouz Boochani's foreword is provided by Houchang Chehabi, a professor of international relations and history in the Frederick S. Pardee School of Global Studies at Boston University.

Behrouz Boochani

پیشگفتار

بهروز بوچانی

در یکی از روزهای گرم جزیره مانوس چندین نفر از نیروهای گارد استرالیایی وارد زندان کمپ پناهندگان شدند و گیتاری را که دسته‌اش شکسته بود از دست موزیسنی جوان قاپیدند و در حالتی پیروزمندانه از کمپ خارج شدند. جوان تمام طول مسیر صد متری داخل زندان را به دنبال آن ها بود و التماس می‌کرد که گیتارش را به او برگردانند، اما هر بار یکی از افسرها با قاطعیت به او می‌گفت که باید گیتارش را فراموش کند، و در پاسخ این سوال که چرا گیتارش را از او گرفته اند این جواب را به او می دادند که «داشتن ساز موسیقی در زندان ممنوع است چون ممکن است که با سیم هایش خودت را حلق آویز کید». این تصویری بسیار سوررئال است از وضعیت زندانی دور افتاده در جزیره‌ای دورافتاده و زندگی نوازنده‌ای جوان که تمام دارایی‌اش یک جفت دمپایی و یک گیتار بود.

در این صحنه تصویری وحشتناک است. سیستمی که کمپ را اداره می‌کند و منبع تمام خشونت های روحی و فیزیکی است، در برابر موسیقی و ابزار موسیقی که زیباترین است خودش را تعریف می‌کند. در واقع در اینجا موسیقی و هنر به عنوان یک ابزار خشونت معرفی می‌شود و محکوم می‌شود. در این تصور موسیقی، که یک عنصر رهایی بخش و زندگی بخش است، به عنوان ابزاری معرفی می‌شود که می‌تواند زندگی را نابود کند. از زاویه ای دیگر این تصویریست وحشتناک از نظام های سیاسی حاکم امروز در دنیا که چگونه خشونت را توجیه می‌کند و هر آنچه را که به زندگی و آزادی مربوط می شود نادیده می‌گیرند، و کسانی را که به آن اعتراض می کنند چگونه در یک نظام ظاهرا منطقی ساکت می‌کند.

در این زندان پناهنده ی جوان از موسیقی به عنوان ابزاری استفاده می کند که به او کمک کند که در برابر سیستمی که موجودیت و فردیت‌اش را نادیده میگیرد و می‌خواهد او را کنترل کند خودش را به عنوان یک انسان بازتعریف کند؛ در اینجا پناهنده‌ای که تمام هویت انسانی، موجودیت و فردیت‌اش نادیده گرفته می‌شود

از موسیقی استفاده می کند که تمام عناصر انسانی اش را حفظ کند. موسیقی در فضایی این چنینی فضایی را خلق می کند که درآن زندانی ها بتوانند بقا پیدا کنند، در فضایی این چنین خشن و غیر انسانی آنچه اهمیت دارد نخست تنازع برای بقاست.

تحولات سال های بعد در کمپ جزیره مانوس این فرصت را ایجاد کرد که نوازنده ها و خواننده هایی که در آنجا زندانی بودند بالاخره این فرصت را پیدا کنند که بتوانند یک گروه موسیقی را سازماندهی کنند. دادگاه عالی پاپوآ گینه نو حکمی را صادر کرد که نگه داشتن پناهنده ها در کمپ بسته غیر قانونیست و همین باعث شد که درهای کمپ باز شود وکسانی که در چهار زندان کمپ این حق را نداشتند که با هم معاشرت کنند بتوانند در کنار هم ساز بزنند و بخوانند. وجود گروهی نوازنده در آن جزیره دورافتاده اتفاق شگفت انگیزی بود و این گروه چند وقت یک بار در تمام داخل کمپ به شکل نوازنده های دوره گرد برای پناهنده های دیگر ساز می زدند. موسیقی در فضای این چنینی نه تنها یک عنصر هویت بخش و زندگی ساز است بلکه عنصری است که یک زندانی می تواند از طریق آن همچنان با گذشته اش و سرزمینی که از آنجا آمده است ارتباط داشته باشد، یک نوع ارتباط که با عنصر خیال و خلق کردن معنا پیدا می کند. این خودش بزرگ ترین غنیمت و هدیه ای است برای پناهنده ای که احساس می کند گم شده ی زمان هاست.

خوشحالم که مقالات کتاب حاضر از نقطه نظرهای مختلف مسایل موزیسین های آواره را بررسی میکنند.

Foreword: Expunging Confusion, Filling Emptiness

Displacement. The word renders images of uncertainty, confusion, even chaos. It signals a sense of loss, of turbulence and turmoil. It results in feelings of imbalance, restlessness, and an emptiness, all of which can maximize and intensify to the brink—to an unraveling of the spirit.

Amid the pain of displacement, music has served to counter and cure some of the suffering and sorrow. Music has found its way into the circumstances of those who have endured violence, withstood traumatic experiences, and survived upheaval from familiar places of relative comfort to situations ranging from bleak to brutal. At times, the music has emerged for the displaced in ways both unprompted and unbidden. More likely, however, it is the skillful facilitation by another that brings on music to fill the hollows and heal the sadnesses. Through the expert undertakings of music educators can come the flow of meaningful musical encounters into the lives of the displaced.

I recall episodes and images of displacement in my own earlier life, and can still hear the music that people made as they, the displaced, resettled themselves. With no personal experience in displacement, I have only empathic glances and glimpses from the outside in. There were the Hungarians who came in droves to my childhood city of Cleveland, Ohio after the 1956 Revolution, the men dressed in full-length wool coats and brown leather work boots and the women in their embroidered vests, or blouses, or skirts; their families joined other Hungarian families altogether in tiny apartment quarters, suffering the anguish of resettlement, and they sang, danced the czárdás, and played the violin. Of my African American fellow students in secondary school, when several had been temporarily displaced from school, suspended for "language" that was sometimes little more than a difference of their local dialect from mainstream English (but also anger in their adolescent awakening to civil injustices), they returned to school singing with all-the-more passion and verve the gospel songs of the Edwin Hawkins Singers. I fondly remember the residents whom we met on weekend "music therapy" visits to the Gallipolis Epileptic Hospital, a 19th century-styled asylum that sat high over the Ohio River; every one of them had been removed from their homes, many involuntarily, for permanent institutional care and so we sang and danced with them, and gave impromptu lessons to them on guitar, banjo, dulcimer, and fiddle. When the first wave of refugees from Laos arrived to the US in the 1970s, I gathered with Lao musicians to co-write grants to support their expressed need to sustain cultural heritage as they resettled into their new St. Louis, Missouri home, and I joined them at *basi* ceremonies to hear the soulful songs of their roots as they sang and played on their two-stringed lutes (*phin*) and free-reed bamboo mouth organs (*khaen*).

Displacement continues now, as ever, and in myriad ways, and still music continues to be a presence, expunging the confusion, filling the emptiness, and providing an outlet of expression from those who most deserve a safe and civil (and artistic) declaration of the everyday challenges. Today's stories of the displaced, in these unprecedented times, are personal, sometimes political, and frequently wrapped into the social circumstances that first triggered the displacement and that later are giving hope for an end to the anguish. These stories are sung (and played) by the displaced, and their songs and instrumental expressions narrate the varied journeys while also spawning remedies for their resolution.

Music education would seem a likely hub from which spring inspiring stories of the search for solace. The field may be, at its base, a repository of potential expressions facilitated by teaching musicians and emerging from the hearts of people coming through hardship, working through troubles, seeking transition to a more peaceful life. After all, the rhetoric in the field of music education claims that a broad umbrella of efforts is open and available for tapping into the capacities of all people to express themselves musically. Yet while the reports are plentiful for in-school music education accomplishments, it has taken a volume like this one to venture into the void of reports beyond school, and to draw together the views of individuals whose voices represent teachers and learners in the midst of meaningful musical experiences.

I've been in search of such a compendium of essays as this volume provides, this chapter book so full of the merits of music as they are acquired and expressed by those at the outer edges of conventional music education practice. There are elsewhere in the professional literature stacks of stats on the positive results of standards-based curricular studies in music for children and youth, ages 5–18, in thoughtfully sequenced elementary and secondary school programs. There are rich descriptions elsewhere of the processes involved in growing the musical skills and understandings of children in music classrooms, and in school bands, choirs, and orchestras. There are writings elsewhere, dense by dissertation design or within the lighter touch of a feature-page quality, that speak to the successful ways in which school music programs have made a difference in the lives of children and youth, and the roles that teachers have played as facilitators of their musically expressive selves. There is a vacuum, however, on the role of music and music education in the lives of the displaced.

These 28 chapters speak to music education writ-large, to the people, the places, and the projects that wrap music into the process of those who grieve, who desire a way to articulate loss, who seek consolation and a modicum of comfort in the struggle of displacement, and who hope to forge a way forward to light and new life. Co-editors and authors Kính T. Vũ and André de Quadros have carefully crafted this collection of reflective writings by musicians and music educators, by the displaced and by those who collaborate with them. They have made space for many voices to share their struggles to maintain some semblance of their past, some hold on their identities, some sense of who they were when they were at home, and who they are becoming in a time of their displacement and in their transition past the uncertainties and confusions. We feel the angst, the anxiety, and even the anger in these heart-rending views of teachers and students, and the hope that comes through music's power to sustain and strengthen the human spirit. I am personally buoyed by the stories and by a realization of why what we do as music educators counts... and should be extended to those at the periphery who have been neglected, overlooked, undesired, and too far removed from life's joys. I am inspired by the stories, and by the constant theme of music's emotive and healing powers, and I sense that there are teaching musicians everywhere who will likewise find inspiration and be emboldened to want to bring music into the lives of those who are displaced and in transition to better times.

Patricia Shehan Campbell
Donald E. Peterson Professor of Music
University of Washington

Acknowledgements

Bringing together such an extraordinary collection of voices has been a labor of love for us, and we are deeply grateful to those who made it possible. Julie White, one of the series editors, was an early supporter, and without her, this book might never have seen publication. All the chapter contributions were part of a peer review process that resulted in considerable reflection that the authors willingly embraced. We are immensely grateful to our peer review team for this work: Emilie Amrein, Michael Birenbaum Quintero, Houchang Chehabi, Casey Clementson, Peggy Dettwiler, Amira Ehrlich, Miguel Felipe, Paula Grissom-Broughton, Joy Hirokawa, Emily Jaworski, Tavis Linsin, Toni Pepe, Allyn Phelps, Eric Shieh, Rachana Vajjhala, Chia Youyee Vang, Janelize van der Merwe, and Mary Yang. As the book neared completion, we benefited from the insight and recommendations for structure that Dave Kelman's review gave us.

We are indebted to our research assistants Allyn Phelps and Georgia Voulgaraki for their tireless work in compiling literature, organizing data, communicating with contributors, and collecting materials of all kinds. The book's completion was facilitated by their careful and excellent work.

For this book, we asked two esteemed individuals to write for us. Each in their own way brings a global citizenship, resistance to the conventional, and the pursuit of justice. We thank Behrouz Boochani and Patricia Shehan Campbell for sharing their exceedingly thoughtful observations about this book. Their support is invaluable and speaks to the importance of looking at displacement through multiple viewpoints, especially music education.

Most importantly, we are indebted to our contributors for their inspiration to imagine and create this important, first-ever collected volume on music education and displacement. It is due in part to their continuous support that the stories of so many people from around the world are shared within these pages.

Illustrations

Figures

Videos

Notes on Contributors

#4459

was inspired to study music by his high school band director. He was involved with various choirs throughout his life; he joined the Oakdale Community Choir in the spring of 2011. In addition to writing songs for the choir, he has developed writing prompts for the choir and has put together a choir newsletter from their responses. He has been involved with the University of Iowa Liberal Arts Beyond Bars program where he shares what he has learned from the broken road to bring hope and encouragement to others.

Efi Averof Michailidou

studied economic and political science at the Institut des Sciences Politiques et Economiques in Paris, design at the New York School of Design, and theory of music at the Athens Conservatoire, and has been working for the last forty years as a music educator in conservatories and music institutions in Greece. Her main activities include the production and presentation of the "Sunday Morning Family Concerts" at the Megaron Athens Concert Hall (2001–2013), active participation in the educational projects of the Friends of Music Society in Athens and other centers throughout Greece, and a collaboration with the Athens Conservatory. She is the founder and President of the Board of Polyphonica, a non-profit company (since 2011).

Kat Bawden

is a photographer, multimedia artist, and teacher based in Los Angeles. Bawden's photographic essays explore grey areas between propriety and transgression, order and chaos, and the duality of our internal and external lives. Bawden's work has appeared in *The Los Angeles Times*, *The Huffington Post*, and *F-Stop Magazine*, among other publications. Her client list includes numerous non-governmental organizations including the Open Society Foundations, and she has exhibited work in galleries across the country. Before a career in art, Bawden worked as a community organizer and teacher in Ecuador, West Virginia, Washington, DC, and North Carolina.

Rachel Beckles Willson

is a Professorial Research Associate at SOAS at the University of London. Her research focuses on music of Hungary, the former Soviet Union and the Arab world, with questions relating to nationalism, imperialism and material culture. Her most recent monograph is *Orientalism and Musical Mission: Palestine and the West* (Cambridge University Press, 2013). For her historical and ethnographic work on travelling instruments, see www.oudmigrations.com. In 2017–2019, Beckles Willson worked in eastern Sicily, undertaking research within musical and broader educational projects with young asylum-seekers (see www.todayisgood.org). She is also an active musician and composer.

Marie Bejstam

is a driven cultural entrepreneur and choral leader. She received her MFA in music education and choral conducting at the College of Music in Örebro. She works as a pedagogue, lecturer, entrepreneur, producer, composer, and conductor within the school system, through choirs for asylum-seekers, and her own children and youth choirs Spektrum, for the Royal Academy of Music as well as within the private sector for churches, TV, etc. She is the CEO and co-founder of the cultural center Kulturfyren. She has been awarded the "Children and youth choir leader of the year 2009" by the Swedish national organization Ungikör for her social and international dedication and engagements in combination with her qualifications within children's choral music.

Rhoda Bernard

is the managing director of the Berklee Institute for Arts Education and Special Needs. Her research interests include arts education and disability, urban music education, and music teacher identity. She regularly presents at conferences throughout the United States and abroad, and provides professional development workshops for educators in local, national, and international forums. Her work has been published in books and journals. She currently serves as Vice Chair for the Arts Education Advisory Council of Americans for the Arts, as well as on their Speakers Bureau.

Behrouz Boochani

is the Kurdish-Iranian asylum-seeker who spent six years seeking his freedom from the Australian detention center on Manus Island, Papua New Guinea. He is a prize-winning author whose memoir, *No Friend but the Mountains*, was written in a series of WhatsApp messages while in detention.

Patricia Shehan Campbell

is the Donald E. Peterson Professor of Music at the University of Washington. She teaches at the nexus of music education and ethnomusicology, and is consultant to Smithsonian Folkways and the Association for Cultural Equity.

Michele Cantoni

is an Italian violinist who has worked intermittently in Palestine since 2004. From 2010 until 2015 he was academic director of the Edward Said National Conservatory of Music and artistic director of the Palestine National Orchestra and Palestine Youth Orchestra. He currently coordinates music projects in Palestine. He is the director of the Palestine Philharmonie and co-founder of the Amwaj children's choir schools (Hebron and Bethlehem).

Mary Cohen

is an associate professor of music education at the University of Iowa. She researches music-making and well-being, songwriting, and collaborative communities. In 2009, she founded the Oakdale Prison Community Choir (see http://oakdalechoir.lib.uiowa.edu/ for original songs, recources and recordings). Her research is published in the *International Journal of Research in Choral Singing*, *Journal of Research in Music Education*, the *Australian Journal of Music Education*, the *Journal of Historical Research in Music Education*, the *Journal of Correctional Education*, the *International Journal of Community Music,* the *International Journal of Music Education,* and numerous book chapters. She is completing *Silenced Voices: Music-Making in Prisons.*

Wayland "X" Coleman

was born in Birmingham, Alabama, on January 18, 1978. His family was very poor. In order to escape the poverty of the south, they moved to Worcester, Massachusetts, in 1988. At age 11, he was given a one-year scholarship to the Worcester Art Museum, because of drawings he had created as a child. While he attended the Art Museum, he was introduced to hustling in the streets. At the age of 13, he became a member of the Leicester Satellite Drum and Bugle Corp, where he played the trumpet for two years. At the time of writing, he is an incarcerated activist and organizer.

André de Quadros

is a professor of music at Boston University, where he holds affiliated positions in African, Asian, Muslim studies, and prison education. His professional work as a scholar, musician, teacher, and activist have taken him to the most diverse settings in more than forty countries. http://www.andredequadros.com

Samantha Dieckmann

is an associate professor of music at the University of Oxford, teaching music education and community music. Her program of research examines how intercultural relations play out in a range of music education settings, with a focus on the musical lives of migrant and former refugee communities in resettlement contexts. She conceives of music education broadly, and her projects have involved looking at music-making across a range of classroom, extracurricular, community music intervention and self-directed community music contexts. Dieckmann has published on these topics in journals and edited volumes across music education, community music, and ethnomusicology.

Irene (Peace) Ebhohon

is 15 years old and a second-generation immigrant from Nigeria. Her hobbies involve singing, playing with other children, while she loves participating in the social activities of the Nigerian community in Athens that include the creation of different hairstyles. Her father is a worker in the airport and a pastor in the local community. Her mother is a cleaning lady and a deaconess. Irene has four brothers and sisters. When she grows up she wants to be an artist or a flight attendant.

Con Fullam

is an internationally recognized and award-winning songwriter, recording artist and media content creator, and producer. In more than 50 years in the field of entertainment he has been nominated for four Emmy Awards, received gold albums, and had his films and television shows broadcast in the US and 50 countries around the world.

Ismael "Q" Garcia-Vega

is an artist (poet, songwriter, and performer) and former student of Boston University's Empowering Song course. Born into an impoverished minority from the South Bronx of New York City before moving throughout the Caribbean, Florida, and Massachusetts, he has struggled to overcome the language barrier, as well as the trauma of physical, psychological, and sexual abuse that led him towards a life of crime. While incarcerated he discovered the healing power of his own artistic voice. With a Bachelor of Liberal Arts degree from Boston University, Quota Mill (aka Q) continues to explore and share his experience, while remembering his journey from a state of indifference and borderline psychopathic to vulnerability.

Erin Guinup

is a conductor, author, composer, soprano, voice teacher, and TEDx speaker. She is the founding director of the Tacoma Refugee Choir and a passionate advocate for community singing, speaking at national conferences for ACDA, NATS, and Chorus America. Specializing in both classical and contemporary technique, her internationally performed one-woman show has been praised as "an amazing tour-de-force" and her students have achieved success on Broadway, regional theatre, operatic stages, and television. Other career highlights include conducting Rob Gardner's *Lamb of God*, performing as *Mary Poppins*, teaching voice workshops at Amazon, and mentoring new teachers.

Micah Hendler

is a musical change maker bringing Israeli and Palestinian youth together in the Jerusalem Youth Chorus (featured on the *Late Show with Stephen Colbert*) to create a powerful singing community based on equality, respect, mutual understanding, and love. The chorus's message has inspired millions through its viral music video *Home*, and its influence is growing to help change the discourse about the kind of place Jerusalem could be. Hendler was named to the Forbes 30 Under 30 List for Music for 2017 for his work in musical conflict transformation.

Hala Jaber

is currently in her third year of an arts practice PhD at the University of Limerick. Her research revolves around how community music workshops can be used to promote integration in the context of post-conflict migration.

Shaylene Johnson

speaks, reads, and writes the Mi'kmaq language and is the female member of The Sons of Membertou, a traditional Mi'kmaq drumming and singing group that performs internationally. She has worked at the Membertou Youth Centre, where she coordinated programs for youth. Johnson has also worked as a research assistant in integrated science with Cheryl Bartlett and with Albert and Murdena Marshall, work for which she was awarded an undergraduate research award from the Natural Sciences and Engineering Research Council of Canada. Johnson is dedicated to her family and to improving the quality of life in Mi'kmaw communities.

Arsène Kapikian

is a former music educator in secondary schools for more than 18 years, a composer, and an arranger. He has developed artistic, technical, and educational skills that led him to the creation of film documentaries. Arsène's documentaries include *Le jeûne* (2018–2019), *A Choir that Saves Lives*, *Séjour de Rupture à Madagascar* (2015), *In Terra Pax* (2011), and others set in Indonesia.

Tou SaiKo Lee

is a spoken word poet, storyteller, hip hop recording artist and community organizer from St. Paul, Minnesota. Lee has organized an annual hip hop event that included a huge urban street dance competition called Boom Bap Village to coincide with Hmong sports tournaments in St. Paul. He now organizes a project called Street Stops and Mountain Tops that connects teaching artists from the US to Hmong children in Southeast Asia. Lee received the Jerome Foundation Travel Study Grant in 2008 and is a 2009 Intermedia Arts VERVE Spoken Word grant recipient. Lee also received the Bush Foundation Leadership Fellowship in 2016 to focus on utilizing creativity and arts to preserve cultural identity.

Sarah Mandie

is a singer, songwriter, performer, choir leader, and teacher from Melbourne, Australia. She has performed a cappella, klezmer, Sephardic, and original songs and leads a diverse range of community choirs. She has directed several successful community singing projects, producing book and CD resources. She currently leads the Swinburne Chorale (www.swinburnechorale.com.au) and the all-abilities High Street Bells Choir (http://www.highstreetbellschoir. org.au/). Along with Voices of Peace, her latest projects include That Girl Song project (http://www.thatgirlsong.com), which combines her songwriting and community project work for the empowerment of culturally diverse women and young girls of Victoria.

David Nnadi

is 14 years old and a second-generation immigrant from Nigeria. He goes to the second intercultural high school of Athens for immigrants and refugees. His parents came to Greece from Nigeria about 14 years ago. He has a younger brother, aged 12. He enjoys singing, drumming, and playing basketball. In his free time, he likes being with his friends.

Marcia Ostashewski

is an associate professor of ethnomusicology and director of the Centre for Sound Communities at Cape Breton University. This state-of-the-art digital arts and humanities facility supports multi-faceted research programs for Ostashewski and affiliated researchers, emergent and technology-enhanced creative, critical community-engaged research collaborations among artists, scholars, students, and wider communities. These programs result in innovative outcomes, including intensive public outreach and the production of diverse digital media, as well as both popular press and academic publications.

Ulrike Präger

is currently a postdoctoral fellow at the Paris Lodron University of Salzburg working on a theoretical and methodological handbook for studies in music and migration. She is also a course developer and instructor in Boston University's graduate program in music education and will teach at the University of Chicago in 2020. She holds a PhD in musicology/ethnomusicology from Boston University and degrees in voice and vocal pedagogy and in music and dance pedagogy from the Mozarteum University Salzburg. Currently, she is working on a book titled *Publicity and Representation: Music in Medializing and Politicizing Processes of (Forced) Migration.*

Kate Richards Geller

has been playing with the elements of music to change our minds and our bodies and our communities since 1997. In the fields of music therapy and vocal improvisation, making music with children and grownups has been her focus. A singer-songwriter, circleSong facilitator, and founder of Sing for Yourself—a music-centered practice that invites curiosity, self-awareness, and transformation—Geller views the body as an instrument, applies musical solutions to most life situations, and gleans life lessons from most musical situations. Playfulness, creativity, and a willingness to say "Yes" are key features of her work. She earned a master's degree in music therapy from New York University, works as a consultant at Musical Health Technologies (SingFit.com), and acts as the associate director and music therapy consultant at Urban Voices Project (UrbanVoicesProject.org)

Charlotte Rider

is a driven culture entrepreneur and choir leader. She received her Bachelor of Music Education degree from the University of Colorado at Boulder and her Master of Fine Arts degree in choral pedagogy from the Royal Academy of Music in Stockholm. She works as a pedagogue, lecturer, producer, and conductor within the school system, through choirs for asylum-seekers, and her own children's and youth choirs Prisma, for the Royal Academy of Music as well as within the private sector. She is co-founder and chairman of the cultural center Kulturfyren in Stockholm. She has been awarded the "Children and youth choir leader of the year 2009" by the Swedish national organization Ungikör for her social and international dedication and engagements in combination with her work in children's choral music.

Matt Sakakeeny

is an associate professor of music at Tulane University in New Orleans, where he has lived since 1997. He is the author of *Roll With It: Brass Bands in the Streets of New Orleans* (Duke University Press, 2013) and articles in several journals, including *Ethnomusicology*, *Black Music Research Journal*, and *Souls*. He has edited two book collections, *Keywords in Sound* (Duke University Press, 2015) and *Remaking New Orleans: Beyond Exceptionalism and Authenticity* (Duke University Press, 2019). Sakakeeny is a board member of the Roots of Music afterschool program and the Dinerral Shavers Educational Fund. His forthcoming book on marching band education in the New Orleans school system is supported by the Spencer Foundation.

Timothy Seelig

is a conductor, singer, teacher, and motivational speaker. In addition to serving as the artistic director of the San Francisco Gay Men's Chorus, he keeps a busy guest conducting schedule throughout the United States and internationally. He is conductor emeritus of the Turtle Creek Chorale, which he conducted for twenty years; co-founded The Women's Chorus of Dallas; and taught on the faculty at Southern Methodist University. Seelig holds four degrees, including a diploma from the Mozarteum University Salzburg and a Doctor of Musical Arts. He has authored seven books and DVDs on choral technique. His recordings have been on Billboard Top Ten and iTunes Top Ten classical charts.

Katherine Seybert

completed her bachelor's degree in music education at Marshall University in Huntington, West Virginia, and her master's degree in music education at the University of Illinois. She has more than five years of experience teaching general music, band, and choir to students from kindergarten to eighth grade.

Brian Sullivan

holds a PhD and is an independent researcher, musician, and educator in Charlotte, North Carolina. His current work includes church and community music leading, group ukulele experiences, and songwriting. Sullivan's research has focused on philosophical inquiry into school wind bands and critical service learning.

Mathilde Vittu

is a French musician and has many areas of expertise, including violin and viola, choral and orchestral conducting, musicology, and arranging. She earned a PhD from the Paris-Sorbonne University and has received many awards from the Conservatoire de Paris and the French Ministry of Culture. She has published mainly about French baroque music. Interested in Arabic culture and music, she taught for a year at Sultan Qaboos University in Muscat and in 2013–2014 at the Edward Said National Conservatory of Music in Palestine. Since September 2014, she has been teaching musicology at the Conservatoire de Paris and been the director of the Amwaj Choir in Palestine.

Kính T. Vũ

is an assistant professor of music at Boston University where he teaches music education courses in general music, instrumental pedagogy, history, and philosophy. Focusing his teaching, learning, and research model on innovation and justice, Kính's pedagogy is community-based with partnerships emerging in Boston and internationally. His current research centers on exploring connections between music education and forced human displacement in Cambodia, and Vũ's homeland Việt Nam, where he was abandoned at the end of the American War.

Derrick Washington

is a 34-year-old Black man who has been incarcerated since the age of 20 in the State of Massachusetts. He was born and raised on the west side of Cleveland. Following the incarceration of family members, he relocated to Massachusetts and was subsequently charged and convicted of first-degree homicide along with two co-defendants and given the mandatory sentence of life without the possibility of parole (LWOP). He is currently challenging the validity of his conviction. In 2012, Washington founded the Emancipation Initiative whose dual goals are to end LWOP and restore universal prisoner suffrage. As a result of his experience, he remains steadfast in his commitment to end 21st-century slavery enabled by the 13th Amendment of the Constitution of the United States.

Henriette Weber

has experience in primary, secondary, tertiary music education as well as community music for over 30 years. She has held appointments in music education and arts management positions at non-profit organizations. She has returned to her alma mater, the University of the Western Cape (UWC) to head the Centre for the Performing Arts (CPA). The CPA's accredited music courses focus on community engagement, lifelong learning, and distance learning thereby providing quality music education to community music practitioners and special needs learners. Weber was acknowledged by local government and UWC for her contribution to youth development, service, leadership, and excellence.

Mai Yang Xiong

is currently a teacher at Maxfield Elementary School teaching fourth and fifth grades. Born and raised in St. Paul, Minnesota, she is also a singer and songwriter. Xiong has had many roles in her life leading to becoming a teacher, including working as a Teaching Artist for Street Stops and Mountain Tops organization in 2016, the founder and coordinator of the Art Saves Us: Beyond the Noise summer music program at the Center for Hmong Arts and Talent in 2013, events coordinator for In Session singer/songwriter competition at Freedom Festival in 2013, and founder and president of the SHE Pab: Voices of Hmong Women student organization at St. Catherine University in 2012.

Keng Chris Yang

is a guitarist, singer, and songwriter born and raised in the Twin Cities, Minnesota. He became involved in music later in life. By the time he picked up a guitar, he was already 18 years old. Yang has two degrees, in design and in music. With his "5 After 6" team, he intends to start a media business that touches all aspects in media such as videos, acting, music, and games. Yang graduated in 2016 with a bachelor's degree in music business and guitar performance at McNally Smith College of Music. He teaches guitar music to Park Center High School students as well as in an after-school guitar program for the Center for Hmong Arts and Talent.

Nelly Yurina

is a second-generation immigrant. She was born in the Ukraine and joined Polyphonica at the age of twelve. Her father has worked in the church. She loves improvising songs on themes such as hope, friendship, sickness, and hardship.

A Note Regarding Media Links

In conceiving this book, we sought to disrupt the silence that oftentimes accompanies publications in the field of music education. We contend that many of the stories presented here would have been incomplete without the sounds and sights that are described throughout this volume. It is our intention that in providing media, readers might gain a more complete understanding about the musical processes and products that have been created to address and attenuate the effects of displacement around the globe.

The living features of this book are presented on our website, which extends the written material of this book by providing more information about each of our contributors, musical examples that illustrate, and verbal commentary of their continuing work (https://www.musicdisplacement.org/). To help readers access the website from the print version, a QR code has been placed at the end of chapters where links have been referenced. Live links have been included in the digital text online. It is our hope that readers might be able to extend their exploration of stories presented throughout this volume by visiting this book's website.

PART 1

The Setting

∵

CHAPTER 1

Charting the Land(s)-scape(s)

André de Quadros and Kính T. Vũ

Displacement, relocation, dissociation, disruption, trauma, otherness. Each of these terms elicits images of mass migration, homelessness, statelessness, or outsider-ness of many kinds, too numerous to name. While these issues might paralyze us, together they are cause for actions that affirm, support, uplift, and honor the people who experience a reality of belonging nowhere, and those who work with them through music.

In this book, we conceptualize displacement as encompassing all those who have been forced away from their locations by political, social, economic, climate, and resource change, injustice, and insecurity. This includes, but is not restricted to: refugees and internally displaced persons; forced migration victims; indigenous communities who have been forced off their traditional lands; people who, because of their gender identity and sexual orientation, have fled discrimination; imprisoned individuals; persons who seek refuge from domestic and social violence; homeless persons and others who live in transient spaces; the disabled, who are relocated involuntarily; and the culturally dispossessed, whose languages and heritage have been stolen from them.

The aim of this edited volume is to create opportunities for scholars, practitioners, and silenced voices to share theories and stories of progressive, transformational, and transgressive music pedagogies that challenge the ways music educators and participants think about and practice their arts relative to displacement. In the context of the first-ever volume on this topic in music education, we connect displacement to what music might have been, be, and become to those peoples who find themselves between spaces, parted from the familiar and the familial. Cooper (2017), who studied the relationship between HIV/AIDS and the erosion of nuclear families in Kenya, recognized that separation from home and kin forces displaced persons to "rely on imagination" (p. 37) as a way to construct a sense of "real home" (p. 41). The contributors to this book, whether they make music with those who have left their real homes behind or have themselves fled persecution, drought, or war, must imagine a new world where dreaming, learning, and music-making are possible again. Through, in, and because of a variety of musical participations, we contend that displaced peoples might find comfort, inclusion, and welcome of some kind(s) either in making new music or remembering and reconfiguring past musical experiences. Central to this collection of articles, narratives, short stories, poems, artwork, and of course, musics, are several questions, some of which are: How might music activities open spaces for self and group belonging in times of political, civil, and social unrest specifically framed within forced migration? How is music conceived as a means of welcome and inclusion? What kinds of evaluations are used to determine the effectiveness of such projects?

To illuminate this discourse, we have included stories from around the globe. The call for contributions was an exercise in itself. We wrote the call to attract the widest range of contributions, publishing it in scholarly journals but also in social media, where we issued the invitation not only in English but also in Arabic, Chinese, French, and Spanish. Some of the contributions are authored by the displaced while some contain the stories of musicians, artists, practitioners, activists, prisoners, children, and scholars who have worked with displaced people. Some authors tell stories about how they came to be displaced and how they interact with their state of past or present displacement using music as a backdrop or backbone for their arts-based practices. Other authors have sought to ameliorate the stressful situation of being displaced for those who identify as refugees, asylum-seekers, immigrants, prisoners, and people enduring homelessness, providing a glimpse into a world heretofore unseen in the field of music education. Together, the contributors highlight the reach of music teaching and learning as well as the benefits and challenges to the musicians who participate in these projects.

From the outset, we knew that our book would be inadequately served if it was yet another book about social justice in which scholars were privileged and the only voice, that the chapters were written by scholars for fellow academics to read. Besides which, we felt strongly that the academic voice over-values a certain rationality, even in stories that are deeply distressing. In "The Space of Academia: Privilege, Agency and the Erasure of Affect," Clegg (2013) critiques the "affectless rationality" of the academy, a kind of emotionless quality that we wished to avoid in this book. The spectrum of contributions, academic and non-academic, challenged us as editors. There is a certain familiar routine to editing academic writing. In many ways, this is like engaging in reading students' research projects, one of our central teaching activities. In short, we know how to expect the compliance of our academic contributors to scholarly protocols. With the non-academic writers, our editing process taught us to think differently, to dismantle the rules, and to see the work as liberatory not only for the writer, but for the book as a whole. With all our writers, whose work moves the human heart as Rosenbaum (2011) describes, our editing sought to be respectful and responsive.

Given the broad scope of diverse contributions that fill the pages of this book, it was difficult to imagine a particular order to the book without running the risk of essentializing the experiences of the contributors. Notwithstanding this challenge, we cohered the book around four principal themes: The Setting, Process/Pedagogy, Belonging, and Land(s) and Culture. All the chapters carry these elements, but the chapters in each individual section share common threads that persuaded us to create these chapter groupings.

Part 1: The Setting

First, we define the landscape[1] with a suite of four chapters authored by us co-editors as a way to foreground the array of scholarly and creative contributions that follow. These introductory chapters (Chapters 1–4) position us in the context of displacement and provide the theoretical grounding for the text, showing our personal stake in the topic of music education and displacement. Chapter 2 is André de Quadros's personal narrative of displacement from India through Australia and the US to multiple sites of musicking, and his struggle and search for meaning in music education. Chapter 3 is the theoretical guidepost for this text; it establishes a case for such a book by showing how we understand the intersection of music education with forced displacement. While displacement has been questioned and theorized outside music, as in the social sciences, and sometimes within it (see, for example, Cohen & Deng, 2012; Jacques, 2012), the topic of displacement has rarely been connected explicitly to music education. De Quadros argues the merits of thinking along the lines of displacement theories and how we might bring them into the practice and scholarship of music teaching and learning. He foreshadows Chapter 4 in which Kính T. Vũ describes the double bind of living with "one hand in the past and one in the present." A disquieted concept of home-yet-not-home underscores his relationship with the family that raised him in the United States. His personal story of abandonment on the streets of Sài Gòn gave the book its title.[2]

Part 2: Process/Pedagogy

A realization of the world through conscientious pedagogy is possible when educators take stock of what has occurred in the learning environment. A sort of reflective practice, this unwrapping of process and pedagogy as it takes form is what inspired this group of contributors to share their stories of teaching and learning in various parts of the world. Each author, some of whom are or have been themselves displaced, brings a special relatedness to this section of the book. The authors attempt to name the forgotten peoples within their stories, a central aspect of critical pedagogy (see, for example, Freire, 1970). Similar to medical anthropologist Paul Farmer's (2005) work in which he discussed the plight of millions of women suffering from HIV/AIDs calling them "hidden away" (p. 188), prisoners, refugees, and allies who musick among or as displaced peoples in their communities are at risk of being lost in the masses of displaced persons—they are at risk of remaining nameless. This section of the book aims to name the bodies and souls of the dispossessed and to provide readers with a glimpse into some of the world's forgotten peoples and places.

Beginning with Rachel Beckles Willson, Chapter 5 shares the importance of songwriting among refugee boys in Sicily, showing the importance of adopting a flexible teaching model in which song leaders demonstrate flexibility in their approach to music pedagogy. #4459, the author of Chapter 6, is a singer in Mary Cohen's choir who shares stories about personal growth and enjoyment while participating in the Oakdale Community Choir. His prisoner identification number has been used as a pseudonym due to ongoing reconciliation efforts on the part of a victims' advisory council. From the central United States, we feature Brian Sullivan, Mary Cohen, and Katherine Seybert who share their music education projects in Iowa prisons (Chapter 7). Their understanding of music education within incarcerated settings is informed by the practice of choral singing, explaining how musical participation has evolved in the process of leading prison choirs.

In Chapter 8, Rhoda Bernard conceives of disability as a kind of displacement for those who are differently abled in our classrooms. She takes readers into the world of disability in which she argues that the voices of musicians with disabilities may be marginalized due to their special talents. Wayland "X" Coleman (Chapter 9), who is imprisoned as of 2019, addresses the inhumane, racist, and unjust conditions within the "Amerikkkan" prison industrial complex, telling readers in text and hand-drawn artwork about moments of joy experienced through participation in a prison-based music program. His spelling of Amerikkka(n) elicits images of the Ku Klux Klan, a white supremacist group known for its crimes against humanity in the United States. In the tenth chapter, Erin Guinup shares her story about starting the Tacoma Refugee Choir in the State of Washington where she contends that these singers are able to amplify their voices rather than being silenced by cultural norms that might otherwise have them be silent. In a highly personal way, she discusses the struggles and accomplishments of her initiative. In America's Upper Midwest,

Tou SaiKo Lee, Mai Yang Xiong, and Keng Chris Yang describe their intercultural partnership in St. Paul, Minnesota, and Chiang Mai, Thailand. They tell their stories about teaching hip-hop to Hmong youth living in Piyawat Orphan House where they teach rap, singing, and guitar to Hmong children who feel no connection to their new home in an urban center in Thailand (Chapter 11).

In Chapter 12, Ulrike Präger discusses the use of mobile devices to source music for dance parties comprised of immigrants in Berlin, Germany. She argues that this process is a means of welcoming newcomers to the capital city. To conclude the section on process and pedagogy, Matt Sakakeeny uncovers the privatization of New Orleans, Louisiana, public schools that foreclosed the opportunity for music-making among schoolchildren. He argues in Chapter 13 that the abandonment of the city during Hurricane Katrina in 2005 was the antecedent to the disbandment of arts programs, especially marching bands, that historically had served many of the city's black youth who called band programs home.

Part 3: Belonging

The third section of this book consists of a collection of stories situated in belonging, of being part of somewhere. In the absence of home, for example, there may arise a yearning to be part of a community. The people represented here find some solace in music-making activities such as group singing, choirs, and other arts-based initiatives. Although these stories come from different parts of the world, the common thread is belongingness.

Kate Richards Geller and Kat Bawden provide readers with a look into one of America's most documented homeless populations: Skid Row in Los Angeles (Chapter 14). Their photo essay is a celebration of Linda, a woman who lived in the elements of Skid Row and whose music-making with neighbors revealed glimmers of hope in what might otherwise be felt as inhospitable. Ismael "Q" Garcia-Vega is a former prisoner who, in Chapter 15, provides readers with a rap and three poems that describe different aspects of his life as an incarcerated man and his thoughts about freedom or lack thereof.

We turn our attention to Melbourne, Australia where Sarah Mandie (Chapter 16) works with the Assyrian Chaldean Syriac Women's community group that composed an anthem speaking to their heritage and thusly made a space to call home. Marie Bejstam and Charlotte Rider show us the musical work they do with refugees living in Sweden in Chapter 17. While their music practices seek to support language acquisition among new immigrants, the greater aspect of their work is a gesture of welcome for youth from war-torn lands.

Across the North Sea, Hala Jaber (Chapter 18) shares her work with Syrian women in Limerick, Ireland, and how her musical work and personal investment in the lives of a mother-daughter pair has made an important contribution to the mother's perception of self and place.

Con Fullam presents his organization, The Pihcintu Multicultural Chorus, a group of young women who are refugees and immigrants living in Portland, Maine, in Chapter 19. These singers affirm that the chorus and its members are a space of home. Chapter 20 is a quartet of essays from Polyphonica, a Greek music program organized by Efi Averof Michailidou. Her efforts to welcome children, including a small number of refugees, from many places offer youth a way to be musical. In their own words, David Nnadi, Irene (Peace) Ebhohon, and Nelly Yurina describe what it is like to participate in Polyphonica. The final essay in this section demonstrates how LBGTQI peoples might be forcibly displaced because of their sexual orientation. In Chapter 21, Timothy Seelig provides a riveting account of being outed by church officials in Texas and subsequently losing everything he had, including family. He tells readers about the turn of events that led him to the San Francisco Gay Men's Chorus as its artistic director and conductor where the singers make the choir a safe and vulnerable space.

Part 4: Land(s) and Culture

The last section of the book is dedicated to interrogating the places in which displaced persons live and work. Where there is incarceration, disputed territory, and forced relocation, for example, there exists a sense of being trapped in limbo. Perhaps, one might argue that these people occupy non-places where they dwell between two or more worlds: both here and there and simultaneously neither here nor there.

Chapter 22, by Samantha Dieckmann, investigates South Sudanese people living in Australia who use music and other arts to keep the memory of home alive despite and because of the conflict that saw Sudan separated into two parts (Republic of Sudan and South Sudan). Mathilde Vittu and Michele Cantoni discuss the Amwaj Choir from Palestine in Chapter 23 and its positive influence on the lives of youth living in the West Bank, one of the world's most contested regions.

In Chapter 24, Arsène Kapikian recounts the making of a documentary in which he follows the Malagasy Gospel Choir at Toliara Penitentiary Centre in Madagascar. Micah Hendler discusses his work leading the Jerusalem Youth Chorus by looking at music's role in conflict resolution among youngsters who have experienced temporary or long-term displacement (Chapter 25). From Canada, Marcia Ostashewski and Shaylene Johnson share their work with First Nations people who used music and theater to tell the story of their community's displacement (Chapter 26).

Henriette Weber, in Chapter 27, provides readers with a look into apartheid and post-apartheid South Africa in which she experienced displacement, but now serves as an advocate for music education in townships that lack local music teachers in schools where Black and Coloured people still reside. The concluding contribution is by an imprisoned man, Derrick Washington (Chapter 28). He gazes deeply into his lived experience through the lens of the Empowering Song classes at his prison. He takes readers through the process of learning about music, but more importantly how he learned about himself as a human being in a brutal and racialized setting.

Taking the First Step

This book represents an effort to welcome a diversity of viewpoints and experiences. Those who responded to the call for contributions include prisoners, children, refugees, music educators, and music scholars who have experienced and/or witnessed the trauma of displacement. While we are aware of the impetus for scholars to tell their stories in an academic style, we honor storytelling that emerges in a variety of ways. Because each contribution stands on its own merit as testimony to the trials of displacement, we exercised care in how we worked with each contributor, encouraging them to share their ideas through words, poetry, artworks, and photographs. Our egalitarian approach is uncommon in academic writing; hence, we welcome feedback from readers and hope that our colleagues might add to and build upon our efforts.

Taken together this collection of stories demonstrates the complex, and oftentimes tangled intersection where music education and displacement meet. These two subjects have been well-documented separately and in two different areas of scholarship and practice; yet, the interstices where they become conjoined have received little attention by music educators. It is with humility, joy, and a stance that seeks justice for the displaced that we share this collection on music education and displacement, with our field and broader community of musicians. We hope that readers—music makers, scholars, activists, and most certainly music educators—will delve into the variety of ideas shared within these pages with a head and heart focused on music education's function in a vastly changing world where human migration is rapidly becoming the norm rather than the exception.

Notes

1 In presenting "Land(s)-scape(s)" we borrow from Appadurai's global cultural flow theory (1990), arguing differently, that "land(s)-scape" is an extension of and related to the ethno-scape that represents the movement of people worldwide. Just as the "scapes" are conceptualized in multiple ways, we see "land(s)-scape(s)" as physical, metaphoric, discursive, and contested. Indeed, "land(s)-scape(s)" can be theorized as provocations and spaces within global flow.

2 An account of Kính T. Vũ's life-narrative can be seen in "Kính T. Vũ's Journey from Vietnam Orphan to BU Music Professor," https://www.bu.edu/articles/2019/kinh-vus-journey-from-vietnam-orphan-to-bu-music-professor/

References

Appadurai, A. (1990). Disjuncture and difference in the global cultural economy. *Public Culture, 2*(1), 1–24. https://doi.org/10.1177%2F026327690007002017

Clegg, S. (2013). The space of academia: Privilege, agency and the erasure of affect. In C. Maxwell & P. Aggleton (Eds.), *Privilege, agency and affect: Understanding the production and effects of action.* London: Palgrave Macmillan.

Cohen, R., & Deng, F. M. (2012). *Masses in flight: The global crisis of internal displacement.* Washington, DC: Brookings Institution Press.

Cooper, E. (2017). Beyond the everyday: Sustaining kinship in western Kenya. *Journal of the Royal Anthropological Institute, 24,* 30–46.

Farmer, P. (2005). *Pathologies of power: Health, human rights, and the new war on the poor.* Los Angeles, CA: University of California Press.

Freire, P. (1970/2011). *Pedagogy of the oppressed.* New York, NY: Continuum.

Jacques, M. (2012). *Armed conflict and displacement: The protection of refugees and displaced persons under international humanitarian law.* Cambridge: Cambridge University Press.

Rosenblatt, R. (2011). *Unless it moves the human heart: The craft and art of writing.* New York, NY: Ecco.

CHAPTER 2

From Boy in a Boat to Searching for Song

André de Quadros

My own displacement story took shape simultaneously with the book's evolution. As I co-formulated the call for contributions, read through the submissions, wrote what is now Chapter 3, reflected on the increasing focus on worldwide displacement and its causes at the hand of unscrupulous government and non-state actors, I began to perceive a resonance in my own family's history, and my personal and professional life trajectory. If one had asked me a couple of years ago whether I saw a personal connection to displacement, I might have scratched my head in puzzlement. Now I see it differently, for, as so often happens, the present allows one to reframe the past, and to reconstitute it in the present. I had not given much thought to my family's history for decades. Now, in this book, this story finds a place. Displacement has diverse impacts, and some are more typical or representative of larger human geographies. Here then, is my story, an isolated one, and atypical.

My parents came ancestrally from Goa, the Portuguese possession on the west coast of India. My mother was born in British India, and my father in Portuguese India. He left Goa to study medicine in British India in the mid-1930s. Then came the partition of British India into the independent countries of India and Pakistan in 1947, resulting in one of the most cataclysmic of displacements in human history, in which over 15 million people were forced to migrate. At the time of Partition, my mother was in Pakistan, and my father in India. She moved across the border for marriage, losing citizenship and living and traveling as a stateless person until well into her fifties when she became an Australian citizen.

My parents married in 1949 in Bombay. Meanwhile, my father's relatives were living in Goa, which, even after Indian independence in 1947, remained a Portuguese colonial possession. Indian freedom-fighters engaged in various armed and non-violent actions for Goan independence from Portugal. My father's brother, the most senior native-born civil servant in the Portuguese colonial administration, was the attorney-general in Goa, and responsible for sentencing freedom-fighters to prison. In the mid-1950s, to prevent him from ruling in a trial of freedom-fighters, the Azad Gomantak Dal, a freedom activist group sent him a book bomb, which exploded upon opening, almost killing him.[1]

© KONINKLIJKE BRILL NV, LEIDEN, 2020 | DOI: 10.1163/9789004430464_002

A couple of years later, in 1957, my nuclear family went across the border of independent India—the Republic of India—to Goa (Portuguese India) for a brief Christmas vacation. The vacation came to an end, and my parents, sisters, and I—we were only very small children—proceeded back to the border to return to India, only to be informed that the family was banned from returning, on the order of the Indian central government. The family was stuck in Goa, my father away from his medical practice, and my mother away from her school teaching job. I heard later that this period was a time of depression and anxiety for my father. In weighing the prospect of starting life from scratch either in Goa or in a third country, my parents hit on an unusual and audacious plan of being smuggled into India. So it was, that one day, we left my uncle's home, disguised in very plain clothes, my mother in a sari that would have been worn by a fisherwoman. I don't remember the road trip or the changing of cars, but I do remember reaching a coastal area and waiting until late at night. I recall being picked up in the arms of a man who must have been a smuggler, and placed in a small rowboat, and I remember vividly the search lights scanning the water and being told to crouch in the boat. Late at night, we reached Bombay, and then sought refuge with family friends. We hid indoors as fugitives, lest the government would find us. After weeks of this self-imposed hiding, the family came out, and I was allowed to return to school. The complex details of the sequence of events and the political back story lie beyond the scope of this chapter.

A few years later, my father, still perhaps reeling from the trauma of the experience mentioned above, enquired about immigration to Australia, at which time he was told that the country had a White Australia Policy,[2] and he could enter Australia only if he had a European ancestor. He had no European ancestors; on the contrary, he believed himself to be of pure Hindu Brahmin descent. Nonetheless, he falsified his birth documents to demonstrate that he had European blood. That was how we were allowed to emigrate, arriving in Melbourne in 1965. I was the only non-White boy I could see in a humanscape of white people. My father, unable to adjust to life in Australia, and to being a non-White doctor in Melbourne, the first such that anyone had ever experienced, decided that we should seek political asylum in Portugal. In 1966, we relocated to Portugal, where we lived briefly before returning to India.

And, in India, in the early 1970s, I fell in love with conducting choirs and orchestras (see Figure 2.1) at about the same time that I was reading Paulo Freire's *Pedagogy of the Oppressed*,[3] and being awoken to anti-imperialist discourse. The sense that Western classical music was somehow part of India's colonial legacy, and a continuing symbol of White superiority did provoke in me an internal conflict.

FIGURE 2.1
André de Quadros's first major concert in Bombay, reported in the Bombay press, 1975.
PHOTOGRAPH: MARISE DE QUADROS

In 1975, imagining a better artistic and material future, and desiring to leave an abusive father and a tormented home, I returned to Australia, by which time the White Australia Policy had been lifted. After a couple of years of working mainly in the Australian corporate world, I felt so alienated that I returned to India in search of meaning.

This was the time when Prime Minister Indira Gandhi had imposed a dictatorship (aka "the Emergency"). One of my closest friends, a music teacher, was imprisoned in a massive roundup of dissenters. On the advice of an associate, I fled the country, buying a one-way ticket to Europe. In Munich, my conducting teacher said to me, "Why don't you go to Salzburg and visit Carl Orff and the Orff-Institut?" I did; I enrolled in a summer course at the institute, and felt very deeply that I had finally found something life-changing. I returned to Australia, and pursued parallel lives in music education, conducting, and community music.

In 2001, continuing my search, I moved to the US, at about the time that 9/11 took place, and my first instinct was to leave a country whose government's foreign and domestic policy committed so many crimes against humanity and violations of common decency. But, for numerous reasons, I decided to stay, and my views on the war on Afghanistan, Eurocentric pedagogies, and other social issues became heightened. Increasingly, I felt a sense of alienation in the US. Having chosen to stay, I thought that, perhaps, my interests in justice would be better served by getting me out of my static critiques to engaging in local communities. This started my journey of working in American prisons that has continued to the present day. Another of the many provocations for my work has been the exclusionary refugee policy in Australia and worldwide. In the last five or six years, my Australian family hosted two Afghan refugee boys who arrived in Australia after surviving hazardous trips on boats from Indonesia. In Chapter 3, I refer to these asylum-seekers in my story about Afghan boys.

Why then, am I telling these stories and how do they connect me to this book? First, although my family has a history of displacement, there is no intergenerational disadvantage at work. While I have no doubt that the events recounted here had traumatic effects on my parents, I have little memory of lived trauma. This already places me in the privilege of understanding the diverse nature of displacement, and provokes me to reflect on my good fortune. Secondly, my professional work in incarceration,[4] in the Arab world,[5] and on the US-Mexican border[6] has given me a view of displacement that few music educators have. Most particularly, I found the experience heartbreaking at the San Diego-Tijuana border wall, when Mexican and American singers from Common Ground Voices/La Frontera[6] looked at each other through the wall, barely touching finger-tips (see Figure 2.2).

FIGURE 2.2   André de Quadros with Common Ground Voices/La Frontera at the Mexico-US border wall in March 2019.
PHOTOGRAPH: ANDRÉ DE QUADROS

I saw the wall as an instrument of exclusionary brutality in many of the contexts in which I work—in prisons, in the Israeli-Palestinian context, in sites of poverty, in racialized situations, and with refugees. These multiple sub-stories in my personal and professional life have opened up a reflective stance of my family's displacement, a desire for greater understanding of diverse displacement situations, a fire of activism against institutionalized injustice, and an enquiry into the potential that music might have for social change.

Notes

1 For a detailed historical account of the attempted assassination of my uncle, José Militão de Quadros, by book bomb, see Risbud (2003) and https://shodhganga.inflibnet.ac.in/bitstream/10603/32202/16/16_chapter%207.pdf

2 For further information on the White Australia Policy, see, for example, Tavan (2005).

3 For further information on my early conducting years, see de Quadros (2019).

4 For further information on my work in incarceration, see de Quadros (2015b).

5 For further information on my work in the Arab world, see de Quadros (2015a).

6 For details on Common Ground Voices/La Frontera, see https://www.cgvlafrontera.org

References

de Quadros, A. (2015a). Rescuing choral music from the realm of the elite. In C. Benedict, P. Schmidt, G. Spruce, & P. Woodford (Eds.), *The Oxford handbook of social justice in music education* (pp. 501–512). New York, NY: Oxford University Press.

de Quadros, A. (2015b). Case illustration: I once was lost but now am found: Music and embodied arts in two American prisons. In S. Clift & P. Camic (Eds.), *Oxford textbook of creative arts, health, and wellbeing* (pp. 187–92). Oxford: Oxford University Press.

de Quadros, A. (2019). *Focus: Choral music in global perspective*. New York, NY: Routledge.

Risbud, S. (2003). *Goa's struggle for freedom 1946 1961: The contribution of National Congress Goa and Azad Gomantak Dal* (PhD thesis). Goa University, Taleigão.

Tavan, G. (2005). *The long, slow death of white Australia*. Melbourne: Scribe Publications.

CHAPTER 3

Displacement and Music Education: Background, Issues, Paradigms

André de Quadros

Bodies—Spaces—Places—Heartbreak

Small boats overflowing with black and brown bodies, families fleeing from war with their possessions on their backs, asylum-seekers detained on the US-Mexico border, drowned children,[1] mountains of discarded life vests littering the Mediterranean coast, refugee boats being turned away from Australia—these images persist and stories abound as we wrestle with what this global movement of human beings means.

The images of displaced people constructed in the "here and now" with attendant narratives and public commentary seem to suggest that displacement is a recent human phenomenon. This erases the very foundations of the ways in which several countries came into existence. The United States, for example, was founded on the migration of English settlers fleeing religious persecution —the Pilgrims, the uprooting of Africans and coercing them into slavery,[2] the banishing of Native Americans from their lands (Dunbar-Ortiz, 2014). Likewise, Australia was founded as a penal colony with the exporting of convicted persons from the UK, and is inscribed with the genocide of Aboriginal people (Tatz et al., 2011). The partition of British India into Muslim-majority Pakistan and Hindu-majority India resulted in the displacement and mass migration of more than 15 million people (Dalrymple, 2015).[3] In short, displacement is not a feature of the twenty-first century. Human civilization has met this problem head-on for better or for worse since earliest times.

The United Nations High Commission for Refugees (UNHCR) reports that there are 70.8 million displaced persons worldwide,[4] comprising 25.9 million refugees, 3.5 million asylum-seekers,[5] and 41.3 million internally displaced persons. The World Health Organization states, "In the context of emergencies, displaced people are people who have had to leave their homes as a result of a natural, technological or deliberate event."[6] Dryden-Peterson (2011) outlines three main ways that children (and their families) are forcibly dislocated— through social unrest, war, and when social/economic life are unsustainable. The University of British Columbia categorizes human displacement into "(1)

Disaster Induced Displacement,[7] (2) Conflict Induced Displacement or (3) Development Induced Displacement."[8] More powerful terms have been used, such as "uprooting" and "forcibly uprooted," directing us to the vast populations who have been violently moved or abducted (see, for example, Colson, 2003).

In defining displacement, the Norwegian Refugee Council (NRC) and the Internal Displacement Monitoring Centre (IDMC) indicate the difficulty in distinguishing between voluntary and forced migration particularly when migration can take place as a pre-emptive and adaptive measure to avoid what appear to be emerging as provocations for displacement. In its document, *Global Estimates 2014*, the NRC and IDMC conclude that in at least 119 countries, the displacement of approximately 22 million people took place in 2013, three times the number of those displaced as a result of violence and conflict.

Yet these figures of refugees, forced migrants, and refugees form only a portion of the displaced peoples in the world, as we have chosen to define them in this book. We conceptualize displacement more broadly than the three UNHCR categories above, because these images of displacement—refugees, asylum-seekers, and internally displaced persons—are limited, and do not account for, as Bhabha (1994) expressed, those who suffer the "fragmented and schizophrenic decentring of the self" and the fractured, oppositional, and conflictual nature of identity and body. Further, the UNHCR's figures obscure other global population migration and micro- and local dislocation, the deported and invisibly displaced, internal displacement at the intersection of other types of oppression, non-locational types of displacement, and those displaced by the rapid onset of climate change.[9]

The highlighting of flight of refugees and asylum-seekers—both in this essay and in broader discussions of displacement—has deflected attention away from the invisibly displaced by deportation and enforced disappearance. Indeed, one sees refugees entering the affluent world but we see little of their fate after they are deported by governments.[10] "When Deported, You Become Nothing"[11] can be said for almost all deportations worldwide. In 2019, I co-directed a musical ensemble, Common Ground Voices/La Frontera,[12] making music and engaging in communities in southern California and in Tijuana, Mexico. It was in Tijuana, that I observed firsthand the horrendous social problems created by US deportations. Thousands of people have been deported to Tijuana, frequently after spending decades in the US, and with no familial ties and connections in Mexico.

Enforced disappearances, defined in Article 2 of the UN's *International Convention for the Protection of All Persons from Enforced Disappearance*[13] as "the arrest, detention, abduction … followed by a refusal to acknowledge the …

whereabouts of the disappeared person"[14] have rarely been considered within the larger framework of displacement. The numbers are difficult to pinpoint, and victims of enforced disappearance are invisible, with absent bodies and voices (Scovazzi & Citroni, 2007)—out of sight and out of mind, tragically.[15] The visibly displaced can be identified in a way that the disappeared cannot be—the abducted are invisible except to their families and local communities (Vidal, 1982, p. 60).

Furthermore, the standard discourse does not take non-locational displacement into account. Such displacement can be spiritual or cultural, and it can immobilize a person involuntarily. Spiritual homelessness frequently takes place when people have been expelled from their spiritual congregations for perceived transgressions, for example; and it is also manifested in denying people access to spiritual life, which, in many cases may be life-sustaining. Although discussions of spiritual homelessness (see, for example, Christensen, 2013) have mostly concentrated on indigenous peoples, some anecdotal narratives of LGBTQ+ people who have been forced out of religious communities indicate that spiritual homelessness is a field to be explored in greater depth.

Cultural displacement is akin to spiritual homelessness. Bammer (1994) discusses culture as place and home, and "cultural displacement" as either the colonizing of a local culture, or the physical dislocation from one's native culture. The eradication of culture by globalization, geopolitical forces, urbanization, and other dynamics means the erasure of traditional forms of expression, and populations can be left in place, but the societal and physical place is eroded and the social fabric stripped of tradition. Of particular relevance to music is the loss of intangible cultural heritage, an area considerably less reported than the loss of ancient architecture and objects—visible and tangible creations of past civilizations. Such loss contributes to and is a consequence of cultural and spiritual dislocation.[16]

In addition to spiritual and cultural displacement, involuntary immobility is another facet of displacement that is insufficiently understood: when one's environment has changed dramatically, perhaps unrecognizably, and one feels no longer at home in what had been familiar, a sense of displacement could be experienced. Spiritual and cultural displacement and involuntary immobility are all manifestations of non-locational displacement, where silencing can take place.

The more I studied displacement and opened several frames of view, I discovered ways of thinking about displacement that extended my preconceptions. One thing led to another and the greater was my realization that there were no hard and fast definitions, but that the displaced peoples of the world encompassed a massive and diverse population. What, one may ask, is the value in constructing displacement so widely? Why not focus on refugees and asylum-seekers, for example? Or, if we cast such a wide net in conceptualizing displacement, do these displacements become simplistic constructions? Or, in stringing them together, is there not a danger in losing the distinctions that belong in each displacement?

Displacement is clearly a wide and deep set of terms, and while it may be confusing to draw all these differences together (e.g., from sexual violence to war refugees, from homelessness to incarceration), I found great merit in constructing a connection between all of these, employing Wittgenstein's (1967) "family resemblance" philosophical idea. Wittgenstein argued that where multiple ideas are connected by a single feature they may indeed be coupled by a chain of interrelating likenesses, where no single feature is shared by all things. He illustrated this by talking about games; they could be played on a field, or on a board, or be between competitive teams or individual players, but in some ways, they have overlapping similarities. Thus, when one draws together these vastly differing displacements, one might argue that there are indeed overlapping likenesses that call us to consider them together, and that space, place, body, and spirit of the displaced are joined by resemblance, allowing for confluence and connectivity in understanding the disadvantage, heartbreak, trauma, struggles, and opportunities in displacement as a whole.

In this tangled and slippery taxonomical and terminological landscape, for the purposes of this book, rather than defining displacement, a collection of key terms may be useful. Drawing from critical refugee studies, I offer these terms to frame our thinking but not to describe and enumerate displaced persons and diminish their agency to make them objects of pity and recipients of charity. Le Espiritu and Duong (2018) expand as follows, "The hyperfocus on suffering, and the outpouring of outrage and concern over dead and injured refugees, has become a substitute for serious analysis of the geopolitical conditions that produced their displacement in the first instance. Constructed for Western consumption, these spectacular(ized) images render invisible and inaudible displaced people's everyday and out-of-sight struggles as well as their triumphs as they manage war's impact on their lives" (Lubkemann, 2008, p. 36; Hyndman, 2010). In assembling this list, I considered what other researchers and practitioners in the field of displacement use as key terms, presented in Figures 3.1, 3.2 and 3.3.

FIGURE 3.1
Key terms 1.
GRAPHIC DESIGNER: ANISSA
MARTÍNEZ LOZANO

FIGURE 3.2
Key terms 2.
GRAPHIC DESIGNER: ANISSA
MARTÍNEZ LOZANO

FIGURE 3.3
Key terms 3.
GRAPHIC DESIGNER: ANISSA
MARTÍNEZ LOZANO

What Does the Literature Tell Us?

In endeavoring to understand how music education might draw on the work of activists and researchers, I examined a wide range of literature outside of the music education field and within it. The material on displacement external to music education falls mainly into: the mental health of the displaced and the emotional impact of displacement; the community health of such populations; forced migration and refugee studies; and specific interventions using education and the arts. In this section, I signal to some of the literature that may be helpful to the way in which music educators might find direction. This literature survey is in no way intended to be comprehensive; such a review would lie outside the scope or purpose of this chapter.

In studying the mental health of displaced persons, Colson (2003) refers to displacement as a chronic and inescapable condition, the health-related manifestation of what Mowafi (2011) identifies as non-communicable diseases, infectious diseases and malnutrition, women's and reproductive health, mental health, and challenges to the health care system. Not only affecting health, Good (1996) finds that displacement may cause extreme disruptions to life: stress, anger, bitterness, loss, physical health problems, depression, anxiety, gender conflicts, power struggles, behavior pathologies, and issues related specifically to the elderly and women. Further complicating mental health, some displaced persons are placed in transitional spaces, such as refugee centers, which Weston and Lenette (2016) call "accidental spaces" where the population is neither connected by affinity or cultural similarity. This concept of accidental space is carried forward into other forced sites, such as prisons, where residents are left to build social networks and other groupings with relative strangers—a task that takes a toll on the mental health of displaced persons.

The negative implications of homesickness are an important aspect of understanding and working with people who are displaced. Studying forced migrants in India, Gupta and Singh (2018) suggest that researchers and practitioners generally focus on situations where the government does not provide support programs. Correspondingly, in India, Snodgrass, Upadhyay, Debnath, and Lacy (2016) compare displaced villagers with people who were allowed to stay in their villages in safe zones and found that those who relocated suffered greater mental health impacts. The overwhelming conclusions from this literature are that displacement results in trauma-related mental illness (see, for example, Bhugra & Gupta, 2011).

There is a relatively larger body of literature in forced migration studies, identified by Chimi (2009) as a natural progression from the field previously described as "refugee studies." Associated with the forced migration literature is the phenomenon of place attachment. Scannell and Gifford (2010) suggest a three-way definition of place (person, process, place): (1) who is attached, (2) how does the attachment manifest, and (3) the object of attachment. And, persons become attached to place to support survival, self-regulation, and continuity (Scannell & Gifford, 2010). In a study of female forced migrants in an asylum living center in Munich, Germany, Witteborn (2011) found that asylum-seekers felt homesick and lacked a sense of new space and place leading to feeling "arrested, stuck, isolated" (p. 1143) highlighting the importance of social connection and mobility in forming new place attachments. In a later study, Witteborn (2015) outlined how forced migrants realize their potential when they were marginalized outsiders. Despite being immobile in their new locations, the migrants utilized technology to learn new languages, to maintain friendships and as an expression of identity. In a systematic study, Camino et al. (2005) investigated how the loss of one's identity forces the constructing of a new identity, and this is a common feature in almost all displacement circumstances. New identities are assumed as well as imposed.

In the edited book *Music and Displacement: Diasporas, Mobilities, and Dislocations in Europe and Beyond*, Levi and Scheding (2010) connect musicology and displacement. In this publication, Petersen (2010) writes about one of the most striking of compositions connecting to displacement, Schoenberg's *A Survivor from Warsaw*. Outside the genre of Western art music, there have been thousands of musical expressions, from formally composed to improvised, that tell the stories of the displaced. Reyes (1999) studied the way in which resettlement was reflected in musical expression by Vietnamese forced migrants in the 1980s and 1990s. Among the many songs written by Nidal Karam, a Syrian refugee, "Safarna Ala Europa"[17] is reportedly known by all Arab refugees.[18]

Specifically, in music education and displacement, the literature of interventions with the populations covered in this book is enormous. Although these studies in incarceration, gender identity, sexual orientation, and refugees are numerous, rarely are they interrogating with displacement as a lens. Hence, the theorizing on this subject is at an early stage. The music education studies that expressly consider displacement are those that focus on asylum-seekers and refugees. Particularly significant among these is a study of music-making undertaken in an Australian detention center by Weston and Lenette (2016). They found that music-making created a unique cultural space that encouraged a commonality of the detention culture. In the same context, Lenette and Procopis (2016) examined the impact on music facilitators who work with asylum-seekers in the Scattered People[19] project based in Australia, discovering the heavy toll it exacted on those who witness the emotional devastation of detention.

In a mixed-methods study in Colombia, Zapata and Hargreaves (2018) discovered that musical participation had a significant impact on the self-esteem of children. Ailbhe Kenny's work with choirs and asylum-seekers in six Irish centers—the Song Seeking project—focuses on integration. Kenny seeks to find commonality between asylum-seekers of different backgrounds, through which she intends to understand the cultural needs of this population.[20] Millar and Warwick (2018) examined the impact of music-making with young Yazidi refugees, finding that such activities have a positive impact on their wellbeing while improving their sense of agency.

There is clearly a need to study displacement in all the various demographics in this book. If we were to take the Wittgenstein approach further, one could argue that the studies of displacement with refugees and asylum-seekers could inform similar place-based studies with homelessness, poverty, and other manifestations of violent exclusion.

Music Education and a Way Forward

The purpose of this book, as indicated in Chapter 1, is to connect multiple dimensions of displacement to music education. In 2017, Kính T. Vũ and I published a peer-reviewed article in the *International Journal of Inclusive*

Education, discussing Swedish choirs as a locus for welcoming forced migrants and refugees (de Quadros & Vu, 2017). The formative work and preparation for the article led us slowly and surely to the realization that, as music educators, we had given little attention to what music education might mean in the particular contexts of displaced populations. Our thinking about refugees and asylum-seekers provoked us to reflect on the politics of place and space making, the countless people who are displaced within and from their own countries, and, significantly, to critical questions in music education. Did they have access to music education? What kind of music education did they encounter? Did their music education experiences emphasize, erase, give voice to their displacement? Was their trauma from displacement recognized as an identity in the classroom and ensemble? How can the music education process be a way of understanding displacement and its relationship to global injustice? And many more such questions.

That is, fundamentally, the way in which this book came about. In the initial conversations, it became evident to us that music educators had only recently started to think about the intersections of poverty, race, sexual orientation and gender identity on the music education environment. The rise of displacement should be a matter of increased concern to music educators, as it is one of the most compelling and urgent issues of our time. And, although we have begun to understand about displacement, as evidenced by the work of many authors in this book, the music education field has yet to develop paradigms of work that consider intersections between music education and displacement in their many forms. In other words, not only are displaced people absent in classrooms, ensembles, and other music education sites but they are missing from the discourse. Our goal is to introduce displacement as *a* lens through which music education can be constructed and conducted so that the identities of displaced persons are recognized and honored.

We argue that, although millions of people are displaced, and because they are routinely deprived, very few find themselves in music education environments. Even when some displaced persons find themselves in music classrooms and ensembles, their identities and traumas may not be noticed, still less given expression. It is not just about access, as I will discuss further below, but also a question of representation and agency.

An important step toward recognizing the diversity of learners represented in Western music classrooms and ensembles and general music was manifested in the multicultural or global music education movement (Moore et al., 2010). Initially, this movement encouraged music educators only to broaden their repertoires away from a white, Eurocentric stance. Partly, the intention of multiculturalism was to build relationships and understandings across cultures, an argument that was situated in the idea that music is a universal language. In this regard, culture is seen as static, historical, idyllic, sometimes exoticized, rather than changing, even disappearing. Conventional multiculturalism also privileges national cultures at the expense of local sub-cultures (Gupta & Ferguson, 1992). Benhabib's (2002) argument, that culture is not a well-defined whole, is a springboard for challenging existing notions of multiculturalism. Her provocations strengthen the need for music educators to appreciate the classroom or the ensemble as a contested, diverse, and heterogeneous space in need of meaning-making (Schippers, 2010). Multiculturalism has now evolved to include discussions about justice, broadly conceived (see, for example Campbell, 2018). In similar fashion, Ladson-Billings (2014), who theorized culturally relevant pedagogy, reflects on her previous work and suggests that since culture is constantly changing, scholarship, theory and practice must change and adjust accordingly. Thus, music educators need to reframe repertoire and process in terms of new realities. It is fundamental that music educators attend to displacement by allowing for diverse place-based cultural worldviews to be represented.

One of the key questions must therefore be: what kind of music education makes sense? Grouping all displaced people together undergoing one type of music education risks making the displaced persons the other, the ones to be included, even welcomed. Classifying them as underserved populations needing music, making them recipients of musical charity, ennobling the providers to forgive them for not producing the beautiful sounds typically expected from the more able, and assuming that being oppressed equates with lacking culture is potentially an act of structural or symbolic violence[21] (Araújo & Cambria, 2013). This symbolic violence is all too prevalent. Indeed, as Bates (2016) points out, "Included within this symbolic violence is the conviction that music education can help impoverished participants develop important personal and social skills, thought to be characteristic of the upper or middle classes, and thereby overcome a "culture of poverty" (n.p.).

To further a discussion of challenges in this work, I provide an illustration of a musical activity from 2016. This example is intended to be self-explanatory to the perceptive reader.

Michael/Ahmad, Hallelujah/Alhamdulillah—Almost Missing the Boat

In 2016, I was directing a musical leadership course in Sweden. As part of this course, I brought a group of course participants—music educators and choral conductors from Sweden and other countries, including the US—to a Swedish middle and high school. As part of an institutional initiative in Sweden, this school had been hosting a group of Afghan refugee boys in daily classes. Our task was to engage and empower these refugee boys through music-making. Our group of music educators entered a room and met about ten Afghan boys whose Swedish was non-existent, and English was minimal. The boys responded to each musical activity in a desultory fashion, lacking enthusiasm but without marked resistance. Imagine these Afghan boys encountering music education in the Western style!

One of the musical leadership course participants proceeded to introduce the song, "Michael, row the boat ashore," and the boys learned the song enough to repeat by rote. At the end of the song, I invited the course participant/song leader to provide an explanation of the song. As she went through the origins of the song, I saw the boys losing concentration and interest. After she finished, seeing an opportunity, I attempted a different path. I had a conversation with the boys that went something like this:

AdQ:	How did you come to Europe?
Afghan boys:	We came by boat.
AdQ:	I know. I have other Afghan friends who came to safety by boat.
Afghan boys:	Really? You know Afghan refugees who were in a boat!
AdQ:	Yes, we have two Afghan boys who are part of my family, and they went to Australia by boat. So, I know how much you wanted to get to land. You were impatient, hungry, restless, worried, right?
Afghan boys:	Yes, it was terrifying, really horrific.
AdQ:	That's what this song is about. It's about getting the boat to shore. Michael is the name of the person who is steering the boat. Let's call him Ahmad. And do you know what "hallelujah" means?
Afghan boys:	No, we don't.
AdQ:	Well, "hallelujah" means the same as "alhamdulillah." So, now let's sing the song with different words: Ahmad, steer the boat ashore, alhamdulillah.

We sang the song again, and it was different, filled with passion and enthusiasm, evoking memory and trauma. Understanding, indeed critiquing, the illustration above in terms of Gay's (2010) culturally responsive teaching helps to vitalize the central purpose of music education, not just the purpose of musicking with the displaced. Gay argues for an approach that is validating, comprehensive, multidimensional, empowering, transformative, and emancipatory. The encounter above can be seen as carrying some of the seeds of the six central features of culturally responsive teaching that Gay describes.

Concluding Remarks

In the summer of 2015, I was co-teaching the Empowering Song course, focusing on progressive and imaginative modes, paradigms, and processes of music education. The Empowering Song approach had its genesis in the prison teaching that my colleagues and I had undertaken since 2012. Kính Vũ visited one of the sessions and, during an improvisation, I observed him curled on the floor in an embryonic, self-protective posture. The participants were scribbling thoughts on the blackboard, and Kính wrote, "My body was left on the street" (see Figure 3.4). At that stage, I had had no understanding of the abandonment that Kính had suffered. The music education classroom is where he told his story and where we listened. Two years later, when we decided to proceed with this book, I asked him to place this sentence as the opening title.

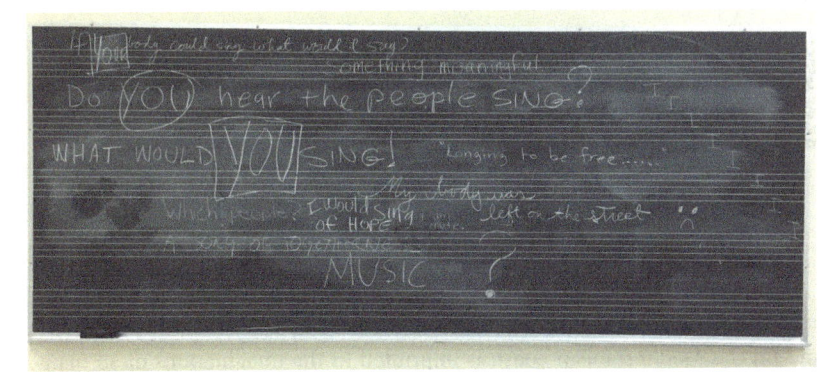

FIGURE 3.4   Text from the Empowering Song course with Kính Vũ's writing.
PHOTOGRAPH: ANDRÉ DE QUADROS

The displaced have stories to tell, and their stories are generally told by journalists, scholars, musical leaders, people like me. But they—the displaced — can tell their own stories, and the music education environment may be where it can take place. As argued earlier, the musical storytelling and repertoires of displaced people in the music education setting may then serve not only to empower the displaced, but to make a major cultural contribution to enlarging music education skills, knowledge, and values, and for us to understand how governments and power elites perpetuate injustice, and commit crimes against humanity. Such understandings are necessary precursors for musical activism.

The way forward for music educators is complex. Transcending narrow identities and understanding the trauma of displacement allow music educators to build a powerfully engaged, integrative and holistic approach. Such an approach would, of necessity, seek to dismantle existing habits of teaching (see, for example, Rendon, 2014), the familiar paradigms of music education that fetishize sonic products and narrow performance outcomes (see, for example, Howe et al., 2020). Additionally, the adherence to sharing a dominant culture as a means of welcome may be an imposition on forced migrants. Contrastingly, educators and community leaders make the assumption that migrants bring with them the culture of their country of origin. Paradoxically, migrant students may not have any familiarity with the music of their origin, given the possible transitory nature of their lives (Karlsen, 2013). The aspiration for an empowering, culturally responsible pedagogy makes the act of music-making essentially a means by which the displaced become writers of their destiny, and their narratives demand being inscribed in the centrality of the way in which music education is conceived and the fabric of society changed.

 VIDEO 3.1   Ndal Kram's album Safarna Ala Europa.
The video accompanying this chapter is freely available online at
https://doi.org/10.6084/m9.figshare.12445625

Notes

1   The image of the three-year old Kurdish boy, Alan Kurdi, whose drowned body was found on the Mediterranean coast, is imprinted in the imaginations of so many. Tima Kurdi (2019) writes about Alan Kurdi and the fate of other Syrian-Kurdish refugees in *The boy on the beach: my family's escape from Syria and our hope for a new home.*

2   Bryan Stevenson (2014) establishes a historic through-line connecting African-American slavery to contemporary incarceration.

3   William Dalrymple (2015) details the calamitous legacy of Indian Partition in the New Yorker; see https://www.newyorker.com/magazine/2015/06/29/
the-great-divide-books-dalrymple

4   UNHCR The UN Refugee Agency tracks international data and reports this in "Figures at a Glance" (see https://www.unhcr.org/figures-at-a-glance.html). The figures reported above are current at the time of going to press.

5 William Blum explains asylum-seekers' motivations in The Anti-Empire Report #158: Why do they flee? https://williamblum.org/aer/read/158

6 See https://www.who.int/environmental_health_emergencies/displaced_people/en/

7 See "Global Estimates 2014: People displaced by disasters," https://reliefweb.int/sites/reliefweb.int/files/resources/201409-global-estimates.pdf

8 See https://wiki.ubc.ca/Human_Displacement#cite_note-5

9 Consider, for example, displacement when women flee domestic violence, when the poor are evicted from housing (see, for example, Desmond, 2016), when women and children are subjected to human trafficking (see, for example, Shelley, 2010), when LGBTQ+ persons escape persecution (see, for example, Freedman et al. 2017; Spijkerboer, 2013). Baldwin and Bettini (2017), discuss global migration as a result of climate change. For further information on disappearing countries, see https://www.activesustainability.com/climate-change/countries-risk-disappearing-climate-change/#8 and the effect on large countries such as India in the World Economic Forum's article "In Why India is most at risk from climate change." See https://www.weforum.org/agenda/2018/03/india-most-vulnerable-country-to-climate-change

10 Sarah Stillman (2018), writing "When Deportation is a Death Sentence" in *The New Yorker*, describes the fate of hundreds of thousands of immigrants deported from the US in https://www.newyorker.com/magazine/2018/01/15/when-deportation-is-a-death-sentence?utm_campaign=cm&utm_source=crm&utm_brand=tny&utm_mailing=TNY_SubMOW_Immigration_032919&utm_medium=email

11 This is an investigative account of deportations, a story that is exceedingly prevalent: https://www.politico.com/magazine/story/2019/04/19/displaced-puebla-deportation-immigration-new-york-photos-226657

12 Co-directed by Emilie Amrein and André de Quadros, Common Ground Voices/La Frontera made music at the border wall and in cities on either side. For further information, see https://www.cgvlafrontera.org/english

13 See https://www.ohchr.org/EN/HRBodies/CED/Pages/ConventionCED.aspx

14 See https://www.amnesty.org/en/what-we-do/disappearances/

15 For further information, see Latin America: The region with the highest number of enforced disappearances, https://latinamericanpost.com/23187-latin-america-the-region-with-the-highest-number-of-enforced-disappearances. The *Stolen Generations* in Australia, where children were removed from their families by government agencies in collaboration with Christian missionaries is another example of legalized enforced disappearance (see, for example, Barta, 2008).

16 Thiesmeyer (2003) argues that knowledge can be displaced into other forms of expression, or simply unexpressed. In looking at forced Christian conversion, and the suppression of native languages, cultural, and spiritual life, Treuer (2019) lends weight to Thiesmeyer's arguments.

17 See https://www.youtube.com/watch?v=knJESy-paXU

18 In 'Every Arab refugee in the world knows this song,' Gautama Mehta describes a music lesson for young refugees in Greece, where the children sang this song. See https://www.politico.eu/article/every-arab-refugee-in-the-world-knows-this-song-safarna-ala-europa-migration-news-music/

19 Scattered People creates conditions for asylum-seekers to tell their stories through music. For further information, see https://australianculturalfund.org.au/projects/scattered-people/

20 For further information, see https://www.mic.ul.ie/news/2018-11-06/mic-lecturer-awarded-eu90000-under-national-creativity-fund-for-song-seeking

21 Bourdieu (1999) and Galtung (1990) used the terms "symbolic power" and "symbolic violence" in discussions of exclusion and privilege within the social order. Christopher Small (1998) connects these terms to Western concert music.

References

Araújo, S., & Cambria, V. (2013). Sound praxis, poverty, and social participation: Perspectives from a collaborative study in Rio de Janeiro. *Yearbook for Traditional Music, 45*, 28–42. doi:10.5921/yeartradmusi.45.2013.0028

Baldwin, A., & Bettini, G. (2017). *Life adrift: Climate change, migration, critique*. Lanham, MD: Rowman & Littlefield.

Bammer, A. (1994). *Displacements: Cultural identities in question*. Bloomington, IN: Indiana University Press.

Barta, T. (2008) Sorry, and not sorry, in Australia: How the apology to the stolen generations buried a history of genocide. *Journal of Genocide Research, 10*(2), 201–214. doi:10.1080/14623520802065438

Bates, V. C. (2016). Foreword: How can music educators address poverty and inequality? *Action, Criticism, and Theory for Music Education, 15*(1), 1–9. Retrieved from act.maydaygroup.org/articles/Bates15_1.pdf

Benhabib, S. (2002). *The claims of culture: Equality and diversity in the global era*. Princeton, NJ: Princeton University Press.

Bhabha, H. K. (1994). *The location of culture*. London: Routledge.

Bhugra, D., & Gupta, S. (2011). *Migration and mental health*. Cambridge: Cambridge University Press.

Bourdieu, P. (1999). *Language and symbolic power*. Cambridge, MA: Harvard University Press.

Camino, L. A., DeVoe P., & Krulfeld, R. M. (2005). *Reconstructing lives, recapturing meaning: Refugee identity, gender, and culture change*. Abingdon: Taylor & Francis.

Campbell, P. S. (2018). *Music, education, and diversity: Bridging cultures and communities*. New York, NY: Teachers College Press.

Chimni, B. S. (2009). The birth of a discipline: From refugee to forced migration studies. *Journal of Refugee Studies, 21*(1), 11–29.

Christensen, J. (2013.) "Our home, our way of life": Spiritual homelessness and the sociocultural dimensions of Indigenous homelessness in the Northwest Territories (NWT), Canada. *Social & Cultural Geography, 14*(7), 804–828. doi:10.1080/14649365.2013.822089

Colson, E. (2003). Forced migration and the anthropological response. *Journal of Refugee Studies, 16*(1), 1–18.

de Quadros, A., & Vu, K. T. (2017). At home, song, and fika—portraits of Swedish choral initiatives amidst the refugee crisis. *International Journal of Inclusive Education, 21*(11), 1113–1127. doi:10.1080/13603116.2017.1350319

Desmond, M. (2016). *Evicted: Poverty and profit in the American city*. New York, NY: Crown.

Dryden-Peterson, S. (2011). Conflict, education and displacement. *Conflict & Education, 1*(1), 1–5.

Dunbar-Ortiz, R. (2014). *An indigenous peoples' history of the United States*. Boston, MA: Beacon Press.

Freedman, J., Kıvılcım, Z., & Özgür, N. (2017). *A gendered approach to the Syrian refugee crisis*. New York, NY: Routledge.

Galtung, J. (1990). Cultural violence. *Journal of Peace Research, 27*(3), 291–305.

Gay, G. (2018). *Culturally responsive teaching: Theory, research, and practice*. New York, NY: Teachers College Press.

Gupta, A., & Ferguson, J. (1991). Beyond "culture": Space, identity, and the politics of difference. *Cultural Anthropology, 7*, 6–23.

Gupta, D., & Singh, P. K. (2018). The hidden cost of development—a review of mental health issues of displaced tribal populations in India. *Journal of Public Health, 26*(6), 717–723. https://doi.org/10.1007/s10389-018-0913-9

Howe, E., de Quadros, A., Vu, K. T., & Clark, A. (2020). The tuning of the music educator: A pedagogy of the "common good" for the twenty-first century. In I. Yob & E. Jorgensen (Eds.), *Humane music education for the common good*. Bloomington, IN: Indiana University Press.

Karlsen, S. (2013). Immigrant students and the "homeland music": Meanings, negotiations and implications. *Research Studies in Music Education, 35*(2), 161–177.

Kurdi, T. (2019). *The boy on the beach: My family's escape from Syria and our hope for a new home*. Toronto: Simon & Schuster.

Ladson-Billings, G. (2014). Culturally relevant pedagogy 2.0: a.k.a. the remix. *Harvard Educational Review, 84*(1), 74–84.

Le Espiritu, Y., & Duong, L. (2018). Feminist refugee epistemology: Reading displacement in Vietnamese and Syrian refugee art. *SIGNS, 43*(3), 587–615. http://dx.doi.org/10.1086/695300

Lenette, C., & Procopis, B. (2016). "They change us": The social and emotional impacts on music facilitators of engaging in music and singing with asylum seekers. *Music and Arts in Action, 5*(2), 55–68.

Levi, E., & Scheding, F. (2010). *Music and displacement: Diasporas, mobilities, and dislocations in Europe and beyond.* Lanham, MD: Scarecrow Press.

Millar, O., & Warwick, I. (2018) Music and refugees' wellbeing in contexts of protracted displacement. *Health Education Journal, 78*(1), 67–80. https://doi.org/10.1177/0017896918785991

Moore, M. C., Ewell, P., & MENC, The National Association for Music Education (U.S.). (2010). *Kaleidoscope of cultures: A celebration of multicultural research and practice: Proceedings of the MENC/University of Tennessee national symposium on multicultural music.* Lanham, MD: Rowman & Littlefield.

Petersen, P. (2010). Dimensions of silencing: On Nazi anti-Semitism in musical displacement. In E. Levi & F. Scheding (Eds.), *Music and displacement: Diasporas, mobilities, and dislocations in Europe and beyond* (pp. 31–42). Lanham, MD: Scarecrow Press.

Rendón, L. I. (2014). *Sentipensante (sensing/thinking) pedagogy: Educating for wholeness, social justice and liberation.* Sterling, VA: Stylus Publishing.

Reyes, A. (1999). *Songs of the caged, songs of the free: Music and the Vietnamese refugee experience.* Philadelphia, PA: Temple University Press.

Scannell, L., & Gifford, R. (2010). Defining place attachment: A tripartite organizing frame-work. *Journal of Environmental Psychology, 30*(1), 1–10. https://doi.org/10.1016/j.jenvp.2009.09.006

Schippers, H. (2010). *Facing the music: Shaping music education from a global perspective.* Oxford: Oxford University Press.

Schoenberg, A., & Monod, J. L. (1979). *A survivor from Warsaw: For narrator, men's chorus, and orchestra, op. 46.* Hillsdale, NY: Boelke-Bomart.

Scovazzi, T., & Citroni, G. (2007). *The struggle against enforced disappearance and the 2007 United Nations convention.* Leiden: Martinus Nijhoff Publishers.

Shelley, L. I. (2010). *Human trafficking: A global perspective.* Cambridge: Cambridge University Press.

Small, C. (1998). *Musicking: The meanings of performing and listening.* Middletown, CT: Wesleyan University Press.

Spijkerboer, T. (2013). *Fleeing homophobia: Sexual orientation, gender identity and asylum.* Abingdon: Routledge.

Stevenson, B. (2015). *Just mercy: A story of justice and redemption.* New York, NY: Spiegel & Grau.

Tatz, C., Monash University, & Castan Centre for Human Rights Law. (2011). *Genocide in Australia: By accident or design?* Melbourne: Monash University.

Thiesmeyer, L. (2003). *Discourse and silencing: Representation and the language of displacement.* Amsterdam: J. Benjamins.

Treuer, D. (2019). *The heartbeat of Wounded Knee: Native America from 1890 to the present.* New York, NY: Riverhead Book.

Vidal, H. (1982). *Dar la Vida por la Vida: La Agrupación Chilena de Familiares de Detenidos-Desaparecidos* (Ensayo de Antropología Simbólica).

Weston, D., & Lenette, C. (2016). Performing freedom: The role of music-making in creating a community in asylum seeker detention centres. *International Journal of Community Music, 9*(2), 121–134.

Witteborn, S. (2011). Constructing the forced migrant and the politics of space and place-making. *Journal of Communication, 61,* 1142–1160.

Witteborn, S. (2015). Becoming (im)perceptible: Forced migrants and virtual practice. *Journal of Refugee Studies, 28*(3), 350–367.

Wittgenstein, L. (1967). *Philosophical investigations.* New York, NY: Macmillan.

Zapata, G., & Hargreaves, D. (2018). The effects of musical activities on the self-esteem of displaced children in Colombia. *Psychology of Music, 46*(4), 540–550.

CHAPTER 4

My Body Was Left on the Street: Making Pathways toward Home

Kính T. Vũ

> I don't know how to grieve. I've never been brave enough or courageous enough to face the demons that might pop out of my suitcase. I did not notice that my country was lost, that my name and nationality were taken from me, that my mother and my homeland were lost. Where are they? They aren't in the bottom of my bag.
>
> KÍNH

∵

"Leave your baggage at the door." That is what my school music teachers told me before band and chorus rehearsals. I contend, however, that music does not always begin from a baggage-free journey or from silence; it oftentimes emerges from the clutter and chaos of our circumstances. Music-making is informed by all the things we carry. The pebbles collected and the people met along our pathways of a life-in-progress make our musical experiences dance with vitality. While I have always struggled to unpack my baggage for the fear of discovering a horrible truth about a mysterious past, the act of music teaching has cleared a space for me to invite students and research friends to consider their baggage, unpack it, and use everything contained inside to inform their artistry. In this chapter, I too will attempt to unpack some of the contents of my baggage as a way to illuminate how displacement informs my practice of music education.

In the small act of creating this chapter, I must disclose that producing it is the most difficult writing process I have ever endeavored. Getting up in the morning to write made me sad. Daily, tears dripped from guilt-ridden eyes that feared looking into the past. Too many times I simply abandoned the effort and moved on with the day. Mustering any amount of courage to write this personal and professional story was a monumental effort that might look on the surface to be nothing more than a self-centered account of events from my birth in Việt Nam to the work I do in present-day Boston. I share this story with readers as a way to show solidarity with those who have been dispossessed, dislocated, and disheartened by the mysteries of their own pasts. Marie McCarthy (2007) argued that "[s]tories woven out of the experiences of teachers…serve to bridge the generations, to pass on the torch and keep the flame alive" (p. 9). Where grieving a lost homeland was once foreclosed to me, writing this story invited me to gaze into the past to ponder how it was that my body was left on the street and what that abandonment means for me as a music educator. As it was articulated in Chapter 3, my first visit to André de Quadros's Empowering Song course provoked a particular way for me to consider my lived experiences, creating further moments to query where and how my personal and professional lives might converge or diverge. Writing also provides a place where I might encourage other teachers around the world to keep going, to keep lighting the world with their music and music teaching.

Abandonment, Evacuation, and Resettlement

Between 2011 and 2019, I spent winter, spring, and summer breaks volunteering at one orphanage in Hồ Chí Minh City playing music for and with children and their caregivers (Vu, Saetta, & Shekleton, 2018). There have been visits during which I had witnessed the intake of an abandoned baby. The place becomes frenetic as the message spreads across each ward. Quickly, women gather around the infant to assess its needs and simultaneously begin shouting commands at onlookers. Once the child is bathed and made comfortable in one of the many beds, constant watch is provided by caregivers working in shifts whose sole responsibility is to look after the baby, the newest member of their family.

Wollons (2009) outlined the age-old practices of abandonment and infanticide describing them as "solutions to poverty, illegitimacy, or family crises" (p. 1). Additionally, the International Committee of the Red Cross (2004) indicated that armed conflicts, for example, may cause children to become "separated from their families" (p. 12). While I may never know the reason for having been abandoned at the end of the American War in Việt Nam, my abandonment cannot be viewed in reductionist terms. It may never have been the intention of parents to permanently disown their newborns. In some cases, as Ward (2017) explained in his companion text to the Public Broadcasting Service (PBS) documentary, *The Vietnam War* (Botstein, Burns, & Novick, 2017), parents deposited their children in orphanages or other care centers to protect them from danger with intentions of retrieving them when the war ended. For an untold number of families, those children could never be reclaimed after the bombs and bullets ceased, because they were evacuated prior to South Việt Nam's fall to its northern neighbor. Leshkowich (2012) used Anna Tsing's *Monster Stories* (1990) to describe mothers who "anonymously abandoned their infants, many of whom ultimately were adopted by foreigners" (p. 503). Leshkowich dispelled this myth noting that "[a]nonymous abandonment is rare" (p. 505).

As fighting troops encroached on Sài Gòn, the southern capital, during the final days of the American War in April 1975, fear of an all-out attack was rampant. I have been told that people barricaded themselves inside their homes or tried to escape what they thought might be a violent assault on the city. Orphanage caregivers were concerned that the Việt Cộng, communist forces based in Sài Gòn, would attack the city as they did during the Tết Offensive in January and February 1968 (Pohle, 1969). In haste, lists of orphanage occupants were fabricated, submitted to the Vietnamese Ministry of Social Services, and children were removed from the war-torn city.

In April 1975, US President Gerald Ford authorized Operation Babylift, a program that assisted American-supported orphanages to remove babies and children and bring them to the United States for future adoption. Some orphanages were not part of the official program; hence, it fell to independent citizens' initiatives to organize their own evacuations of orphans. This was the case of my departure from Sài Gòn.

The orphanage where I was abandoned received support from a woman named Betty Tisdale, the wife of an American military surgeon, and personal secretary to the late Senator Jacob Javits of New York. Saving her money and eating at hot dog stands while working in New York City, she began traveling to Việt Nam in the 1960s to volunteer at An Lạc Orphanage—Happy Place. I had an opportunity to meet *Miss Betty*, as the children called her, during visits with her in Seattle and Tết (New Year) festivals in Little Saigon, a largely Vietnamese community in Orange County, California. She told me stories about her work to support the orphanage's director Madam Vũ Thị Ngải (from whom I received my surname). Like staff at other care centers, Madam Ngải and Miss Betty were concerned about the likelihood of war permeating Sài Gòn's perimeter.

On April 4, 1975, the first of several Operation Babylift cargo planes crashed just after takeoff from Sài Gòn's commercial airport Tân Sơn Nhất. Approximately half the children and some staffers were killed when the plane made impact in a nearby rice field. This event scared government officials and orphanage caregivers; speculation abounded that a ground-to-air missile had caused the plane's destruction. It was later discovered that the rear cargo hatch somehow opened causing the plane to fall from the sky. Knowing the risks of

FIGURE 4.1
Kính at former orphanage gate
where he was abandoned in
1974/75.
PHOTOGRAPH: YEN NGUYỄN

departing the warzone, An Lạc officials had to make a choice: risk evacuation
or hunker down and weather the possibility of a violent takeover. In haste, Miss
Betty and other staffers drafted a manifest listing nearly 400 children's names
and submitted them to the Ministry. Miss Betty was told that no one over 10
years old could be included in the evacuation. On April 10, just 20 days before
the Fall of Sài Gòn, 219 children primarily from An Lạc, as well as a handful of
orphans from other care centers, were airlifted to the United States and subsequently adopted into American families (Canfield & Hansen, 1993).

Adoption is not meant to be the focus of this chapter; however, it is part of
my displacement story and pathway back to home, back to Việt Nam. While
I believe that adoption provides children with homes, families, and much-
needed love, I join Kathryn Joyce (2013) in a critique of adoption. Joyce's (2013)
book, *The Child Catchers: Rescue, Trafficking, and the New Gospel of Adoption*,
is an exposé on the "humanitarian cause" (p. 132) and "international salvation" (p. 279) of Christian adoption practices. She explained that when children came to new homes in the United States, usually with white parents who
expected gratitude for their kindness, a common narrative among adoptees
became one of loss for homeland rather than one of thankfulness for adoptive

parents. According to Kevin Vollmers, founder of Minnesota-based blog Land of Gazillion Adoptees, this savior attitude created a "power dynamic" between the people who did the saving and those children who were "saved" (Joyce, 2013, p. 280).

Los Angeles Times writer Martha Groves[1] reported my coming-to-America story when I gave a series of talks at the David Geffen School of Medicine and Mattel Children's Hospital at UCLA in 2010. It was there where I met the doctor who saved my life upon entering America in 1975. Until that UCLA visit, I had very little information about my past or the history of the war. I grew up in an American household and received excellent care by an adoptive family whose motive for adoption had its provenance with a Christian organization in the US Mid-Atlantic region. While I do not doubt that these parents loved me, they did not realize the advanced degree of my angst living as a person of color in rural and white America. To be perfectly clear, I am certain that I never asked them for information about my Việt past. What I learned about my Asian-ness came from school. In Nguyễn-Duy's 2019 play *Amputees*, the story about a Vietnamese family struggling to live in America after the war, he shared a sentiment with which I have struggled for years. Sam, the main character, recalls in his opening monologue: "I got taught my ancestral roots in fifth grade by a class seminar on how to use chopsticks. We made sounds like bing-bong and ching-chong, holding them between our gums like walruses" (p. 3). As my cultural roots were being exploited, the tension between an actual experience (i.e., living white) and one that I imagined (i.e., being Asian) created what I now look back on as two isolating/isolated spaces.

The first of these was the house environment in which I lived. To the parents who raised me, the world was a dangerous place in which people from the Middle East were terrorists, prisoners deserved what they got, and newcomers, specifically the Philadelphia "influx" (read Black/African American), were to be feared. The second space was the school and town community. There were very few people of color—any color. While this may read like a trope for many rural and suburban regions of America, the absence of diversity informed my sense of self. Having been told very little about my past, I thought that I was white. Otherness, however, emerged from the isolation which was further reified by the people who had the potential to influence me most: family unit, teachers, and peers. My sense of white personhood further deteriorated as I endured racial slurs by youth and adults. Now I was caught somewhere between being American or being Vietnamese—both and neither together.

When I return to the homeland, Việt friends and acquaintances call me Việt Kiều. This term is commonly understood among the Vietnamese community as persons who were born in Việt Nam, but were raised in other countries for myriad reasons. Fawng Daw (2012), a Vietnamese/German/American rapper living in Europe expressed the double bind of being torn between what is and what might have been in his song *I'm a Viet Kieu* (2012):

> *Born in the east, raised in the west*
> *Heart of the motherland pounding in my chest (yeah)*
> *I'm a Viet Kieu, I'm a Viet Kieu, Kieu, Kieu, Kieu. (See Video 4.1)*

The importance of these lyrics is twofold. Fawng Daw expressed a powerful sense of being one thing and wanting another while simultaneously naming something important about his identity through music. I feel both sentiments, but have never been able to express them for myself in song, word, or deed.

My Voice Was Stolen

Perhaps the price of my abandonment and subsequent adoption is the loss of the mother tongue. The language is difficult to learn, with its many tones and inflections. When I visit the homeland, I project American through my dress, speech, and attitude. While I am heartily welcomed by orphans and their care-givers, the division between us hinges on my (in)ability to speak Vietnamese, a language that perhaps is lost to me forever. During my youth and early adult-hood, singing art songs, playing euphonium, and conducting bands became an important aspect of my musical self. Each of these acts has contributed to part of who I am as a teacher. Today, I have come to consider how my Amer-ican childhood, and particularly my school-based music education might have obfuscated my Vietnamese voice, one that, had the circumstances been different, could have spoken the Tiếng Việt (language) or sung its traditional songs.

Forced loss of voice can be demonstrated by examining Disney princesses (see, for example, Downey, 1996; Tonn, 2008). The Little Mermaid, for instance, was the victim of vocal theft by the conniving sea witch Ursula. The initial benefit to the nemesis was that she could potentially enslave her victim Ariel forever. Yet, the consequence to the mermaid for relinquishing her voice in exchange for legs might have been disastrous were it not for Disney's clever storytelling in which writers made her the spokes-merfolk for mer-girl power. While it may be difficult to conjecture how Ariel felt about her bargain, it may be fair to state that regret was the least of her worries. Ursula described in her song "Poor Unfortunate Soul" an assimilation scheme to which Ariel would have to adhere in order to please her man and conform to social norms of a foreign land (literally land rather than ocean). Additionally, she would have to give up her home, abandoning visitation rights with her sisters and father.

Ariel gained one thing and surrendered another. Assimilation became a survival strategy, but at what cost?[2]

I never considered how a music education could be an assimilation strategy with the potential to colonize its participants until enrolling in a doctoral program. In her essay on fallibility, Jorgensen (2003) noted that public education is a "profoundly political process" (p. 67). The price of becoming American was my silence—my assimilation. The cost of leaving and forgetting about home was deafening silence. While I do not consider the dominant culture an inherently bad one, its stealthy understructure erased my home and effectively silenced me by stealing my voice, my Tiếng Việt. What remains of Việt Nam is a nagging awareness of not truly being Vietnamese and worse, I am left with survivor's guilt.

In Patricia McCormick's 2012 novel *Never Fall Down*, she focused on Arn Chorn Pond, a survivor of Cambodia's Khmer Rouge government (1975–1979). Arn Chorn was a child prisoner who was forced to play music for officials of the Pol Pot regime. Arn repeatedly observed atrocities that no person, especially a child, should ever have to witness. After escaping the terror, he was adopted by an American family and resettled in New Hampshire. These are Arn Chorn Pond's words regarding survivor's guilt as expressed to McCormick:

> I try now to go back to sleep, think about all the good thing here in this good place, this rescue place call New Hampshire, United State, and think: after all the things I been through, now being rescue is something I also have to survive. (p. 195)

I can hardly compare myself to Arn Chorn Pond. Unlike him, I have only witnessed one murder. The victim was a gypsy who I saw executed by a Romanian "police" officer. At the time, I was volunteering in the streets of Bucharest. I had quit my music teaching job in Western Pennsylvania and decided to travel to Eastern Europe to serve children who had been abandoned on city streets. It was my first encounter with orphans, orphanages, and street culture. Nothing about my music training had prepared me to work in this setting. I saw abject poverty, rampant drug use, as well as silent and violent death. I felt helpless standing in the street looking at children whose bodies were left on the street. Some were living; some were not. What had I been doing with my life aside from earning a spot in an elite choir, learning modal variations on a b-flat scale, or winning marching band trophies? In a flash, the importance of music and music education died.

Returning to the United States I was unable to bear the scenes I had observed on the streets of Bucharest. Perhaps my motives in Romania were altruistic, but what the street children underscored for me was a heightened awareness about the mystery of my abandonment. A realization of self-as-Vietnamese, self-as-orphan, self-as-music teacher, and self-as-human being in a complicated and oftentimes terrifying world signaled a beginning to the complex process of wayfinding back to music and music teaching.

Having nowhere to live after Romania, I moved in with friends on the Pennsylvania-New York border and took a job as a church secretary and choir director. Part of that work entailed visiting hospice patients, nursing home residents, and prisoners, all of whom were displaced in their own ways. Unbeknownst to me, these people opened doors to what I consider a slow miracle that revitalized my energies to become a music educator once again, to give back in a small way. My work prior to Romania and New York included preparing my students for marching band competitions and honors ensemble auditions. The busy-ness of these activities disguised how deeply my students and I could be affected by our participation in teaching, learning, singing, playing, problematizing, uncovering, challenging, feeling, and caring through music-making. Romania- and US-based humanitarian work changed me; until having those opportunities, I had never conceived of music teaching as a critical act of being human.

Giving serious thought and action to a special profession like music education, I have made a deep commitment to a particular pathway. Walking that pathway is one way to be alive and more importantly *a way to be alive with others*. Along the road, fellow sojourners join my song and make up their own as they quest for a meaningful life. For some people, music or music education becomes a life course, a lifestyle where they have found out who they are or what they want to become. While I cannot know how I will follow this path in the future, I believe music teaching and learning is the journey in which I can have the most influence on the people I encounter and be/become the best person possible. Perhaps the critical nature of being human is not in the music education so much as it is in the connections made with others as an educator-artist-activist who is traveling from a state of abandonment to one of banding together in song.

Having been abandoned and eventually working with abandoned children (a point of connection), I began to understand my purpose as a music teacher in the United States. What I had observed overseas in Romania and Việt Nam as a young teacher was a tragedy that I could no longer ignore. I struggled to make sense of a world where child abandonment, for example, was a normal practice. Survivor's guilt crept in as a side effect of dealing with my own abandonment and evacuation. Converting that experience into something purposeful became and remains a lifelong challenge, one that has the potential to make a small and positive difference in the lives of the people I teach and research.

Singing songs with and for the people who cannot or will not sing their own songs, especially the orphan children with whom I have made music in Việt Nam, is vital to me. This is one way I attempt to enact music education as a form of compassion for others; it is a way to give back. Where I have failed to show compassion, patience, or love, however, is with myself. In *Compassionate Music Teaching*, Karin Hendricks (2018) shared that we must "know and show compassion for ourselves" as a pathway toward "showing genuine compassion to others" (p. 33). Perhaps being a voice with others has been and will continue to be one musical link to a possible future for myself. Where I have been diligent in my attempts to show compassion for and make music with Vietnamese orphans, American schoolchildren, and research friends, I have neglected to show compassion for myself. That means singing my own songs. Now more than ever, I yearn to sing, to play, to dance, and to shout.

Pathway Home

Known worldwide for his peace initiatives and mindfulness practices, Thích Nhất Hạnh (2016) conjectured "Your true home is something you have to create for yourself" (p. 178). The point he seemed to make is that home cannot be wholly defined by geophysical boundaries or nationality; home is something inside you. For an adult with so many questions about his own abandonment and resettlement, being at home means making room for my personal expression as well as creating channels for others to speak and sing their stories. While home is sometimes a physical place, oftentimes enacting home is about shaping an emotional and liminal space that is somewhere between here and there, home and not home, "one hand in the past and one in the present" (Nguyễn-Duy, 2019, p. 1). In her song *Hello Viet Nam*, Phạm Quỳnh Anh (2006) sings:

> *One day, I'll touch your soil*
> *One day, I'll finally know your soul*
> *One day, I'll come to you*
> *To say hello Viet Nam*
> *To say xin chao Viet Nam. (See Video 4.2)*

Sometimes we leave because there is no choice except to leave, or worse, to escape. We go away, we forget, we try to remember, we grieve, we atone.

Wandering the earth, we pack and unpack our bags over and over again. For me, a Việt Kiều, returning home to Việt Nam means making amends for having left so many people behind (see Figure 4.2). I want to beg for forgiveness, to fall in love with a land and a people I have never truly known. Survivor's guilt has been a protracted experience, and my atonement—my music making and music teaching—might never be enough. Yet, music and music teaching are what I have to offer the people in my life in Việt Nam and America.

I wander the earth; free of house, without a home.

Flying above it

I refuse to dig my heels into its soil.
Yet, somehow an indelible mark is left on every stone
    every stone
          every stone

What do these imprints mean and when will they lead me home?
Why can't I simply turn around and follow them like a breadcrumb t r a i l?

Why are they fading into   distant   memory?

FIGURE 4.2   Home, by Kính T. Vũ

In this chapter, I have shared my experience of abandonment, what it means to carry baggage, and how I conceive of my life as an educator, artist, scholar, and activist. In music education, I argue that teachers have opportunities to carry their baggage into the classroom and onto the streets as a way to inform their pedagogies and to explore a critical way of being human. More importantly, I consider how vital it has been to help other people carry their bags, to pack and unpack them, and to use the contents as inspiration toward a deeply personal music-making life where each of us can grieve, laugh, give back, and celebrate our lives well-lived both alone and together. Perhaps it's time for me to unpack my bags and stay awhile.

VIDEO 4.1   Fawng Daw performs his song Việt Kiều.
        The video accompanying this chapter is freely available online at
        https://doi.org/10.6084/m9.figshare.12445775

VIDEO 4.2   Hello Viet Nam is sung by Phạm Quỳnh Anh.
        The video accompanying this chapter is freely available online at
        https://doi.org/10.6084/m9.figshare.12445793

Notes

1   For the full story, see https://www.latimes.com/local/la-me-baby-lift25-2010mar25-story.html
2   It is at this point in the story where I am unable and unwilling to disclose how assimilation is part of my personal narrative. While it might be helpful for readers to know how assimilation relates to the intersection of self and music pedagogy, I am not ready to write about it. In the meanwhile, let it suffice to say that the cost to my wellbeing was and is high.

References

Botstein, S., Burns, K., & Novick, L. (Producers), Burns, K., & Novick, L. (Directors). (2017). *The Vietnam War* [Documentary]. United States: PBS.

Canfield, J., & Hansen, M. V. (1993). She saved 2019 lives. In J. Canfield & M. V. Hansen (Eds.), *Chicken soup for the soul* (pp. 367–371). Deerfield Beach, FL: Health Communications, Inc.

Daw, F. [Viet Phuong Dao]. (2012, November 9). *Viet kieu*. Retrieved from https://www.youtube.com/watch?v=WJ_V2JFKr50

Downey, S. D. (1996). Feminine empowerment in Disney's Beauty and the Beast. *Women's Studies in Communication, 19*(2), 185–212.

Groves, M. (2010, March). 35 years later, a joyous reunion. *Los Angeles Times*, pp. AA1, AA3.

Hanh, T. N. (2016). *At home in the world: Stories and essential teachings from a monk's life*. Berkeley, CA: Parallax Press.

Hendricks, K. S. (2018). *Compassionate music teaching: A framework for motivation and engagement in the 21st century*. Lanham, MD: Rowman & Littlefield.

Jorgensen, E. R. (2003). *Transforming music education*. Bloomington, IN: Indiana University Press.

Joyce, K. (2013). *The child catchers: Rescue, trafficking, and the new gospel of adoption*. New York, NY: Public Affairs.

Kellenberger, J. (2004). *Inter-agency guiding principles on unaccompanied and separated children*. International Committee of the Red Cross. Retrieved from https://www.unicef.org/protection/IAG_UASCs.pdf

Leshkowich, A. M. (2012). Rendering infant abandonment technical and moral: Expertise, neoliberal logics, and class differentiation in Ho Chi Minh City. *Positions, 20*(2), 495–526. doi:10.1215/10679847-1538497

McCarthy, M. (2007). Narrative inquiry as a way of knowing in music education. *Research Studies in Music Education, 29*, 3–12.

McCormick, P., & Chorn-Pond, A. (2012). *Never fall down.* New York, NY: Balzer + Bray.

Nguyễn-Duy, Q. (2019). *Amputees.* Unpublished play.

O'Brien, T. (1990). *The things they carried.* New York, NY: Houghton Mifflin.

Pham, A. Q. [quynhvalentine]. (2009, November 8). *Hello Vietnam.* Retrieved from https://www.youtube.com/watch?v=94y6svVU4so

Pohle, V. (1969). *The Viet Cong in Saigon: Tactics and objectives during the Tet Offensive.* Santa Monica, CA: RAND.

Tonn, T. (2008). *Disney's influence on female perception of gender and love* (Master's thesis). University of Wisconsin, Stout.

Tsing, A. L. (1990). Monster stories: Women charged with perinatal endangerment. In F. Ginsberg & A. L. Tsing (Eds.), *Uncertain terms: Negotiating gender in American culture* (pp. 282–299). Boston, MA: Beacon Press.

Vu, K. T., Saetta, J., & Shekleton, A. (2018). The heartwork in the artwork: In-service music educator professional development in Việt Nam. *Visions of Research in Music Education, 32.* Retrieved from http://www.rider.edu/-vrme

Ward, G. C. (2017). *The Vietnam war: An intimate history.* New York, NY: Alfred A. Knopf.

Wollons, R. (2009). Abandonment and infanticide. In T. R. Bidell, A. C. Dailey, S. D. Dixon, P. J. Miller, & J. Modell (Eds.), *The child: An encyclopedic companion* (pp. 1–4). Chicago, IL: University of Chicago Press.

PART 2

Process/Pedagogy

∵

Forced uprooting

FORCED MIGRATION

immobility

Resettlement

DÉPORTATION

DISPLACEMENT

Enforced Disappearances

Dislocation

immobility

DISPLACEMENT

Forced upro

Resettlement

Key terms 1.

CHAPTER 5

The Individual outside the Community:
Music Education for Fraught Spaces

Rachel Beckles Willson

Abdoulie left The Gambia as a teenager for political reasons. He travelled across Mali and Algeria before being imprisoned and tortured for several months in Libya. He lost all his possessions there, but saved his life by managing to board a boat to Europe. He arrived at the port of Augusta in Sicily, early in 2017, and applied for asylum. Two episodes from Abdoulie's life are given here.

Story I

> Abdoulie has moved into the center of the circle of men and picked up a small goblet drum from the floor. Holding it under his left arm, he raises his right hand. He speaks gently, turning around as he does so. The men gradually stop clapping, chatting, and rattling shakers. Now he's starting to sing and turn again. As he comes full circle he points to one person in the circle who takes up the melody. Others join; one adds a shaker and others copy him. All are singing it over and over, moving as they do. The sound builds, and they begin to dance.

Story II

> Abdoulie is in a recording studio conversing with the producer. He has his latest earnings in his pocket. "But I can pay you," he says. The producer shakes his head. "Your song is not ready," he reiterates for the third time. He continues, "My studio has a reputation. You have a lot to learn. You have to learn how to write a proper song." Abdoulie is ready with a response: "Can you teach me?" The producer laughs. "Let's look," he responds, "show it to me." Abdoulie gets out his notebook, and they start to work.

Of the two stories, the second took place earlier. Based on my interview with Abdoulie in March 2018, the story recounts his first attempt to record music in The Gambia in 2014. This exchange with the producer led to his only training

© KONINKLIJKE BRILL NV, LEIDEN, 2020 | DOI: 10.1163/9789004430464_005

in songwriting, namely informal meetings in which he learned to form rhyming lines of text and, by copying the producer line by line, to sing them as a melody. The next time he wrote a song, he wrote his own melody for the words and chose another studio to record it. When he left The Gambia, he had seven songs on a zip-drive along with his long-term plan to release them on a CD. He also uploaded them on a YouTube channel. He lost the thumb drive in Libya, however, and deleted the YouTube channel for his own protection.

Story I describes a moment in one of the music workshops—offered by myself and a volunteer musician, Francesco Iannuzzelli—in a hostel for male unaccompanied minors near the town of Priolo, eastern Sicily, in the summer of 2017. Along with humanitarian work, I was mapping out a research project. I was learning the legal system as it regards under-age immigrants to Italy and grasping the lay of the land in terms of hostels. I was also working out how best to make contact with African teenagers (greeting each one individually and shaking their hands was very important, for instance). My music-related questions had two facets. First, I was probing which kinds of musical activities could make sense educationally in this context of displacement, that is, hostels for Asian and African men ages 14–18. Second, in what ways could music education enable these new immigrants to find their voices in Europe?

Regrettably, well-intentioned musical aid practices frequently reproduce the power structures they seek to overcome, creating problematic continuities between colonial and neoliberal structures in music education and performance. Music may foster oppressive, manipulative or humiliating practices, performances may mask rather than address acute political problems, and financial inequalities may be perpetuated rather than addressed (Baker, 2014; Baker & Frega, 2018; Beckles Willson, 2011, 2013; Al-Ghadban & Strohm, 2013). In this project, my work was built around my understanding of immigrants as not strangers, but as heirs to our shared history (Danewid, 2017), one that has long been structured by slavery and exploitation and that is now also shaped by the policies of the World Bank, the International Monetary Fund, and the ongoing white supremacy that bars the movement of some people and not others (Dannreuther & Kessler, 2017; Greenhill, 2012, 2016). My perspective was less as a (white) helper and more that of a person experiencing and contributing to a working through of present and future creativity.

As a music facilitator, my approach was thus cautious and wide open, insofar as I made no prerequisites for participation and laid down no groundwork (Wiggins, 2015) on which the men were to learn. I was keen to elicit the participants' experiences and interests in order to discover on what basis we could all meet, and I started with a "socially textured" group activity (DeNora, 2013, p. 261) that I describe below, which was open to a range of participatory styles.

I wanted through these activities to discover which "cultural tools" (Viig, 2017) would enable community music-making in the hostel, but also to learn how music-making could empower new arrivals. My practice of scaffolding, familiar in music education discourses, was thus what Wiggins & Espeland term "artful" (2012): it was fluid, responsive, and undertaken with my primary consideration for the participants' future lives.

As a researcher, I approached with a light touch. When I first offered workshops, I informed the staff that part of my interest was as a researcher. To the immigrants, I presented myself only as a musician. After observation in workshops, I made notes and began interviewing others only several months after I had established good relationships with several of them. I have briefly discussed these workshops from the perspective of refugee activism and global politics (Beckles Willson, 2019). Here I describe the activities from the specific perspective of education in the context of displacement, and I offer some suggestions of ways forward.

Contexts

During 2015, unprecedented numbers of unaccompanied minors arrived across the Mediterranean from sub-Saharan Africa, after passing through the militia-run, collapsed state of Libya.[1] They joined people from other countries similarly stuck in Libya, from Bangladesh, Morocco, Pakistan, or elsewhere. Those arriving in Italy were housed in hostels for minors funded through the Italian Home Office with the support of the European Union. Usually located outside urban centers, these hostels make little or no attempt toward integration. Hostels are run with varying levels of efficiency by associations of social workers, psychologists, and tutors. Residents are provided with food and lodging and, when hostels are well managed, pocket money, but educational offerings are meagre and rely on volunteers. Many refugees attempt to pass through Sicily and Italy to richer countries, but some stay and hope to gain proficiency in European languages, professional skills, or an apprenticeship to build an independent life in Italy, if only as a first step toward another place with greater potential.

To enter a hostel is to engage in a labyrinth of fragments of past lives, journeys, painful arrivals, and dreamed-of futures. In such a space one encounters numerous languages including Italian, English, French, pidgins, the (often) religious language of Arabic, Urdu, and a range of African languages such as Wolof and Tigrinya. These languages intermingle and alternately bridge and divide the young people. It is a world of intense bureaucracy. For these people between the ages of 14 and 21, many hours of paperwork and court rulings lie ahead.[2] Their bureaucratic limbo exists within a larger limbo: figures vary, but the Italian economy is stagnant and unemployment is high.

I ran music activities in three hostels, one for women and two for young men. The work described here refers to a hostel for men from which a core of interested, even passionate, people emerged. The hostel staff encouraged residents to attend, without making the activities obligatory. When sessions worked well, it was due to staff interest: the resident psychologist frequently took part in our sessions, for instance, and other staff also attended. It was also a result of the individual participants with burgeoning talent and ambition. Their energy kept the project going, although, as I describe below, their ambition also created tension at times, and raised questions about styles of social interaction.

Open Workshops and Encounter: Phase 1

Phase 1 consisted of musicking workshops with whatever group (it varied from eight to 30 people) amassed in a space cleared in the dining room. The basic shape of the workshops more or less followed this pattern:

Stage 1:
– an initial warm-up in a circle with hand clapping and vocal games
– the creation of some rhythmic loops with body percussion
– distribution of percussion instruments
– the addition of a guitar cycle of chords
– singing of basic melodic loops such as Solomon Linda's *Mbube*
– the addition of saxophone improvisation by myself
– spontaneous dancing often emerged

Stage 2:
– group learning of a song such as Bob Marley's *Get Up, Stand Up*
– general jam (emerging spontaneously as the participants gradually took over the space with their own songs, improvisations and dances)

Prior to establishing this pattern, we visited the hostel and tried to discover what music the boys themselves were listening to. (I refer to them as boys to adhere to their status as legal minors, although the majority were over 15.) We imagined running workshops focusing on this repertoire as a good starting point, but this approach succeeded only to a limited extent, mainly because none of the boys saw themselves reproducing music they liked listening to. In addition, repertoires divided the groups linguistically and nationally: although most boys liked rap, they did not listen to the same rappers or in the same languages, therefore working on one song engaged only a small subset of the group.[3] Although we did learn some songs they knew and liked, I had no sense that our learning their repertoire allowed them to feel met, let alone have own-ership of the workshops.

In the general jam session, on the other hand, an explosion of engagement and enormous energy often occurred, including some individual raps as well as individual song presentations. The excitement was stoked by boys entering the dining room to dance and then disappear. At these moments, participants took over, and the dancing was sometimes extremely wild, as was yelling and beating the drum. On a number of occasions, the switch into general jam hap-pened quite quickly, so that we jumped from the first part of Stage 1 to the last element of Stage 2. We did not attempt to establish order or rehash repertoire, but tried instead to contribute to whatever the boys were doing. Our strategy was in line with the relaxed line taken by staff at the hostel, who were attracted by the noise and enjoyed the evident energy and pleasure. For some, dance seemed to be an obvious way to participate, even briefly. We did not have skills to foster this activity, but it was triggered by the music we were making. It sometimes seemed to become the real point of the session. One boy's dance with a chair became so overtly sexual that it became the focus of everyone's gaze and so cathartic as to become the culminating event of the workshop. The music had been pushed into the background.

In slightly less rampant moments, our attention was caught by Abdoulie's contributions, because his voice was so melodic and he had his own appeal-ing songs. We were also impressed by the rapping. It gradually became clear that the music culture most active boys understood was not reproductive but rather productive. In other words, they were not interested in covering a repertoire, but wanted to create their own. In the same period, we discovered that two boys had performed in a local community event in which they had sung their songs with digital tracks as backing. The only available tracks were recordings of Abdoulie's songs that he had made in The Gambia and uploaded to YouTube. Volunteers tried to find a backing track on the internet that could serve for these songs in order that Adboulie not have to sing in counterpoint against his own voice.

We offered our own studio technology to create a backing track similar to the original ones and we even helped record and edit his songs.[4] Using WhatsApp to communicate between workshops, we were able to put together a basic recording of his voice with a new beat built with the music creation software package Cubase. Other boys soon started to share their own songs with us, singing privately as we packed up our instruments or sending us their songs on phones via WhatsApp. They also showed us their song notebooks and asked us several times whether we knew a studio to make recordings.

I had some qualms, given that we were geared towards group work and wanted to draw the creative impulse into a group compositional activity. One day I called out, "Let's make a song about today," and we moved into the middle of the percussion circle and asked what we could say about today. Obaydul, from Bangladesh, offered "Today is good," which turned into a chant everyone repeated and held in rhythm by the ongoing hand-clapping and guitar. Another voice yelled out, "What's that?," and a response followed rapidly from the same Bangladeshi: "We are singing." The basic question and answer continued for some time, generating some variation with a "We are dancing" response. When I played the saxophone in each phrase, the work became more of a song than a shout. In due course, a boy sitting at the edge of the circle was coaxed into offering something, and he came up with a Nigerian expression "Osadeba" ("God is with us"); others took up in a call. This fragment was strikingly melodic. After a few rounds, solidified by guitar and saxophone, one of the boys stood forward and started to rap on the theme of today. When we had finished, there came a roar of "Osadeba" and a return to "Today is Good." "Today is Good" became a core motto for the music activities, and we repeated the song frequently with varying rappers and raps.

We tried numerous times to reproduce this group compositional activity with only mixed success. While it was entertaining, it seemed to have much less relevance to the boys than did the individual songs. Several of them had realized we might become their future producers and requested our assistance with increasing insistence. What strongly appealed to them was the fact that we responded to their needs, gave them a channel, helped their voices be heard outside the hostel, which kept them in touch with friends back home. The activity also seemed to provide a meeting point between us more meaningful to them than anything we had devised earlier.

I was still not comfortable with the idea that our work could help these boys package themselves as individual heroes in a market I viewed as aggressively commercial and misogynist. Nor was I comfortable with their potentially passive role in the process (even while, for singers, commercial song production often succeeds according to this model). It was necessary to shift our questions. How could we combine support for their desire to enter the music world in a particular way with didacticism geared to the development of skills? How should we handle some of the ethical questions arising from their texts? How could we influence their choices without feeling as though we were new colonial missionaries? Another concern with individual work was the risk of losing other boys at the workshops. Some had never sung in their lives and they attended sporadically, slipping shyly in and out of the room, sometimes making their presence felt before running away in embarrassment, unable to join the space fully or consistently. We did not wish to dampen their cautious enthusiasm.

Phase 2: Individual Projects

To respond to these emerging new questions, we began to divide our time, to work with some boys individually in the first part of each session and then to move to group activities. This involved setting up a computer and microphone and recording their voices. It also meant that we worked separately with boys on various aspects of song-preparation. Finally, we built and mixed a track for them, either drawing from a pre-made track online or starting from scratch using digital libraries imported into Cubase.

Our recording hub triggered such interest that sometimes a group of four or five boys sat close by, captivated by the technology. One Moroccan boy recorded his voice in two songs, another a message for his sister. In the hostel, he had little opportunity to speak Arabic, his mother tongue. Although we sent him a recording of the mixed song on WhatsApp, he was transferred to another hostel shortly afterward, therefore we gleaned no sense of the benefit he had derived. In an interview, the psychologist stated that working on songs gave them a way to work through their psychological struggles. Some songs were love songs, some about mothers, while others addressed the journey from Africa or life on the street as an African in Italy. Some were in English, others multi-lingual. To the young men, the meaning was of central importance; aesthetic aspects were peripheral.

A small cluster of boys was hugely enthusiastic about the recording project, and we started to feel a certain amount of pressure to deliver tracks for them, or edit our suggested tracks to reflect their taste. This pressure was partly due to the challenging sound material with which we were entrusted. Two boys had had no musical experience prior to our workshops. One had never danced. Many boys lacked an awareness of tempo and rhythm and were frequently out of tune, or their pitch meandered. In some cases, densely written prose (covering a notebook page) constituted a song, chanted rapidly without pauses or changes in delivery style. Clearly, several steps needed to be taken for such a song to function within even a moderately structured backing track, let alone in a performance with others.

During one-to-one sessions with the songwriters, I taught in a way not unlike Story II above. I demonstrated to two boys how to rewrite their song texts on paper that would show both the sectional structure, the line structure of verses, and even the positioning of words on rhythmic beats. With the help of another volunteer, one boy created an Italian text for a song originally written in English. I also made them speak the words in a rhythmic pattern, copying me, accompanied by their own body percussion—clapping, clicking fingers or slapping their leg. In cases where the song was only partly a rap, I encouraged them to transform their speaking into something more melodic.

Their rhythmic awareness started to improve, and I learned some of the vocabulary important for them: "hot," for instance, was a positive quality in a backing track; it translated as fast and energetic, often accompanied by a strong bass. Its antonym was "cool," used for softer, ballad-like songs and often somewhat ambivalently.

Pitch awareness was difficult to develop. Some boys focused essentially on words (and gradually added rhythm) and had little interest in pitch. Many were in the habit of recording themselves on their phones and listening repeatedly to their voices, potentially reinforcing their memory of the words, but also normalizing notes frequently out of tune. Some started singing in a key completely at odds with the track (and occasionally maintained their own key throughout). In other words, pitch was irrelevant to them, and yet in order to help their voices reach audiences, pitch awareness and control would become a valuable tool. I recorded myself singing their songs mixed with the backing tracks. The boys listened to these recordings and substantially improved in both rhythm and intonation. This created another temporary problem, namely that one of the boys started to sing an octave higher than was comfortable, in my female register!

Although some aspects of this work were potentially communal, the boys sought out—indeed seemed to need—individual attention from me or my co-leader. Not interested in the songs of others, the boys who were not (yet!) songwriters, nevertheless sometimes hung around listening. Because our activity had been set up as an open project, without obligation, we did not want to introduce a disciplinary framework. I therefore tried to encourage group activity around the compositions but did not force the issue. The result was that boys remained focused entirely on the needs of their song(s). Those needs became an increasing concern, as did the fact that our time was getting completely eaten up by individual projects. We wanted to reconnect to the group activity, therefore the next question was how to draw the individual projects into a shared space.

Phase 3: Returning to the Group

As a first step, we gathered as many boys as possible and introduced them to the songs by those we had worked with. We taught the group a refrain text both by repetition and by guiding them through written texts displayed on large sheets of paper. In the course of this activity, the boys in the backing group seemed pleased to recognize the achievement of the individuals and to join in it. The sessions also stimulated others to talk about creating their own songs and, after a few weeks, a song had emerged, the account of Amadou's journey from Africa, written in Italian and delivering a pointed message to Italians.[5]

The soundscape that emerged in these group sessions that worked on the boys' own songs had a particularly creative quality in a community sense: echo calls, shouts of appreciation and pleasure, and enthusiastic percussion accompaniments. The result was an unpredictable but dynamic backing of multiple vocals, like an enhanced version of those found in several commercially produced songs by African rappers (see Video 5.1). Encouraging this helped incorporate the broader group. The group went beyond the structured refrain sections and allowed the spontaneity and fluidity of their community to enter the fabric of the song.

We also created spaces for additional raps in the songs and aimed to keep them porous enough to expand the space for the contributions of others. Sometimes we could see that singer songwriters could themselves become facilitators and offer peer support. This development, we hoped, would eventually enable a further set of cultural tools to be acquired. Pressing concerns about authorship, however, emerged simultaneously. One of the songwriting young men wrote me a message saying that he did not like it when his songs were done by others, because "Boys use to rewrite it." Some weeks earlier he had found another boy reading the notebook he left in the dining room and exploded in a rage about his stealing ideas. The fight between them shattered what had been a productive friendship, and it seemed to make it impossible for them to take part in the workshops together. Clearly, the nurturing of individual talent needed to be accompanied by some strategies for managing ambitions, responsibility, and addressing questions of copyright.

Discussion

Responding to the energies of the group, our workshops had shifted rapidly from reproduction to production. They had also shifted from group musicking into bespoke composition while voice instruction combined with recording and production. Our previously envisioned community building work was increasingly strained by the urgency of individual projects and the tensions among the strongest contributors.

Toward the end of the year-long project, in April 2018, we found three opportunities to publicly perform our co-created repertoire. We also launched a structured recording project that resulted in a CD release. We used "Today is Good" as the title song and constructed a companion website.[6] Collaborative work towards public presentation and dissemination has opened up a space to address style and vocabulary, as well as to shape the vocabulary and the style of songs in ways that could find audiences in Europe. The CD also triggered invitations to perform in the region and opportunities to help songwriters prepare themselves for public performance and audience engagement. In other words, the educational goals have shifted, and the cultural tools being shared are now specifically geared to helping the songwriters shape their voices to be heard in Europe and beyond. "Today is Good" has facilitated new types of community work: at any concert, all performers are usually on stage throughout, supporting each other's work with chorus parts or percussion. A further group of songs was published on the Internet early in 2019. Any profits will go to the songwriters, or, in the case of the CD launched in 2018, to a fund supporting further music projects.[7]

Pedagogically, the project inspires several reflections. The first relates to this specific community of displaced people, which has its eyes firmly fixed on the future and on building a life in Europe. The creative needs of these boys were to some extent connected to what they had left behind, insofar as, on occasion, songs referred to mothers and rehearsing what their mothers had said (Beckles Willson, 2019), or to their journeys to reach Europe. There was no space for nostalgia, certainly not any restorative nostalgia (Boym, 2008), activities meant to reconstruct the past. Musical strategies needed to provide forward-looking cultural tools with a view to reaching outward.

Second, while our workshops were appreciated as entertainment and socialization, those who had experience or ambition saw their musical future in writing words and singing or rapping them. They imagined doing this in a studio with a producer who would do everything else for them. In several cases, they also thought the producer would transform their voices to create the vocal sound dominant in popular music. (This despite the fact that the commonly used audio manipulation tool, Melodyne, was introduced initially to cover up intonation problems.) Music educational work aiming to meet the interests of such a group needs to reflect the reality of the digital world, just as does the classroom today (Finney & Burnard, 2010). The incorporation of recording and dissemination strategies has obvious value, as does training in recording and editing.

Nevertheless, these two reflections trigger further questions, particularly bearing in mind my concerns about reproducing colonial structures, alongside my ambivalence about masculinist, individualistic music cultures. It became clear during the project that for some participants, the only desirable reaching out into the futures was a reaching into the world of rap, inherently and consistently a subculture. This reinforced the resistance many had towards the study of music, because they understood schooled music as part of 'the system' that their musical identities were there to subvert. In this context, all I could do was to attempt to show the value of increasing one's skillset (for any practicing musician), and, when possible, open discussions about gender relations and the use of profane language in the context of their interest in reaching large audiences.

Finally, and perhaps most importantly, it became clear that the need to rebuild an individual subject may be particularly strong in a setting of displacement. Music can contribute usefully to what DeNora terms, after Goffmann, the "crafting of self" (DeNora, 2013, pp. 265–267). This point is given less attention in literature on music education than is the value of musicking as a shared, collaborative activity. It warrants investment and thought, albeit in relational terms, given that musical self-definition is always contextual and rarely simple; for displaced people, it may be particularly complex, and displaced teenagers—discussed here—may represent a truly extreme case. Music can be a space to channel violence just as it can foster peaceful collaboration, so it requires a supportive environment for emerging tensions and struggles to be managed productively. Ultimately, as I have shown, a great potential exists for integrating individual work into group activity. Indeed, the former may enable the latter to grow.

 VIDEO 5.1   Wiz Khalifa's We Dem Boyz.
The video accompanying this chapter is freely available online at
https://doi.org/10.6084/m9.figshare.12445802

Notes

1   The number of unaccompanied minors arriving in Italy doubled between 2015 and 2016 (reaching 25,846 in 2016); the majority remains in the south, Sicily in particular. See Open Migration: undated.
2   Individuals can apply to remain in Italy as *neomaggiorenni* (neo-adults), a status that can last for three years after 18, the legal age of maturity. See Open Migration, 2017, point 4.
3   The artists most often mentioned were Iba One, Takana Zion and Wiz Khalifa.
4   Two of his songs can be heard here: https://www.todayisgood.org/artists/sisqo-blender/

5   The song can be heard here. https://www.todayisgood.org/ho-lasciato-il-mio-paese/
6   See www.todayisgood.org
7   See the detailed financial policy at www.todayisgood.org/policy

References

Baker, G. (2014). *El Sistema: Orchestrating Venezuela's youth.* New York, NY: Oxford University Press.

Baker, G., & Frega, A. L. (2018). 'Producing musicians like sausages': New perspectives on the history and historiography of Venezuela's El Sistema. *Music Education Research, 20*(4), 502–516.

Beckles Willson, R. (2011). Music teachers as missionaries: Understanding Europe's recent dispatches to Ramallah. *Ethnomusicology Forum, 20*(3), 301–325.

Beckles Willson, R. (2013). *Orientalism and musical mission: Palestine and the West.* Cambridge: Cambridge University Press.

Beckles Willson, R. (2019). Listening through the warzone of Europe. *Ethnomusicology, 63*(2), 289–295.

Boym, S. (2008). *The future of nostalgia.* New York, NY: Basic Books.

Caruso, F. (2018). Sperimentare e superare i confini attraverso la musica [Experiencing and crossing borders with music]. In A. R. Calabrò (Ed.), *Disegnare, attraversare, cancellare i confini. Una prospettiva interdisciplinare [Drawing, crossing and erasing the borders: An interdisciplinary perspective]* (pp. 272–281). Torino, Italy: Giappichelli.

Danewid, I. (2017) White innocence in the Black Mediterranean: Hospitality and the erasure of history. *Third World Quarterly, 38*(7), 1674–1689.

Dannreuther, C., & Kessler, O. (2017). Racialised futures: On risk, race and finance. *Millenium: Journal of International Studies, 45*(3), 356–379.

DeNora, T. (2013). Music space as healing space. In G. Born (Ed.), *Music, sound and space: Transformations of public and private experience* (pp. 259–274). Cambridge: Cambridge University Press.

El-Ghadban, Y., & Strohm, K. (2013). Ghosts of resistance: Dispatches from Palestinian art and music. In M. Kanaaneh, S. Thorsén, H. Bursheh, & D. A. McDonald (Eds.), *Palestinian music and song expression and resistance since 1900* (pp. 175–200). Bloomington, IN: Indiana University Press.

Finney, J., & Burnard, P. (2010). *Music education with digital technology.* London: Bloomsbury Publishing.

Greenhill, K. M. (2010). *Weapons of mass migration: Forced displacement, coercion and foreign policy.* Ithaca, NY: Cornell University Press (Cornell Studies in Security Affairs).

Greenhill, K. M. (2016). Open arms behind barred doors: Fear, hypocrisy and policy schizophrenia in the European migration crisis. *European Law Journal, 22*(3), 317–332.

Viig, T. G. (2017). Multiple modes of facilitation in a Norwegian creative musicking project. *Research Studies in Music Education, 39*(2), 247–264.

Wiggins, J., & Espeland, M. I. (2012). Creating in music learning contexts. In G. E. McPherson & G. F. Welch (Eds.), *The Oxford handbook of music education* (1st ed., Vol. 1, pp. 341–360). New York, NY: Oxford University Press.

CHAPTER 6

Traveling the Broken Road: Displacement and Songwriting in a Prison Setting

#4459

The Pitfall of Perfectionism

When you take up the noble task of teaching, what is your aim? Some set out to teach to the test, to meet the minimum required, to shuffle kids on like cattle to reach the next level higher.[1] Others feel called to pursue a much higher task, they teach students to learn, to learn how to ask. They light a fire and inspire a lifetime of searching, reaching and growing. The same can be said of every great coach. Winning one game is not their approach; they draw out the character inside, so that win, lose, or draw, the athlete stands with pride.

An important question might be: What are you inspiring them towards? Pedagogical processes that pursue perfectly pure pitches can pull you into the pitfall of perfectionism. Of course, having one so driven to work hard and achieve excellence can seem a good goal. On the flip side, however, is something rather perverse. Deep-rooted perfectionism leaves no room for error. It strikes down anything less than the best. Eventually, it can silence the one who doesn't feel he or she measures up.

We discussed perfectionism at an Oakdale Community Choir practice. A few years ago, we sang "The Learning" by James Schattauer with the original lyrics, "There is no wrong, there is only the learning, to find out love is all we have to give." These well-intended words didn't fit with the reality of a room full of those who have been accused of "doing" something wrong, and "being" so wrong they must be removed and kept away from society. Rather than bringing healing, the original words also deny the pain of victims. Instead of ignoring the proverbial elephant in the room, it seemed best to acknowledge it: There has been wrong. Now what can we learn from it? We changed the words to "Where there is wrong, there is hope for learning to find out love is all there is to give." The lesson may not be easy, and seldom is comfortable. It may require change and hard work. But now we can be confident in the words: Where there is wrong, there is hope for learning, even in the music classroom.

© KONINKLIJKE BRILL NV, LEIDEN, 2020 | DOI: 10.1163/9789004430464_006

Impact of Displacement

Anyone who is displaced, who is forced from what is comfortable or known, will experience loss. For those in prison, the loss is compounded. Not only do many carry the baggage from the troubled homes they grew up in and the loss of being cut off from family and friends, but there is the additional aspect of being publicly labeled. It is much harder to overcome failure that follows you everywhere. What would it be like if everyone's worst choice was made public? It is also harder to succeed when the Department of Corrections' (DOC) policies seemed stacked against you. Without the intervention of outside volunteers, many are doomed to continue down the same broken road.

How then should we view those in prison? I learned to take a new perspective, in part by coming to prison. This was further enhanced in 2012 when I was invited to do a little research and write an article about the history of the Iowa Medical and Classification Center. I found out that in the 1960s the state chose to build a mental hospital on top of a former landfill, which was later expanded as a classification center for all the prisons in Iowa. In 2007 the state added a new unit with medical and mental units. Think about that for a moment. Where society once threw away their trash, now they throw away men.

How do you view trash? Most just want it removed from their sight. In the small town I came from, I knew those who gathered the trash. I also knew, being open to look, from time to time they found small treasures. With these images in mind, and examining the history of Oakdale, I learned that in the 1960s the state built a mental hospital on top of a former landfill. I wrote the song "Treasures Hidden," which was sung by the Oakdale Community Choir. If recycling can cut down the waste of paper and plastics, what about men's lives?

Recently, I read a book about Charles Colson and his work later in life to reform prisons. The author John Perry quotes an unnamed warden with thirty years of criminal justice experience, "The prison system is broken and everybody knows it" (Perry, 2006, pp. 4–6). Despite compelling evidence of an enormously expensive failure, like a large machine it continues to grind down all those who pass through its teeth.[2] The author went on to give four reasons for this. The first involves those in the DOC. Even if our system of justice is broken, everyone is trained to keep doing what he or she has always done. The second reason involves politicians who could enact change, but don't. Most have learned that appearing tough on prisoners, pushing for longer sentences, will win more votes than any effort to rehabilitate offenders. This is true despite the fact that rehabilitating those in prison will greatly reduce the overall cost to the state and over time will increase security releasing those who are more community minded. The third reason involves the average citizen who does not know anyone in prison. The waste of lives and resources in prisons is not on their radar. So, who is left to take up this cause? The final reason that inhibits any effort to change is that for a long time there was no other option. What can be done differently?

There's Something about Mary

Dr. Mary Cohen, who joined the faculty of the University of Iowa in 2007, developed an innovative idea from her experience in Kansas. What if we created a choir inside the prison? What if we brought community and caring to those who have been cast aside? She caught a glimpse of changed lives in Kansas. Could it happen in Iowa? In 2009, she received the green light to begin this journey. From season to season, the choir grew in numbers, in ability, and in supporters who liked to be around success. Indeed, through the success of the choir, many other groups rose up.[3] Each in its own way calls for the individual to rise above his situation, to strive for excellence and to give back to others. Dr. Cohen did not come just to start a choir, so a few men locked up could sing. She came to change her world and the way we view those locked up. Each season she expands the special invitation list to include the influential in the area of justice such as judges, prosecuting attorneys, head of Victim's Services, area politicians, and leaders from the University of Iowa to see what changed lives and a caring community can look like.

In 2018, the relationship with the University of Iowa expanded. Prior to this, most of the educational effort here at Oakdale was focused on those who never graduated or had a lower than sixth-grade reading level. Beyond that, you could pick up outdated workbooks to learn the basics of Microsoft programs on your own. The few people diligent enough to complete those programs could sign up to learn basic Spanish through Rosetta Stone. Dr. Cohen's success brought the University of Iowa into the prison as well. Each semester, opportunities have expanded with new classes, challenging us to think about our future and start working toward it today. States spend millions of dollars for programs that produce questionable results to deter future criminal activity. How much does a choir cost? Rather than treating locked up men as enemy combatants or caged animals, how much does it cost to treat one like a person, to prepare them to be part of a community that cares?[4]

It's inspiring to be around those who look at you for who you can be, rather than looking down on what you once were. We can never pay back the volunteers sufficiently for the humanity they restore during that hour and a half each Tuesday evening. In a small way, however, we can pay it forward by living changed lives. As we go on to succeed, the choir succeeds. We have a growing number of inside choir members who have completed their time. They are now outside the prison walls continuing the path they started here. They return for concerts and always express their gratitude to the warden, Dr. Cohen, and the volunteers. Music, dedication, and care can positively impact lives.

Spring 2015 was a special choir season. Dan Kolen, the son of an outside choir member received permission to collect video footage for a documentary on the choir. After attending a choir concert, he went from questioning his mother's safety entering the prison each week, to wanting to tell the choir's story. He was given the opportunity to walk around and see where we live and work and asked several of us how the choir impacted our lives. For some, the choir concert is the only time we get a visit during the year and it gives families a positive experience to share.

During previous concerts, there had been requests for an encore, but nothing was ever prepared, and under the previous warden we were always under a tight schedule to get done and get all the people out before any contact could be made with the inside singers.[5] Within that context I wrote a special song; a secret encore to honor Dr. Cohen's efforts among us. While she always liked to emphasize the community aspect of the choir, the members all know that it is her energy and devotion that inspire us. I developed the song from a weekly writing prompt that asked, "If your life was put to music, what kind of song would you be?" With the help of another choir member, we set the words to a simple blues style melody that was easy for the choir to pick up. It tells a story that needs to be told:

There's Something about Mary (excerpt)

There's something about Mary
What song would she be?
The tempo would move briskly
Busy as a bee.
She can get your attention
Not saying a word,
But what her life is teaching
It needs to be heard.

She reaches across fences
All that would divide
She builds up community

Standing side by side.
There's something about Mary
Both deep and profound
To take all these offenders
And make such a sound.

Singers Become Songwriters: The Songs of the Displaced

Within the Iowa DOC, I am a number, serving out a sentence. Like so many
gathered here on this side of the fence, I could tell stories of abuse and abandonment. I was a quiet kid who would have slipped by, until a high school band
director created a family and community, and inspired us to be something more.
In college, I took many of the classes to become a band director. Though my life
took a different course, no one would have guessed prison for my future. While
I can't go back and undo the past, I can commit to making the most of the time
I am given. I have been able to take up several writing projects that I didn't have
time for on the outside, to help and encourage others. I have also been able to
do more with music. Over the past seven years I have written twenty songs.
Some were lyrics set to a given melody, and most included an original melody.
Seven of the songs were recorded during summer songwriter concerts and the
choir has sung five during the 16 seasons I have been a member.

Where does inspiration for a song come from? It comes from the soul and
the experiences of life. Several of the songs I have written express the troubled
situations I have found myself in and the hope just ahead. Sometimes I portray
these tragedies and triumphs through lives portrayed in the pages of Scripture.
There I see real people who reached out for something forbidden and ended
up broken and displaced, people I can learn from.

Displacement can take many forms. Until you have walked in those shoes,
few can fully grasp what it is like to leave behind all that is known and loved.
When you find yourself displaced, do you spend more time looking back,
dwelling on what might have been, or can you catch a glimpse of the next sun-
rise? As one travels down the broken road to a place one never intended to be,
it takes courage to find a voice to sing, to share a song that could inspire a soul
and change the world.

The choir gets three months to prepare about fifteen songs for its concert.
About a third are original songs written by members of the choir, and the rest
are songs or choral arrangements that Dr. Cohen has picked up along the way
at different conferences that communicate the choir's message. Choir members can also request songs. We perform one concert for the inside community

and any available staff and a second concert for up to 300 outside guests. While some members do not see themselves as skilled singers, Dr. Cohen prepares us to deliver a quality presentation. Afterward, visitors speak of being overcome by the sound, the sense of community, and the sincerity shown through the introductions and original songs. For us, it is an incredible experience to lay aside our labels and present a gift to those willing to receive it. Eventually we will have to go back to our rooms, cut off from the world, but as those who have performed know, there is nothing like concert night. There is an abundance of community and caring, peace, and joy. And for a moment, there is a breath of freedom, to live a new life.

Every practice and concert of the Oakdale Community Choir begins with the song "Beauty before Me" and ends with the blessing "May You Walk in Beauty." There is an intentionality here to see beauty around us. Toward the beginning of our spring 2018 season, we witnessed a beautiful thing when an international group came to visit. They wanted to learn about promoting social justice through the arts. Though they came from a half dozen different countries and spoke different languages, before the night was over we shared a common bond that was astounding. Elidady Msangi was a choir director from Tanzania who led us through remarkable vocal warm-ups and body percussion. He played a mbira. Quang Vinh Dong from Vietnam played a bamboo flute, and Gustavo Orihuela Calvo from Bolivia played violin. They had never practiced together before that night and yet they made the most beautiful music as they blended with our voices.

We learned that night how music can be a universal language. It reaches beyond the walls that divide and the borders we create. It reaches into the heart of everyone who is open. Though we may have things in our past that we wish we could undo, there can be something beautiful down the broken road. What new relationships will we make and learn to treasure? As you consider taking up the noble task to teach, don't be deterred from sharing your gift. And wherever your task may lead you, "May you walk in beauty."

Epilogue

The following statements were written by two women, Dorothy Whiston and Nancy Halder, who have been an integral part of the Oakdale Prison programming. Their voices are presented here as a way to expand on #4459's experiences of the Oakdale Community Choir.

Dorothy Whiston was a volunteer in the Oakdale Prison ten years prior to the start of the Oakdale Prison Choir. She served as a consultant to help

Mary Cohen connect effectively with prison administrators. She joined the choir in 2018 and has been a leader with the Inside Out Reentry Community. She writes:

Humans are a lot more alike than different in almost every way. Singing in a prison choir is a wonderful way to recognize our common humanity. Participation in our choir encourages members to be vulnerable to one another. We get to know one another through exercises and conversation to whatever degree is comfortable, and that grows over time. We stretch our limits in terms of doing silent meditation together, silly warm-ups, the occasional game, and our musical skills grow. We depend on one another in order to prepare and perform to hundreds of visitors.

While a prison choir or other arts program cannot substitute for good counseling or other therapeutic programming in prisons, it can certainly augment them, both for individuals and for the prison community as a whole. The kinds of relationships developed in a prison choir help change the prison environment and culture in ways that I believe make people feel safer and readier for healing work.

Human transformation can and does happen inside the walls of American prisons, but sadly almost despite the conditions. For such dramatic changes to happen more frequently I believe we need to conceptualize and create a fundamentally different way of approaching criminal justice so it is more healing for those directly involved and healthier for the wider community. Criminal behavior has social and individual roots, so progressing through the challenges of criminal behavior needs both social and individual healing.

Nancy Halder is one of the outside singers who knows #4459. In this brief list by Halder, she describes her understanding of displacement during her first time inside the Oakdale Prison and the first Oakdale Choir rehearsal.

1.   57-year-old woman enters prison for the first time in her privileged life. The door clangs shut; she waits with other choir volunteers for the next door to open. Repeat. With that first and second clang she wonders what did she get herself into?

2.   At the same time, 22 male residents of the prison wait in the classroom for the arrival of volunteers with whom they will form a choir. Yeah, right, why would any people who can make a choice choose to come inside to be with them? they wonder, as they wait, expecting no one and nothing.

3.   The choir director appears in the doorway. Next, completely shocking the awaiting insiders, an outsider arrives, followed by another and another and another...

4.   44 tentative people eye and greet each other, sing together, say goodbye: insiders amazed to converse with people from the outside, outsiders to sing in prison, and to meet insiders who surprisingly, were not so different.
5.   57-year old woman returns home with a smile on her face, and the reflection that this was not that different from being "homeroom parents" for their high school children's show choir competition days.
6.   10 years later: greater understanding is achieved by singing together, writing and reading prompt responses, forming a community of caring and compassion, connecting with returned citizen choir members, learning about incarceration in the US.
7.   Antonym for displacement: singing in the Oakdale Community Choir directed by Professor Mary Cohen.

Notes

1 There are many good teachers out there who offer a great gift to their students. This opening is intended to express the contrast.

2 A few years ago, the choir performed an original song, "Grain of Sand." It developed a metaphor of the DOC as a large machine, and the need for grains of sand in the form of kindness through volunteers' interactions or prison staff saying a kind word to inmates for a job well done, with the hope that those grains of sand will destroy the machine that could chew up every life.

3 We now have a songwriters' workshop, a writers' workshop, a Job Club, a Chess Club, a Pen and Paper Club as well as a Runners Club and Toastmasters Group. These clubs inspire works of art and develop their own games.

4 A documentary explored the differences between the maximum-security Halden prison in Norway and two in the US (see http://www.netflix.com/title/80217333). At Attica, NY, they referred to guards as soldiers rounding up homemade weapons, as though they were in a war against the enemy combatants. In North Dakota, one guard complained that unless locked up for more than 30 days in confinement, offenders could not learn anything. At Halden Prison the men are viewed as future neighbors, who need to learn both what they did was wrong and how to live as part of the community.

5 The current warden allows opportunities to demonstrate responsibility. He brought in a dog program that started with a core group of therapy dogs, then worked with the area animal shelter, preparing dogs for adoption and now is training special dogs for Vets with PTSD and children on the autism spectrum. Also building on

the theme of community of caring, he allowed the concert audiences to grow from 80 to around 300, providing a reception afterward allowing inside singers and visitors to mingle. Through the concerts, not a single untoward incident has come up, because we know what it was like before and we don't want to mess up.

References

Lindh, T. (Director), & Spark, J. (Producer). (2017). *Breaking the cycle* [Documentary]. Helsinki, Finland: YLE. Retrieved from http://www.netflix.com/title/80217333

Perry, J. (2006). *God behind bars: The inspiring story of prison fellowship.* Nashville, TN: Thomas Nelson.

CHAPTER 7

Liminal Spaces: Music-Making in Correctional Contexts

Brian Sullivan, Mary Cohen and Katherine Seybert

Introduction

Correctional facilities are physical manifestations of displacement. Steel doors, stone walls, and razor wire mark the threshold of inside/outside, leaving indelible marks on all who cross them by force or by choice. Life on the inside is displacement from society. The US incarcerates more people than any other country. The total correctional population was 6,613,500 on December 31, 2016, according to the Bureau of Justice Statistics (Kaeble & Cowhig, 2018). According to John Pfaff (2017), there are 3,144 different criminal justice systems in the US—one for each county, plus the federal system. Pfaff argues that this "vast patchwork" (p. 13) varies tremendously. Human rights issues in prison contexts include the need for more healing and affirming approaches for system-impacted youth, sentencing reform, abolishing capital punishment, 13th Amendment reform, restoration of voting rights for people inside and released from prison, and decreased use of solitary confinement. Pfaff (2017) suggests straightforward reform such as changing the language we use when referring to people in prison "('people convicted of violent crimes,' not 'violent offenders')" (p. 235).

Some music educators have created structured musical learning opportunities inside correctional facilities as a step toward reform, including ensembles (for example, Cohen, 2012b; Cohen & Silverman, 2013), songwriting (Cohen, 2020; Cohen & Wilson, 2017), musical composition (Cohen & Hickey, 2012), piano (Hamilton, 2014) and guitar lessons (Marcum, 2014; Martin, 2007), creative arts expression (de Quadros, 2016), and musical theater (Cohen & Palidofsky, 2013). There is a strong need for more positive youth development programs in youth facilities, and we hope this chapter inspires music educators to increase research and practice in these realms. Leaders of such programs are supported by non-profit organizations or are university faculty engaging in creative scholarship and teacher education programs (for example, Sullivan & Nichols, 2016). Messerschmidt (2017) reported that participation by outsiders in prison choirs can positively change attitudes about people behind bars.

Perry Miller, a formerly incarcerated man, described the value of fellowship and friendship he found participating in two choirs, a writers' workshop, and a songwriting workshop during his incarceration (Miller & Cohen, 2017).

In this chapter, we discuss our experiences as music educators in two different correctional contexts. Both programs bring outsiders—community members and university students—into a facility to make music and build connections with individuals on the inside. We could write many stories about overcoming adversity, experiencing transcendent moments of artistic communion, and dealing with failure and frustration. Here, we focus on lessons we learned that we feel have the most to offer music educators.

Love Lives On: The Oakdale Community Choir

Mary: Separate Groups Singing Together

It was February 3, 2009, the first rehearsal of the Oakdale Community Choir inside the testing room of the Iowa Medical and Classification Center (IMCC), commonly known as Oakdale Prison, in Coralville, Iowa. Twenty-two choir members gathered comprised of men in prison and women and men from the community. After six years of research preparing for this new initiative, I was quite nervous, as most of us were. After a brief vocal warm-up, I began rehearsal with Kristopher Erik Lindquist's "Beauty before Me." We rehearsed selections such as "Homeward Bound," "Old Irish Blessing," and "Ose Shalom," and concluded in a large circle singing our closing song "May You Walk in Beauty." After we exited the secure area of the prison and returned to a room where we left our coats, the activity specialist suggested I have everyone introduce themselves to one another at the next rehearsal. Here we were at our initial rehearsal of a mixed inside-outside choir that as of December 2018 has performed 20 themed concerts and one learning exchange inside the prison gym for over 2,700 people, and developed a remarkable community of caring, and we forgot to introduce ourselves at the first practice!

The Oakdale choir rehearses weekly inside the IMCC, a medium security state male prison located in Coralville, Iowa. The facility includes medical and reception units with an average daily population of 950 men. The choir has gradually grown in size with the fall 2018 season including 40 inside and 35 outside singers. A total of 166 inside singers and 132 outside singers have participated in at least one concert. The choir is rooted in the South African concept, Ubuntu: a person is a person through other people. In addition to singing together, members exchange reflective writing (Cohen, 2012c). I distribute weekly writing prompts related to the lyrics we are singing, ideas about singing, seasonal content, and topics relevant to the group. I use select writing pieces for introductions at two concerts. During spring 2009 (Stephen King's *On Writing*), fall 2009 (Bo Lozoff's *We're All Doing Time*), and spring 2010 (Christopher Small's *Musicking*) seasons we paired readings from these books with the writing prompts. We create newsletters comprised of writing samples and distribute these to all the members of the group.[1]

The Summer Songwriters' Workshop at IMCC grew out of the choir's reflective writing. Original songs such as "Love Lives On,"[2] uncover members' ideas and feelings. As of December 2018, 75 of the 142 original songs have been performed by the choir. These songs provide a musical bridge for both disparate groups to perform as one original communal voice. Audience members regularly comment on how meaningful it is for them to hear the original songs. Themes often relate to families. For example, Jorge (a pseudonym) sang "Four Times Bonita" to his wife sitting in the front row with their grown daughters. The love and care expressed through song was extra special.

Being "With": The Champaign County Juvenile Detention Center Arts Project

Brian: Moving Bodies, Shifting Trust

The last bars of the swing music reverberate around the brightly lit gymnasium. Nervous laughter mingles with the familiar opening of Michael Jackson's "Thriller" (1982) as I look to my partner, a young man in a threadbare grey uniform. His mask of distrust is broken by his bright smile, and his openness melting the knot of doubt that had been in my gut since I arrived. We turn away from each other to take in the scene. A small group of university students—mostly female—mingle among a larger group of youth in uniform—mostly male. Up until a moment ago we were dancing across the room in pairs, the awkward joy of shared movement crowding out doubts about our capacity to challenge gender roles and social norms. One university student—the leader for the evening—guides us into rows for the next dance.

The Champaign County Juvenile Detention Center (CCJDC) is a utilitarian brick building, two miles from downtown Urbana, Illinois. The CCJDC can house 40 youth, but staffing allocations in 2018 only allow for 25. Most of the youth are housed on a short-term basis (2–3 weeks), awaiting legal proceedings. A very small number may be housed post-trial, either as part of a short-term sentence before being released back to the community, or moved to the adult facility upon aging out.

The CCJDC Arts program started with the efforts of one undergraduate music education major at the University of Illinois—Alex Moroz—who wanted to teach music in prison. One of his professors—Dr. Jeananne

Nichols—introduced Alex to Mary Cohen, and he visited Mary at Oakdale in the summer of 2011. Upon returning home, Alex reached out to the ccjdc and began offering weekly music sessions. He spoke with Jeananne about continuing the project into the future, and she obtained a grant from Action Research Illinois to start the service-learning course described herein. Brian served as teaching assistant for the first few semesters. Katherine served a similar assistant role two years later.

Every week the university group developed experiential arts sessions. Each session began with 45 minutes of discussing articles about the justice and educational systems, planning for the next few weeks, and preparing for the session ahead. The number of youth ranged from 2–10 per session, depending on the eligible population of the facility. Activities included found-sound scores and performances, covers of pop songs using guitars, drums, ukuleles, and brass instruments, exploration, dancing, beatboxing, and iPad composition. We had a visual art component for several semesters, which we cut because the youth responded better to the music portions. The nights ended with short reflections and debriefing.

Bringing the Inside Out: Lessons We Learned

Our primary experiences have been inside schools and universities. Our participation in correctional contexts was sparked by our concern for the problems of the criminal justice system, and our awareness of how music-making can allow us to explore, affirm, and celebrate our sense of ideal relationships (Small, 1998). Displacement is often framed as deficit, and other selections in this book highlight the challenges of being displaced from one's primary context. The same issues exist in these projects for incarcerated individuals and their families. Our analyses of these respective music education experiences highlight the possibility of growth and potential for positive thinking in the midst of displacement. These two programs have given us a broader view of the educative potential of music-making to create liminal spaces of engagement with the displaced, as well as the challenges rooted in our differing levels of freedom and power. We maintain that music programs in correctional contexts uniquely highlight (a) the potential for personal growth for all participants in shared musical experiences—changing our previous notions of who we are as people and as musicians, (b) the potential for social growth for incarcerated and outsiders, and (c) transformation of people in the general public when they watch a performance or learn about the program and start to think about people in prison in a more humane and positive light (Cohen, 2007).

Liminal Spaces

Mary: Doing Slow Laps on a Short Track

"Inside the Fences" is an original song, with lyrics by an inside singer and musical setting by me, performed by the Oakdale Community Choir.[3] The song symbolizes how all people hold feelings and identities inside themselves. One section of the song states:

> *I'm doing slow laps on a short track, watching time go by,*
> *I'm doing slow laps on a short track, watching the world go by,*
> *As we work to change, from the inside. The inside, From the inside.*

A curious part about being human is the tension between our individual experiences unique to each life's personal contexts, and our desire and need to connect with others. We have certain types of experiences that group us together and allow us to connect with others. For example, people who are incarcerated share a sense of displacement from society outside of prison. How can we connect with others when we are displaced in multiple ways and levels, especially when the two groups trying to connect do not share common experiences?

People inside US correctional facilities have little freedom in their daily lives. Some describe it as a "forced pause," where they can reflect on their lives in new ways. We found that both projects offered all participants an experience of what we are calling "liminal spaces," as each musical activity—choral rehearsal, songwriting session, experiential workshop—provided an educative opportunity for all participants to step outside their primary context and connect with one another through music.

We experienced the musical activities as liminal spaces—neither outside nor inside—created in the act of making music together. These experiences were qualitatively different than other forms of music-making we've encountered. Perhaps it was the unique setting, and the physical and emotional distances that participants must cross in order to come together. Perhaps it was the disparity between the austere correctional environments and the potential beauty of each musical moment. Perhaps it was the intention/motivations behind our actions. For me, it is about learning more about myself through the process, creating spaces for people to build communities of caring individually and communally as well as outside prison walls. For Brian, it was about stepping outside of his comfort zone, learning from individuals whom society had placed at a deficit, to grow in empathy and agency. For Katherine it was about learning strategies to be a more conscious educator in the public-school environment, specifically reaching those students who were court-involved.

As an outgrowth of these liminal spaces, both projects featured a certain degree of democratic engagement and power-sharing. In traditional classrooms, teachers are beholden to stakeholders such as administrators and community members, with a large amount of freedom to move and change. In a correctional facility, they lose some of that agency, and must reckon with a higher degree of constraint. This disparity highlights the power inherent in the act of teaching. In both settings, the primary control lies with the prison administrators. The setting itself was neither completely inside nor outside. Through our musical interactions, we stepped away from our primary social and musical contexts. We recognized this change into liminal spaces from the earliest design stages and made pedagogical and curricular decisions informed by this change in power dynamics by focusing on democratic choice within every lesson in the CCJDC. The CCJDC project minimized the university facilitator's role as authority figure and created opportunities for the youth to lead. In the Oakdale choir, the reflective writing exchange and inclusion of original songs provided a more balanced power dynamic.

Building Trust: The Unpredictable Nature of Institutions and Individuals

Katherine: Drumming to Ease Tensions
The doors to the CCJDC gymnasium opened admitting a group of eight incarcerated youth. As soon as the second and final staff member entered the room, the door slammed shut making many of us jump. There I was, a master's student and teaching assistant for the CCJDC arts project, and I was as nervous as everyone else in the room. The youth, primarily African American boys aged 13 to 18, showed their distrust by their slouched body language and nervous eyes. The university students, primarily Caucasian females, showed their nerves by awkward smiles and small talk. Even the guards seemed ill at ease to have so many youth walking freely around so many "outsiders." The center of the gymnasium held a circle of chairs with drums in front of each seat. I smiled and invited all to find a seat and dived right into drumming using echo patterns, steady beat, and improvisation. Within five to ten minutes, most of the youth had relaxed their tense shoulders, smiled, and opened up communication through their drumming. The drum circle opened communication among all by creating a space for listening and responding to one another through games such as speaking our names while playing the syllables on our drums, playing

call and response phrases, and improvising during those call and response activities. These musical activities led to a greater respect of one another.

Trust is an essential component of positive musical exchanges, and another facet of what makes the liminal space at the heart of these projects so powerful. As described above, building trust was no small feat. During the first four years of the Oakdale choir Mary required all new outside volunteer singers to read "Common Sense and Common Ground" by William Cleveland (1993) in order to guide the group toward mutually respectful relationships with staff and administrators. Mary carefully interacted with all prison staff and administrators, and sent instructions to audience members about showing respect to the prison staff. The Oakdale choir activities required additional duties for staff, so she showed gratitude and followed all protocol and their directives to earn and build trust.

Musical activities hinge on how far each participant is willing to trust and engage. For example, to write and share a song requires courage. The songwriter must feel a sense of psychological safety to uncover personal feelings and express them in song. Through the Liz Lerman Critical Response Process (Borstel & Lerman, 2003), we created a safe space in the workshop processes. This strength-based process allows the songwriter to discuss their concerns before anyone provides constructive comments (Cohen, 2020). Each time the choir learns and performs an original song, those feelings, once hidden deep inside a choir member, are embodied by a communal voice. Audience members note that the original songs are deeply meaningful and provide a heartfelt connection between performers and audience. These musical experiences within the prison create a facet of empathy, bringing audience members directly into this creative and caring community.

Trust between the youth and the university students restarted weekly at CCJDC. The university students focused on a "zero barrier" model where all youth could participate no matter their interests or skill level. The youth noticed outsiders' feelings about activities and they mirrored our energy. We started each session by introducing ourselves and connecting, through sharing a story about a pet or a favorite activity. Over time, we learned to more quickly read and respond to the youth.

Building trust in the Oakdale choir was easier, because the same choir members met weekly. Mary included relationship-building activities—learning each other's names and fun information about each other. After an entire season of these activities—or many years as is the case for some choir members—a community of trust grew.

Empathy

Brian: Complex and Conflicted

His face lit up when we brought the guitars out of the storage closet. He was quiet, exceedingly respectful, and a natural talent. He had been there a while, one of the rare ones to stay more than a week or two. As soon as the guitar hit his hands he was engrossed in the moment. We played together in a corner of the room and quickly learned our part for the cover song of the evening. After talking about his favorite musical styles, it was clear that we felt a connection. When the evening finally came to a close, he was reluctant to pass the guitar back. "Thank you all so much for doing this with us," he said earnestly, "I just love this." As we packed up and walked out of the facility one of the undergraduate students casually remarked, "So we stumbled upon a news article about the guitar kid," she said, "do you know what he's in for?" She told me. I was in shock. What would drive such a genuine and seemingly kind kid to such actions? What must he have felt then, and now? I was overwhelmed by emotion for him as a perpetrator, for the survivors of his actions, for the systems that had shaped his life to this point. Could I look him in the eye again the same way? How did this influence the music we might make next week?

Empathy is an embodied response to the emotions and experiences of another person (Lieberman, 2007). Each of us has experienced these moments of response through music-making in these projects. As I mention above, empathy is seldom simple. We are aware of the complex issues of the correctional system, and the persistent problems of representation and treatment of those on the inside (for example, Alexander, 2012; Dreisinger, 2016; Rideau, 2010; Stern, 1998). There is a difference between a general sense of care for those behind bars, and the visceral empathy that develops through creating music together.

Outside participants spoke of the empathy they developed as they considered their freedom to walk out of the facility each night while the inside participants remained locked away. They became more aware of the many difficulties in the current patchwork of the criminal justice systems in America. Music plays an especially important role as the group interaction itself has the potential to increase our capacity for empathy, and can motivate us toward social action (Cross, Laurence, & Rabinowitch, 2012). When the choir gathers to sing, or when the youth meet together with the university students, they engage in a unique collaborative activity that opens up new possibilities for social, personal, and musical growth. Katherine found this to be true in her experiences with both projects. Participating in synchronizing activities at the CCJDC such as drum circles, song circles, and organized dance created an ideal environment to feel empathy among one another. Rehearsals at Oakdale promoted an environment of empathy as the choir is working together matching pitch, creating harmonies, synchronizing rhythm, and making eye-contact between its members. We think developing empathy with our learners helps create more positive relationships, a core component for a classroom environment ripe for learning.

Opportunities for developing empathy occur in the Oakdale choir concerts. Choir members and leaders invite prosecuting attorneys, community leaders, and survivors of crimes. Many audience members come inside a prison for the first and possibly only time in their lives. These individuals walk away with a new, more humanized perspective of "prisoner." Pre-service teachers who visited the CCJDC project described how their perspectives were broadened. These projects reframed enculturated (mis)understandings of all we interacted with, and provided learning opportunities inside the walls.

Connections and Conclusions

Katherine: Community within Prison Walls, Connecting Programs
Oakdale Prison, Fall 2017: An upbeat energy filled the air as outside community members gathered in the lobby of the Oakdale Prison before the first rehearsal of the season. After receiving our nametags, community members proceeded through a metal detector followed by two sets of secure sliding doors. In a silent line, we walked through the hallways leading to our rehearsal room where we were greeted by the smiling faces of the "inside singers." As a new member, I nervously took a seat in the front row. I was greeted by an inside singer who introduced himself and welcomed me. Unlike in the CCJDC there were no staff members present. It was clear that a sense of community had been formed and I immediately knew I had joined a very special group.

Ultimately, we undertook these projects to use music education as a means toward reshaping broken systems, creating more healing approaches to justice, and cultivating more communities of caring. Through connections between people in the community and the Oakdale Prison, the Oakdale choir inspired the University of Iowa Liberal Arts Beyond Bars program, a credit-bearing college program. Former inside singers have returned to watch a choir performance and reconnect. One former inside singer completed volunteer training to help with the songwriting workshop and join the choir. We performed a longer version of his song, "Love Lives On,"[4] initially debuted in the first choir season in spring 2009 when he was incarcerated. The spring 2019 version, "Building Perfect Peace," included two new sections written by Paul

Soderdahl, the accompanist, and me symbolizing how the process of rebuilding our lives requires communal support. The inside singers describe how outside volunteers' presence through coming into the prison consistently each week, has supported growth of their sense of self-worth (Cohen, 2012a). They felt acknowledged and human through their shared space of choral singing—a space for them to create empathy and caring for one another.

University graduates of the CCJDC arts program report that they trace some of their current practice to the lessons they learned in the facility. Some have gone on to seek out similar work in detention centers and alternative schools, others have reshaped their school music programs to be more trusting, empathetic, welcoming, and democratic. I notice it in my work in public school, where I often draw on pedagogical and social lessons to engage with court-involved students—students impacted by the legal system.

We encourage all educators to consider dismantling their sedimented social understandings by exploring and musically engaging with communities and people who are new to them. Music educators can create conduits for social cohesion and healing. Educators might consider how to build trust through original performance pieces that highlight community strengths, and discover new ways to support one another through care and empathy (Cohen & Duncan, 2015). For example, Scaling Walls a Note at a Time provides music education experiences for children of adults who are incarcerated. How can music teachers support their students whose parents are incarcerated?[5] To what extent do music teachers understand the musical practices of their students' previous generations? We believe such engagement and understanding lead to greater empathy and more musical learning for all, creating more healthy and vibrant communities.

Notes

1   For more information about the Oakdale Community Choir, see http://oakdalechoir.lib.uiowa.edu/

2   For score and recording of "Love Lives On," see http://oakdalechoir.lib.uiowa.edu/original-works/

3   An audio recording of the 2018 performance of this song is available on the Oakdale choir website: http://oakdalechoir.lib.uiowa.edu/

4   For score and recording of "Love Lives On," see http://oakdalechoir.lib.uiowa.edu/original-works/

5   SWAN: Scaling Walls One Note at a Time is an organization that provides support for children whose parents are incarcerated. They offer free music lessons, ensembles, and performance opportunities for the youth: http://www.swan4kids.org/

References

Alexander, M. (2012). *The new Jim Crow: Mass incarceration in the age of color-blindness.* New York, NY: The New Press.

Borstel, J., & Lerman, L. (2003). *Liz Lerman's critical response process: A method for getting useful feedback on anything you make, from dance to dessert.* Dance Exchange.

Cleveland, W. (1993). Common sense and common ground: Survival skills for artists working in communities and social institutions. *High Performance, 61.* Retrieved from http://www.artandcommunity.com/csac/articles-and-essays.html

Cohen, M. L. (2007). *Christopher Small's concept of musicking: Toward a theory of choral singing pedagogy in prison contexts* (Doctoral dissertation). Retrieved from ProQuest Dissertations & Theses database (UMI No. 3277678).

Cohen, M. L. (2012a). Harmony within the walls: Perceptions of worthiness and competence in a community prison choir. *International Journal of Music Education, 30*(1), 47–57. doi:10.1177/0255761411431394

Cohen, M. L. (2012b). Safe havens: The formation and practice of prison choirs in the US. In L. Cheliotis (Ed.), *The arts of imprisonment: Control, resistance, and empowerment* (pp. 227–234). Aldershot: Ashgate Publishers.

Cohen, M. L. (2012c). Writing between rehearsals: A tool for assessment and building camaraderie. *Music Educators Journal, 98*(3). 43–48.

Cohen, M. L. (2020). Songwriting in prisons: Liz Lerman's critical response process as a means for positive structured conversations. In J. Borstel (Ed.), *Critique is creative: Liz Lerman's critical response process in theory and action.* Middletown, CT: Wesleyan Press.

Cohen, M. L., & Duncan, S. P. (2015). Restorative and transformative justice and its relationship to music education within and beyond prison contexts. In C. Benedict, P. Schmidt, G. Spruce, & P. Woodford (Eds.), *Oxford handbook of social justice in music education* (pp. 554–566). New York, NY: Oxford University Press.

Cohen, M. L., & Henley, J. (2018). Music-making behind bars: The many dimensions of community music in prisons. In B. Bartleet & L. Higgins (Eds.), *The Oxford handbook of community music* (pp. 153–171). New York, NY: Oxford University Press.

Cohen, M. L., & Hickey, M. H. (2012). Function-based music education: A framework for facilitating musical learning and developing human relationships through analyses of two prison case studies. In L. K. Thompson & M. R. Campbell (Eds.), *Situating inquiry: Expanded venues for music education research. Advances in music education book series* (pp. 99–118). Charlotte, NC: Information Age Publishing.

Cohen, M. L., & Palidofsky, M. (2013). Changing lives: Incarcerated female youth create and perform with the storycatchers theatre and the Chicago Symphony Orchestra. *American Music, 31*(3), 63–182.

Cohen, M. L., & Silverman, M. (2013). Personal growth through music-making: The Oakdale Prison Community Choir and homeless men in a therapeutic program in

New York City. In K. K. Veblen, S. J. Messenger, M. Silverman, & D. Elliott (Eds.), *Community music today* (pp. 199–216). Lanham, MD: Rowman & Littlefield.

Cohen, M. L., & Wilson, C. (2017). Inside the fences: The processes and purposes of songwriting in an adult male U.S. prison. *International Journal of Music Education, 35*(4), 543–551.

Cross, I., Laurence, F., & Rabinowitch, T. (2012). Empathic creativity in musical group practices. In G. McPherson & G. Welch (Eds.), *The Oxford handbook of music education* (pp. 337–353). New York, NY: Oxford University Press.

De Quadros, A. (2016). Case study: 'I once was lost but now am found'—music and embodied arts in two American prisons. In S. Clift & P. M. Camic (Eds.), *Oxford textbook of creative arts, health, and wellbeing: International perspectives on practice, policy, and research* (pp. 187–191). New York, NY: Oxford University Press.

Dreisinger, B. (2016). *Incarceration nations: A journey to justice in prisons around the world.* New York: Other Press.

Hamilton, A. (2014). The gift of music: Teaching piano in a women's correctional institution. *Clavier Companion, 5*(14), 12.

Kaeble, D., & Cowhig, M. (2018, April). *Correctional populations in the United States, 2016.* NCJ 251211, U.S. Department of Justice, Office of Justice Programs, Bureau of Justice Statistics. Retrieved from https://www.bjs.gov/content/pub/pdf/cpus16.pdf

King, S. (2010). *On writing: A memoir of the craft.* New York, NY: Scribner.

Lieberman, M. D. (2007). Social cognitive neuroscience: A review of core processes. *Annual Review of Psychology, 58,* 259–289.

Lozoff, B. (1998). *We're all doing time: A guide for getting free.* Durham, NC: Human Kindness Foundation.

Marcum, T. (2014, December). Artistry in lockdown: Transformative music experiences for students in juvenile detention. *Music Educators Journal, 101*(2), 32–36. doi:10.1177/0027432114552568

Martin, B. (2007). *Don't shoot: I'm the guitar man!* New York, NY: Berkley Books.

Messerschmidt, T. D. (2017). *Change is gonna come: A mixed methods examination of people's attitudes toward prisoners after experiences with a prison choir* (Doctoral dissertation) Boston University, Boston, MA.

Miller, P., & Cohen, M. L. (2017). "Dear younger me": Writing, songwriting, and choral singing while incarcerated as a means to build identities and bridge communities. In M. Reason & N. Lowe (Eds.). *Applied practice: Evidence and impact in theatre, music and art* (pp. 195–201). London: Bloomsbury Methuen Drama.

Mitchell, T. D. (2008). Traditional vs. critical service learning: Engaging the literature to differentiate two models. *Michigan Journal of Community Service Learning, 14*(2), 50–65.

Nichols, J., & Sullivan, B. (2016). Learning through dissonance: Critical service learning in a juvenile detention center as field experiences in music teacher education. *Research Studies in Music Education, 38*(2), 155–171.

Pfaff, J. F. (2017). *Locked in: The true causes of mass incarceration and how to achieve real reform.* New York, NY: Basic Books.

Rideau, W. (2010). *In the place of justice: A story of punishment and deliverance.* New York, NY: Knopf Publishing.

Small, C. (1998). *Musicking: The meanings of performing and listening.* Middletown, CT: Wesleyan University Press.

Stern, V. (1998). *A sin against the future: Imprisonment in the world.* Boston, MA: Northeastern University Press.

Thriller [Recorded by M. Jackson]. (1982). On *Thriller* [LP]. Los Angeles, CA: Epic.

CHAPTER 8

Shattering Barriers: Exposing and Understanding the Narratives and Rhetorics about Musicians with Disabilities

Rhoda Bernard

Individuals with disabilities often find themselves excluded from music education opportunities in the US. This exclusion may take two forms. In some cases, students with disabilities do not have the opportunity to attend music class—usually due to logistical issues, such as building schedules and paraprofessional coverage. In other, more common situations, students with disabilities do attend music class but, because of a lack of training and support for their music educator, these students do not have the opportunity to participate fully in the music-making in the classroom, nor are they welcome to join school-based music ensembles. There are numerous instances of students with disabilities playing classroom percussion instruments or engaging in movement activities while the rest of the chorus or band students play their parts. As another example, students with disabilities might be handed a kazoo, seated in one of the louder sections of an instrumental ensemble, and be told to hum whatever they wish, with their teacher figuring that the student won't be heard by the audience, anyway (Jellison, 2015). While such students are members of the music class and are present for music instruction, in practice they are excluded from music education. In this way, school music education in the US has displaced young people with disabilities from opportunities to learn and experience music.

Most music educators deeply desire to reach every student. Some music educators do effectively include disabled students in their classes and ensembles, but these individuals are a rare breed in music education (see Figure 8.1). The educators may have developed particularly strong instincts, or they may have sought support from special educators and paraprofessionals. Their extraordinary efforts should certainly be applauded, but should not constitute the exception.

The music education system in the US, including policy makers, music teacher educators, school administrators, and others, is to blame for this extremely unfortunate and downright intolerable state of affairs. Music educators, generally speaking, take at most one course about teaching students

FIGURE 8.1   Students with disabilities in the ABLE (Arts Better the Lives of Everyone) summer
music program at Berklee College of Music play *Proud Mary* at their concert
rehearsal.
PHOTOGRAPH: WILL HOUCHIN

with disabilities in their pre-service training, and many are able to graduate without taking any such courses (Bernard, 2016; Bernard & Hammel, in press; Hourigan, 2009; Morrier, Hess, & Heflin, 2011; VanWeelden & Whipple, 2014; Whipple & VanWeelden, 2012). Furthermore, they receive virtually no relevant in-service professional development or support (Bernard & Hammel, 2018; Hammel, 2001; VanWeelden & Meehan, 2015). As a result, music educators find themselves unable to reach and include their disabled students.

In recent years, the field has made great efforts to address the issue. The National Association for Music Education in the US created a task force for music education and special learners that has sponsored seminars prior to the organization's in-service conferences. Two first-of-their-kind graduate programs—in Music Education and Autism at Boston Conservatory at Berklee and the Berklee Institute for Arts Education and Special Needs—provide specialized graduate study and professional development programs, including an annual conference, for music educators in teaching students with special needs (Bernard, 2016). The number of workshops, online courses, and seminars offered for music educators in this area continues to grow across the US. It appears we might be moving in the right direction as a field, but we have a considerably long way to go to prepare and support music educators' ability to include students with disabilities.

At the same time that students with disabilities are displaced from US school music education, they also face challenges in relating to the world of professional music. While students without disabilities can learn about dozens of successful musicians without disabilities, young people with disabilities have relatively few role models of successful disabled musicians. This means that it is much more difficult for disabled students to see themselves in the musical profession.

Compounding the issue further, society at large has a limited understanding of what it means to be a musician with a disability. Well-known successful musicians with disabilities are out there performing, for example Stevie Wonder and Evelyn Glennie. What we think we know about musicians with disabilities has been told to us by non-disabled people. Even when a musician with a disability has been interviewed, that interview is presented by a reporter. The master narratives about disabled musicians who are in the public were not written by the musicians themselves (Fulford, Ginsborg, & Goldbart, 2011; Honisc, 2009; Hoppe, 2017; Muzikar, 2015; Sulewki, Boeltzig, & Hasnain, 2012).

Music educators work daily under the master narratives about musicians with disabilities. Disabled young people relate to music under these same master narratives. In order for the music education profession to better serve the population of students with disabilities, we must examine and understand these narratives' social and political implications. In addition, we need to provide opportunities for musicians with disabilities to relate their own stories in order that we might better support their experiences and development as musicians.

Master Narratives about Musicians with Disabilities

Every culture perpetuates certain master narratives about various populations—who they are, how they relate to society at large, and so forth. Regarding musicians with disabilities, such stories involve two aspects considered exceptional: people who are musicians and people who have disabilities. From the perspective of society, musicians with disabilities seem profoundly different (Darrow & Hairston, 2016).

Individuals with disabilities appear different, behave differently, move differently, or require other kinds of supports in aspects of their lives. Whether or not one can perceive a person's disability—it may be visible or invisible—the difference(s) associated with it displace the person from the general public. This individual is not like "the rest of us" because the majority of our society is not disabled (although we should remember that every human is only temporarily able, given the inevitability of aging and the occurrence of injuries and other challenges).

When it comes to the master narratives about musicians with disabilities, the tellers of these stories tend to be neither musicians nor people with disabilities. Their stories about disabled musicians emphasize difference and increase distance, as well as magnify the power differential between musicians with disabilities and "the rest of us."

Disability theorist Rosemarie Garland-Thomson (2001) provides a framework—four visual rhetorics—for the portrayals of individuals with disabilities in photographic images. Commonly, more than one rhetoric is at play in a particular photograph of a disabled person.

The four visual rhetorics that Garland-Thomson proposes provide a useful frame for understanding the master narratives about musicians with disabilities in Western society. The first three of Garland-Thomson's rhetorics accurately present the main master narratives told about musicians with disabilities. The fourth describes a lesser-heard narrative about musicians with disabilities— and one that, the data from this study shows, musicians with disabilities tell about themselves when they have the opportunity to devise their own stories.

Rhetoric One: Wondrous

Garland-Thomson's first visual rhetoric, the wondrous, presents the person with a disability as an object that inspires awe. The spectator without a disability looks up to the individual with a disability with wonder and adulation. The disabled person inspires the spectator by performing exceptional acts that most people feel unable to accomplish.

The wondrous rhetoric serves a particular set of political and social purposes that benefit individuals without disabilities. By underscoring the ways that the disabled individual is extraordinary, the wondrous rhetoric validates the spectator's ordinariness. Feeding the human desire to belong, the wondrous rhetoric makes the belonging of the non-disabled secure by illuminating the non-belonging of the disabled.

The wondrous rhetoric also creates distance between the disabled individual and spectators. By setting the person with a disability apart and placing her on a pedestal, and by portraying that individual as an exception while the spectators constitute the rule, the wondrous rhetoric maintains a distance between the disabled and the non-disabled. This distance makes it impossible for true equality to exist between the two.

The Wondrous Musician with a Disability: Gaelynn Lea

Violinist and songwriter *Gaelynn Lea* burst onto the international scene as the unanimous winner in a field of more than 6,000 entries in the 2016 NPR Tiny Desk Contest. Although classically trained, Lea draws from Americana, folk, rock, blues, and popular traditions in her original compositions. Lea has a congenital disability known as Brittle Bone Disease. Her disability is quite visible in her videos. Because of her physical challenges, Lea has altered her technique on the violin, holding and playing it like a cello.

Gaelynn Lea's story demonstrates the wondrous rhetoric because of the awe that she inspires in those who watch her videos and hear her music. They find themselves amazed by her technique, by her playing and singing abilities, and by the beauty and expressivity of her music. Seeing her navigate the violin inspires non-disabled spectators, who wonder at the ways that she has overcome her physical challenges in order to create music, play music, and express herself in her art.

Rhetoric Two: Sentimental

In contrast to the wondrous rhetoric, in which the individual with a disability is positioned above the non-disabled spectators, Garland-Thomson's sentimental rhetoric positions the disabled person below the spectators. This individual is seen as helpless and portrayed so as to invoke pity on the part of the non-disabled person.

From a social and political standpoint, the sentimental rhetoric serves to characterize the non-disabled as benevolent rescuer and the disabled as grateful recipient. These characterizations disempower the disabled and empower the spectators, maintaining their position of power and authority in society.

The Sentimental Musician with a Disability: Jagger Lavely

The story of *Jagger Lavely,* an adolescent with autism, exemplifies Garland-Thomson's sentimental rhetoric. Lavely, a singer, was performing at a talent show at his school outside of Boston. As he started singing, he forgot the words to the song. A moment later, the audience began to sing the song, and he was able to join them. They sang together for the remainder of his performance. ABC *News* produced a segment about Lavely's story, which received millions of hits on social media (Thorbecke, 2016).

In this case, the non-disabled spectators rescued the musician with a disability. On the one hand, the story demonstrates the kindness of the audience members. At the same time, however, what took place perpetuates the power and ability differential between the non-disabled and the disabled. The disabled musician was rendered powerless by his memory lapse, while "the rest of us" were able to save this young man by singing for and with him.

Rhetoric Three: Exotic

While in the wondrous rhetoric the spectator looks up to the individual with a disability, and in the sentimental rhetoric the spectator looks down, in the case of Garland-Thomson's exotic rhetoric, the spectator sees the disabled individual from a distance. The exotic rhetoric presents this person as alien, and this can come across as sensationalized, eroticized, or entertaining. The individual without a disability becomes an ethnographer of a foreign culture, while the person with a disability becomes the object of curiosity.

The exotic rhetoric underscores the distance and differences between the disabled and the non-disabled. In Garland-Thomson's exotic rhetoric, the spectators encounter the disabled as far removed from the ordinary. By objectifying and distancing the disabled, the non-disabled solidify their position of power and their grasp on the ordinary at the expense of the disabled.

The Exotic Musician with a Disability: Derek Paravicini

Thanks to numerous publications, a *60 Minutes* profile, recordings, and several international tours, British pianist *Derek Paravicini* is well known throughout the world (CBS News, 2010). Born prematurely, Paravicini is blind and has learning disabilities. He is a prodigious pianist with a repertoire of many thousands of pieces, can play any music by ear, and he can adapt on the spot any music in any key or style.

Paravicini and his extraordinary musical abilities fascinate all who witness his performances. He is often asked to execute musical tricks, such as playing requested songs in remote keys or in the style of classical composers and popular musicians. Displayed as a musical curiosity, Paravicini is alien from the rest of us because of his outstanding feats.

While spectators marvel at Paravicini's musical abilities, they also derive entertainment from the tricks he is able to perform and view him as a curiosity, profoundly different from "the rest of us."

Rhetoric Four: Realistic

Unlike the three previous rhetorics, Garland-Thomson's final rhetoric, the realistic, brings together the disabled individual and the spectator. This rhetoric normalizes the presentation of disability. Rather than position the individual with a disability as exceptional and outside of the parameters of normal, the realistic rhetoric establishes a connection and closes the gap between such a person and the spectator.

In the realistic rhetoric, the non-disabled and the disabled are positioned as equals. Disability is made to seem ordinary. The realistic rhetoric aims to topple the hierarchy between disabled and non-disabled so that the person without a disability can identify with the disabled person. By promoting an alliance between the non-disabled and the disabled, the realistic rhetoric challenges the current world order and provides an alternative to the ways that the disabled are understood in Western culture. Unlike the three other rhetorics, the realistic rhetoric provides the disabled political power, as well as the agency to construct their identities as they wish.

The Realistic Musician with a Disability: A Question of Authorship

When musicians with disabilities have the opportunity to write their own stories, those stories present powerful examples of the realistic rhetoric. Sometimes they appear in the communications of those arts organizations whose mission is to provide opportunities for the disabled to make and participate in music.

United Sound, an Arizona-based organization that provides peer mentoring opportunities so that middle school and high school students with disabilities can participate in instrumental ensembles, features a video on its website "Who Belongs in Music?" in which a dozen students with disabilities, one after the other, declare, "I belong in music." This message aligns with Garland-Thomson's realistic rhetoric: musicians with disabilities are just like "the rest of us."

Unfortunately, few published first-person narratives about the experiences of musicians with disabilities exist (Fulford, Ginsborg, & Goldbart, 2011; Honisc, 2009; Hoppe, 2017; Muzikar, 2015; Sulewki, Boeltzig, & Hasnain, 2012). This means that the majority of the stories told and heard by the general population are those written and communicated by others.

Narratives Told by Six Musicians with Disabilities

I interviewed six musicians with autism and other cognitive disabilities about their music and about what it means to them to be a musician. In keeping with Garland-Thomson's realist rhetoric, and in the interest of providing opportunities for disabled musicians to tell their own stories, I engaged the interviewees deeply in multiple phases of the process of my writing. They reviewed the transcripts from our conversations and provided edits, clarifications, and feedback. They read drafts and spoke with me about their reactions. I made numerous edits based on their feedback. While, ultimately, I am the author of this chapter, the musicians with disabilities participated in the research, writing, and editing processes. In this way, the participants had control over the ways that their voices and narratives were heard. As will be discussed below, the respondents' stories provide strong examples of Garland-Thomson's realistic rhetoric in action.

The interviews shared one important feature: none of the participants spoke about their disabilities during the interview sessions. None of the interviewees distanced themselves from the interviewer or from other musicians by mentioning the challenges they face because of their disability. Rather, all six of the musicians spoke only about their music and about what it means to them to be a musician. They were thinking about themselves only as musicians and not as people with a disability.

Two themes resonated throughout the responses: communication and ability. Some of the participants spoke about the ways a musician communicates through music. For Julieta, a singer with autism, creating music is not sufficient to make someone a musician. Communication is just as important: "The word musician means someone who creates music and uses it to communicate." Barbara, a concert pianist on the autism spectrum with severe cognitive challenges, agrees. Speaking about her music, she says, "It controls my feelings, my expressions."

Other participants focused on musical skills and talent when they described what it means to be a musician. For Christopher, a singer with autism and other cognitive disabilities, a musician is "someone who is good with music and is— well, a good singer and talented." According to Theo, a singer/actor/pianist on the autism spectrum, a musician is "a person who really likes music and really wants to learn how to sing and not just sing, also to play an instrument."

Helena, a singer/actress with autism, incorporates both themes in her response:

> I think, you can really call yourself a musician—you can say that you're good at what you do, you could say "Oh, I'm really good at playing the trumpet. I'm good at playing piano. I'm an expert at playing guitar." But I think you would only call yourself a musician if you really give—put yourself—if you really give yourself, your all. You really invest yourself in what you're doing. You could say, "I'm a really good singer. I can sing really high notes." But for me, I could sing the high notes, and I'm a really good singer because I invest in what I do. I really get involved with the music and what it means and what the story is. I try to put myself in that story.

Speaking of musical ability, three of the participants have perfect pitch and are prodigious musicians with highly developed musical skills. They echoed the other participants, however, in emphasizing what they have in common with other musicians. Just as they did not speak about their disabilities, nor did they speak about their exceptional musical abilities.

Nathaniel, a jazz pianist and composer with autism, has made numerous recordings and tours internationally. He knew that he was a musician "when I had learned enough songs to give my first concert." Rather than focus on what he is able to do musically, Nathaniel emphasized the ways that he is "just like" other musicians—preparing enough material for a concert.

The narratives these individuals with cognitive challenges posit about their music, their musical experiences, and what it means to them to be musicians demonstrate Garland-Thomson's realistic rhetoric. They bring themselves closer to their non-disabled listener by speaking as musicians, rather than as musicians with disabilities. The focus is on aspects of musicianship they share with other musicians, rather than aspects that make them different. The story that these musicians with disabilities want to tell is a story that others can relate to, a story of sameness that brings them closer to others.

These individuals related their stories to me, a musician and a music educator, someone who leads an organization that provides arts education programs to individuals with disabilities. Because narrative interviews are a mode of self-presentation for the participants (Linde, 1993), we must consider the role of the interviewees' audience. In this case, they did not have to explain musical vocabulary or justify the importance of music in their lives. They also knew that their disabilities would not make me uncomfortable or affect our interview sessions in any way. Their responses certainly would have been different were they speaking with someone not a musician or music educator or with someone who does not work with people with disabilities and the arts.

Cultural Barriers with Implications for Music Education

The master narratives about musicians with disabilities in Western culture perpetuate what is known as the medical model of disability: A disability is an illness or condition that must be cured and the problem of disability lies within the disabled person. This perspective stands in stark contrast to the social model of disability, which locates disability in the environmental, social, and attitudinal barriers society creates for disabled people. In the social model of disability, eradicating those barriers and educating members of society is necessary in order to improve the lives of all people (Shakespeare, 2017).

These narratives also perpetuate the limited positions available to musicians with disabilities. In their culture-as-disability perspective, McDermott and Varenne (1995) argue that every culture provides certain positions to individuals, and the position into which a person is placed affects the way he or she is treated. Western culture severely limits the positions available to individuals with disabilities (Belcher & Maich, 2014). The first three of Garland-Thomson's visual rhetorics illustrate the positions available to musicians with disabilities through the master narratives of Western culture: the wondrous, the sentimental, and the exotic. In reality, however, musicians with disabilities do not fit neatly into such limited categories; rather, who they are, the role of music in their lives, their musical abilities, and their identities as musicians encompass a wide range of deeply personal forms that shatter the barriers they face due to their positioning in Western culture.

As was the case in the interviews in this study, when musicians with disabilities have the opportunity to devise their own stories, they can change the cultural conversation and expand Western society's understanding of what it means to be a musician with a disability. They can put forward a realistic rhetoric that closes the distance between the disabled and the non-disabled. They can also provide opportunities for young people with disabilities who have been displaced from school music education to forge meaningful personal connections with the music profession. I therefore argue that in order to make strides in society at large, as well as in the field of music education, and to put an end to the displacement of young students with disabilities in the US from music education opportunities, we must give voice to the stories of musicians with disabilities. Stories about musicians with disabilities, expressed by musicians with disabilities, must become one of the narrative streams in the cultural conversation about such musicians. In the spirit of "nothing about us without us," a foundational principle from the disability advocacy movement (Charlton, 2000) that owes its origin to Central European political history, the non-disabled must no longer speak *for* musicians with disabilities. Rather, the non-disabled must engage in conversation *with* musicians with disabilities and make it possible for them to represent their own experiences. Only then can the stories of musicians with disabilities be heard as clearly as their music.

For the field of music education and the attitudes of music teachers, I join with Darrow (2015) and Laes and Westerlund (2017) in calling for the development of courses and experiences for pre-service and in-service music educators that increase ability awareness, an expansion of the study of disability in music education programs, the addition of musicians and music educators with disabilities as role models, and the employment of musicians and music teachers with disabilities in all educational settings. I have written elsewhere (Bernard, 2016) about some promising practices now underway. Taking these steps will make it possible for the field of music education to begin to shatter some of the barriers that disabled musicians face, as well as to educate society in order that disabled musicians participate meaningfully in music and music education. These steps can help the field to move away from the displacement of disabled students, toward their meaningful inclusion in music education.

Note

1   See https://www.berklee.edu/berklee-institute-arts-education-and-special-needs for further information on this institute.

References

Belcher, C., & Maich, K. (2014). Autism spectrum disorder in popular media: Storied reflections of societal views. *Brock Education, 23*(2), 97–115.

Bernard, R. (2016). Disciplinary discord: The implications of teacher training for K–12 music education. In J. H. Davis (Ed.), *Discourse and disjuncture between the arts and higher education* (pp. 53–74). New York, NY: Palgrave Macmillan US.

Bernard, R., & Hammel, A. (2018). *Good teaching on steroids: Assessments of music teaching and learning with students on the autism spectrum.* Chicago, IL: GIA.

CBS News. (2010, March). *Derek Paravicini's extraordinary gift.* Retrieved from https://www.cbsnews.com/news/derek-paravicinis-extraordinary-gift-12-03-2010/

Darrow, A. A. (2015). Ableism and social justice: Rethinking disability in music education. In C. Benedict, P. Schmidt, G. Spruce, & P. Woodford (Eds.), *The Oxford handbook of social justice in music education* (204–220). Oxford: Oxford University Press.

Darrow, A. A., & Hairston, M. (2016). Inspiration porn: A qualitative analysis of comments on musicians with disabilities found on international YouTube posts. In M. Belgrave (Ed.), *Proceedings of the 21st International Seminar of the ISME Commission on special education and music therapy* (pp. 49–57). National Library of Australia: International Society for Music Education.

Fulford, R., Ginsborg, J., & Goldbart, J. (2011). Learning not to listen: The experiences of musicians with hearing imparments. *Music Education Research, 13*(4), 447–464.

Garland-Thomson, R. (2001). Seeing the disabled: Visual rhetorics of disability in popular photography. In P. K. Longmore & L. Umansky (Eds.), *The new disability history: American perspectives* (pp. 335–374). New York, NY: New York University Press.

Hammel, A. M. (2001). Special learners in elementary music classrooms: A study of essential teacher competencies. *Update, Fall/Winter,* 9–13.

Honisch, S. S. (2009). The road to marginalisation is paved with good intentions: In pursuit of the re-humanisation of physically impaired musicians. *International Journal of Inclusive Education, 13*(7), 767–783.

Hoppe, E. (2017). Perspectives of young artists with disabilities: Negotiating identity. In J. B. Crockett & S. B. Malley (Eds.), *Handbook of arts education and special education: Policy, research, and practices* (pp. 248–266). London: Routledge.

Hourigan, R. M. (2009). Preservice music teachers' perceptions of fieldwork experiences in a special needs classroom. *Journal of Research in Music Education, 57*(2), 152–168.

Jellison, J. A. (2015). *Including everyone: Creating music classrooms where all children learn.* New York, NY: Oxford University Press.

Laes, T., & Westerlund, H. (2017). Performing disability in music teacher education: Moving beyond inclusion through expanded professionalism. *International Journal of Music Education, 36*(1), 34–46.

Linde, C. (1993). *Life stories: The creation of coherence.* London: Oxford University Press.

McDermott, R., & Varenne, H. (1995). Culture as disability. *Anthropology and Education Quarterly, 26*(3), 324–348.

Morrier, M., Hess, K. L., & Heflin, L. J. (2011). Teacher training for implementation of teaching strategies for students with autism spectrum disorders. *Teacher Education and Special Education, 34*(2), 119–132.

Muzikar, D. (2015). New research relies on first-person accounts from autistic children about sensory issues. *The Art of Autism.* Retrieved from http://the-art-of-autism.com/new-research-relies-on-first-person-accounts-from-autistic-children-about-sensory-issues/

Shakespeare, T. (2017). The social model of disability. In L. J. Davis (Ed.), *The disability studies reader* (5th ed., pp. 195–203). New York, NY: Routledge.

Sulewski, J., Boeltzig, H., & Hasnain, R. (2012). Art and disability: Intersecting identities among young artists with disabilities. *Disability Studies Quarterly, 32*(1). Retrieved from http://dsq-sds.org/article/view/3034/3065

Thorbecke, C. (2016, April). *Teen with autism performs "let it go" with the help of the audience.* Retrieved from https://abcnews.go.com/US/teen-autism-performs-audience/story?id=38330495

VanWeelden, K., & Meehan, L. (2015). Teaching children with disabilities: Preparation through state music educator association conferences. *Update, 35*(1), 1–8.

VanWeelden, K., & Whipple, J. (2014). Music educators' perceptions of preparation and supports available for inclusion. *Journal of Music Teacher Education, 23*(2), 33–51.

Wener, B. (1999, February 3). Stories (and sales) behind the music. *The Orange County Register.* Anaheim, CA.

Whipple, J., & VanWeelden, K. (2012). Educational supports for students with special needs: Preservice music educators' perceptions. *Update, 30*(2), 32–45.

Zara, C. (2012). *Tortured artists: From Picasso and Monroe to Warhol and Winehouse, the twisted secrets of the world's most creative minds.* Avon, MA: Adams Media.

CHAPTER 9

Remember Me for the Love That I Have in Me

Wayland "X" Coleman

This chapter addresses issues of displacement of citizens in Amerikkka via the Amerikkkan prison industrial complex, and the role of music in a contemporary system of oppression.

In the United States of Amerikkka, more than two million citizens are displaced throughout the country's prison industrial complex. The displacement and relocation of so many of Amerikkka's citizens is caused by a corrupt criminal justice empire that uses discriminatory policing tactics to target lower-class, poor, and primarily black communities; a racially unbalanced economic system that ensures that whites will own property and will receive better healthcare; an equally unbalanced education system that somehow benefits from luring children from lower-class communities into the prison system; perpetuating a racist political structure that creates laws to ensure white supremacy and the continued existence of state-sanctioned violence.

The relocation of black men from our communities weakens our social structure. For example, the mass removal of men from our communities creates an increase in single-parent households, which weakens families, and creates a system where young black children—especially boys—can be criminally targeted by white police officers, and for black women to have to depend on the white male figure—essentially the white male power structure, i.e., the same police who targets their children—for protection. In addition, the single parent is burdened by the necessity of being the lone bread winner, which results in the child having to spend more time away from both parents, and which could ultimately lead him or her into the streets. This raises the likelihood of police stop and frisks, harassment, and arrest. Since the sociological factors of displacement play a major role in minimizing the life chances of black youth, it is an unfortunate reality that many of our youth today will become the future incarcerated members of society, and they will have to suffer the oppression and violence of an inhumane system of abuse and control.

Doing time in a prison subjects a person to a variety of abuses. The abrupt separation of incarcerated people from their families creates mental and emotional stress, which leads to depression. This separation from our loved ones, coupled with the strategy of oppressing citizens via violent repression incorporates the element of physical abuse and trauma and exacerbates the psychological abuse that leads to extremely poor mental health. The strategy of repression, emotional and psychological abuse, is prevalent throughout the prison empire, and—interestingly—those of us who suffer similar oppression frequently find solace, humanity, and voice elsewhere.

Music has been a vehicle to soothe the pressures of suffering within oppressive and inhumane conditions and to fight or rebel against such conditions. Throughout slavery, music was a spiritual tool that served many purposes. Songs would be sung in the blistering hot cotton fields in order to remove the oppressed and repressed workers from the burden of their tumultuous and sordid labor. As their bodies slaved under the inhumane heat of the sun and the brutal whips of the slave drivers, their minds were probably able to find moments of peace and humanity from the voices of their neighbors. As long as there was song in the air, there existed a temporary escape from the harsh reality of their living conditions. In addition to the solace found in the flow of the slave song, the captured people found an avenue to communicate their social issues and struggles, as well as possibly their plans to attain freedom, by coding relevant information into song. In a blog post titled, "Singing in Slavery: Songs of Survival, Songs of Freedom," Johnson Reagon noted, "Slaves from different countries, tribes and cultures used singing as a way to communicate during the voyage. They were able to look for kin, countrymen and women through song" (Berry, 2017). Music, in these examples, was thus a primary tool for activists organizing against the system of oppression and repression.

During the civil rights movement, music was used to confront violent racism and fear. Throughout the marches to end segregation, protestors in Alabama, Georgia, and Mississippi used music, not only as a means of calming their own fears of state retaliation by racist power wielders, but also to project a message of peace and humanity in ugly situations. Songs such as "We Shall Overcome"—whose roots in activism date back to the labor struggles of the 1940s—were sung as police kicked protestors, spat on them, and commanded dogs to attack them. Freedom songs were the musical soul of the movement and played a tremendous role in the building of unity and bravery among the activists. Bernice Johnson Reagon, a student activist during the movement, who described the Albany, Georgia, movement as a "singing movement," stated that "after the song, the differences among us would not be as great" (1976, pp. 1–2). The resolve of those brave men and women was able to expose the brutal and repressive nature of the country, and to bring major public—and international—awareness of the cruelty and embarrassment to the political and social power structures.

If we accept music as an important component of struggle, based on its history, and we accept that prisons are contemporary institutions of oppression that preserve slavery and white supremacy, and abuse people's physical and mental health, we can argue that music is an essential need when doing time. The impact and function of music in prisons are consistent with its historical applications in times of slavery and throughout the civil rights movement. One of the most important items for an incarcerated person to have is a Walkman, radio, or tablet, that will provide them some kind of access to music. People who cannot afford these items will often borrow them from friends (at the risk of the lender being punished for sharing) during moments of emotional stress, boredom, or during times of loss. The perpetual noises of incarceration can drive us insane, and therefore, we often use music as a means to drown out those noises, so that we can find or create our own personal space. The effect that music has on the mind and on the emotional content of the listener is a phenomenon that allows the incarcerated person to tap into the depths of memory, dreams, or fantasy. This remarkable phenomenon provides a gateway for us to escape from the harsh realities of our inhumane living conditions, and from the depressing reality of being isolated from our families and our communities.

I am an activist, incarcerated for 22 years in the state of Massachusetts. There is a deep-rooted connection between prison and the preservation of slavery, human breaking, negative labeling, and forced control. I choose to use bold language in my desire to show society these connections. In my use of the word *nigger*, I may offend some of the readers, and if that is the case, I do not apologize. The United States of Amerikkka has used negative, dehumanizing labeling as a strategy to control and kill throughout its entire history. Africans were labeled "niggers," which made it acceptable to capture, oppress, enslave, sell, rape, and murder them. Incarcerated people are labeled "inmates," which makes it justifiable for the state to oppress, dehumanize, abuse, enslave, sell, rape (especially incarcerated women), and murder us. It is a goal of mine to eliminate the negative, dehumanizing label "inmate," and to make it as equally offensive as the word *nigger*. So, if you are offended by the use of that word, then I say to you, call me a "person," not an "inmate."

In 2012, André de Quadros, Jamie Hillman, and Emily Howe, introduced a music course into [xxx],[1] via the [xxx] Prison Education Program. Their unique, and unorthodox approach to teaching introduced us to a world of creative expression and interaction absent in the overall structure of incarceration.

The music course—which would eventually become the Empowering Song approach—encouraged us to tap into our deepest creative compartments through the use of music, art, and drama. It also emphasized, and redeveloped our sense of personhood by introducing the incarcerated students to a variety of guest artists, musicians, and actors. These guests were willing to enter a prison environment—without knowing what to expect—and interact with us without judgement or concern for the reasons of our incarceration. This facilitated an atmosphere of human bonding through music, which began to rehumanize the incarcerated participants and annihilate the negative stigma that the prison industrial complex places on people in prison. In other words, it showed the parties of our external society that there was something else going on inside of the prisons not commonly realized by the citizens of this country. While we sang, held hands, and looked each other in the eyes, we all understood that the differences among us were not great.

The inevitable phenomenon that music has on the human soul expressed itself through the tears of the incarcerated people who expressed sorrow, regret, remorse, optimism, hopelessness, and, at times, mourning. Tears were also liberated from the eyes of some of our guests, who discovered within themselves, a human connection to us, and a genuine feeling of love, appreciation, sympathy, and—possibly—forgiveness.

It is difficult to pinpoint specific incidents that were transformational in the Empowering Song class because everything counted. All of the seemingly little things that were explained above collectively created platforms for transformation that affected different people in a variety of ways. For me, the transformational experience was not behavioral. I was given a new way to look at where I stood in relation to the world, to society, and to people individually.

When the courts condemned me to a lifetime of incarceration, I felt abandoned by people in general. I had just experienced the loss of my life through injustice, and I became angry that society had approved—however blindly— of such a system to exist. I was angry with people for a long time. In prison, I began to experience oppression and repression at the hands of prison guards, and I became a victim of authorized abuse. For a long time, I believed that society did not care about what goes on in its prisons. They did not care about what happened to us. In a sense, they (society) wanted us all dead anyway. I knew that I could not just die, despite whatever society believed me to be, so I began to educate myself and to advocate for better living conditions for incarcerated people. I rebelled against foul treatment and demanded that incarcerated persons be respected and treated as human beings. At some point, I began to think, what if it's not that society doesn't care? What if they just don't know? In theory—if the latter was true—if society were to become educated about the inhumane practices inside prisons, their awareness should then cure the oppression. My generalized anger towards people became hope and inspiration, and, with that, I began to write hundreds of letters to strangers, fishing for anyone who would listen. After years of letter writing to no avail, my original belief was reinforced, and my anger was restored. The pain was in feeling that no one in the free world would ever see a human being when they looked at me. They'd only see an INMATE. Empowering Song proved me to be very wrong. As explained above, the people who came in to interact with us refused to judge us and saw only the human quality. After meeting André, Jamie, Emily, Jen, and Judy (Kính, Andy, Jason, Anna, Yui, and others would come into my life later, and completely bury my old theory, that people did not care), I had to concede my anger with the world. They clearly wished me no harm or hardship.

The greatest transformational incident for me was being introduced to Dido's Lament, "When I am laid in earth." Jamie Hillman had initially introduced the song to the class. During that semester, we had taken the song on as a theme for the course and, as we deciphered, pondered, expressed, and discussed the lyrics and their meaning, I was becoming more absorbed and connected to the piece. "When I am laid in earth, may my wrongs create no trouble in thy breast." "Remember me, but ah! forget my fate." These words spoke to the core of what I always wanted. This was the explanation of my inner struggle. I was condemned and labeled. My name was stripped of its relevance, and I was given an identification number. I was isolated from society, and I was adjudged to die and to perish. I did not want to die as irrelevant. Unknown to the world. Unlawfully judged. Prejudiced by the only life choices available to me in my adolescence. I wanted more than that. I wanted the quality of my human character to be remembered. I wanted to love and to be loved, and I hoped that I could accomplish enough to unburden my mother's heart when I perish.

> "May my wrongs create no trouble in thy breast." "Remember me," for the love that I have in me, and for every attempt that I would make to express that. Remember my kindness, and selflessness, but DAMMIT! Don't judge me for making the best of my limited choices.

I remember one of the classes in which a drama leader named Mike attended. In this class, we had to individually express ourselves using only the words *remember* and *me*. Mike had performed the two words in a way that represented him as having spent time reaching out in order to get the people to remember him beyond his bad choices. He started out extremely optimistic. Surely if he reached out to the people (represented by the class), they would see the good in him and forget his fate. As he went on to express the words *remember* and *me*, his emotions and body movements changed. He became less optimistic and more frustrated, begging to be remembered come his demise. He pleaded more and more aggressively, but to no avail. Finally, at the peak of his frustration with the world, he yelled, "Remember me!" And then, literally, screamed at the top of his lungs, while punching towards heaven and yelling upwards at God, "WELL WHY THE FUCK NOT?!!" I was done. Discovered. I had never seen anything that expressed so clearly and accurately what I had felt inside for so many years of my incarceration. He had reached into the very core of me and held it up for everyone to see. I just stared at him, holding back everything that I felt. I was both happy and terrified of his realization. Mike's performance had so much anger in it. So much rage and frustration and yet so much positive desire. How could he have possibly understood that? How could he have known what was inside of me? And how could he have expressed it so perfectly?

For the rest of the semester, Emily Howe sang the lyrics of Dido's Lament further into my soul, and it has become a part of my own understanding of what I have been after for so long. It gave me some clarity. I could no longer beg society to see me as a human. Instead, I must expose the good that exists in people, despite our immediate circumstances. A friend once told me that a person should not be judged by his or her worst decision, and the Empowering Song class introduced us to people willing to love us and let us into their hearts without such judgements. People are willing to forget our fates and to not be troubled by our wrongs. This is an act of forgiveness.

As I pondered Dido's Lament—even outside of the classroom—my faith in people grew strong. People do care. Because this is true, I have not strayed from this way of thinking, and I will continue to project the good in me, and expose the good in others, even when it seems that society is turning a blind eye.

A Brief Poem

I don't want to die an "Inmate."
A negative dehumanizing label designed to remove one's human

relevance.
Remember me as a "Person,"
But ah, forget my fate.

The Empowering Song approach did such a remarkable job of rehumanizing incarcerated persons that the course became a threat to the traditional culture of institutionalized oppression and dehumanization. This course began to be scrutinized by the prison administration and staff more aggressively than any other course offered through [xxx] Prison Education Program. The prison administration began to interfere with the course by limiting what the professors could bring in (for example, the administration barred the professors from bringing in art supplies, books, and other course material), what they could accept from us as homework, and what they could return to us as graded material. The system wanted control over anything that could cause us to understand our human value. The prison administration had a growing concern that the professors and guests were not objectifying us enough—since any human bonding is forbidden and goes against the weight of the prison regulations and the interests of the authorities. The Empowering Song approach was pulling emotions and substance out of us, that held the potential to create an awareness of our depth of isolation and oppression, and that carried with it a potential spark that could ignite activism. In other words, they were teaching the niggers how to read, and this could warrant an objection from the authorities. In spite of the prison administration's power to threaten, harass, inconvenience, and even bar the professors and guests from entering the prison, the Empowering Song method continued to flourish, and to bring—through that old Negro soul of music—healing, activism, and change, into an environment of oppression, repression, and inhumanity.

Music has established its relevance throughout the history of struggle in Amerikkka. It has been a key component of resistance by creating bonds between people who have suffered, and continue to suffer, the same oppressive experiences; by inspiring those who suffer to stand up against the forces of their suffering; by providing a means of communication that would result in liberation; and by exposing the human quality of the condemned. Since prisons are recognized as inhumane institutions of contemporary displacement, oppression, and repression, and since the United States is the world's leader in displacing its citizens through incarceration, music has a fundamental place in our prison environment. For it is the soul of our movement, a voice for the displaced, a common human ground, and the spark to our activism (see Figure 9.1).

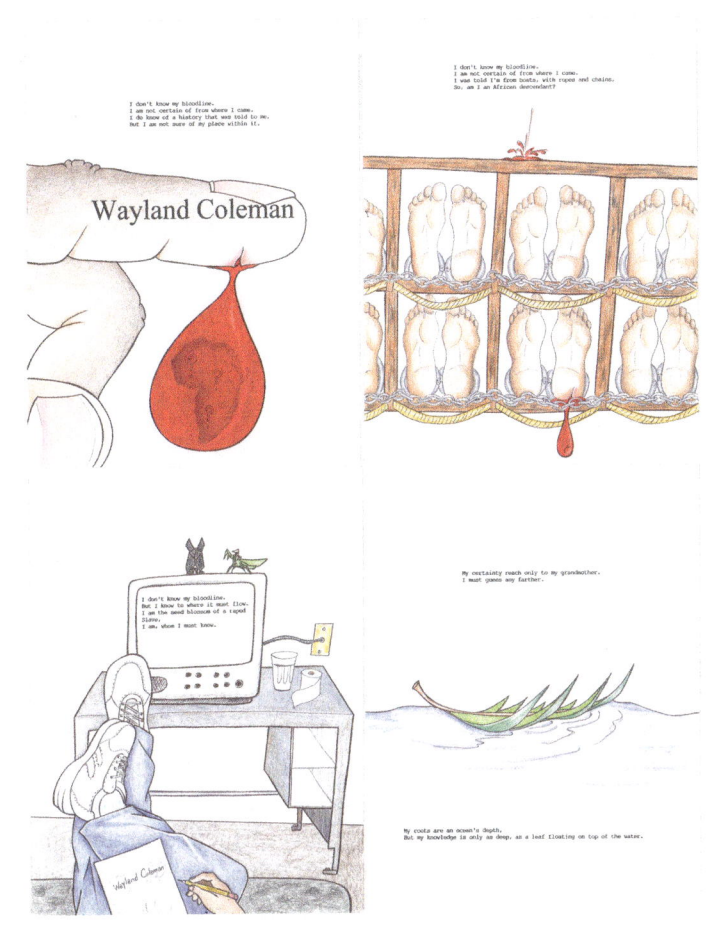

FIGURE 9.1 "I don't know my bloodline."

Note

1 [xxx] represents blacked out words, censured ideas, and forced silences. In some cases, the [xxx] represents locations that should be left unnamed in order to protect people affiliated with such spaces.

Reference

Berry, K. (2017). *Singing in slavery: Songs of survival, songs of freedom.* Retrieved from http://www.pbs.org/mercy-street/blogs/mercy-street-revealed/songs-of-survival-and-songs-of-freedom-during-slavery/

Reagon, B. J. (1976, January–February). In our hands: Thoughts on Black music. *Sing Out!*, 24, 1–2.

CHAPTER 10

What If Their Story Were Your Story? Lessons from Starting a Refugee Choir

Erin Guinup

> What if their story were your story?[1]
> LINDA K. BURTON

∵

I first heard this quote at a church conference about refugees in April 2016, and it haunted me for weeks. Though my family has been in America for generations, I couldn't shake the realization that my present comforts were a result of the kindnesses of others when my own ancestors had been displaced by war and persecution. I felt a great responsibility to do something for refugees in our community and ultimately decided to start the Tacoma Refugee Choir.[2]

I was naïve about how difficult this venture would be. Although the Tacoma Refugee Choir has grown rapidly and seen a strong positive impact on choir members and the community, the venture has also been fraught with complex challenges not faced in traditional choral settings. We experienced a tremendous learning curve as we adapted to meet the unique needs of the populations we served. We faced deep levels of mistrust among some communities, and it was an uphill battle to recruit singers among refugees who are already facing intense struggles to survive. The strategies I had used with other choirs were simply not effective with this ensemble and these challenges forced me to reevaluate everything I thought about music-making and my own privilege. There have been many moments of feeling like hurdles were insurmountable, and I frequently considered whether our goal was even possible.

Despite these difficulties, directing the Tacoma Refugee Choir has been a deeply rewarding experience. Choir members consistently refer to the group as their family and they try to support one another in their struggles. Powerful new friendships have developed as we exchange songs and dances, create new songs together, and share our feelings about the challenges we face. Over 500 people from 48 countries, including Cambodia, Democratic Republic of

© KONINKLIJKE BRILL NV, LEIDEN, 2020 | DOI: 10.1163/9789004430464_010

Congo, Honduras, Iran, Iraq, Sudan, and Ukraine have participated in rehearsals and the choir has performed for over 24,000 people at events including TEDxSeattle, WE Day (a youth empowerment event) and the National Race and Pedagogy Conference. Participants in the choir benefit from the opportunity to make music and friends, better understand other cultures, witness bravery and determination, advocate for fairness and a kinder community, and amplify the voices of those who might otherwise be silenced. The mission statement of the choir[3] emphasizes the value of belonging and hope in creating a welcoming community. The strength of one's social network is shown to be a key indicator of health (Reblin & Uchino, 2008) and success (Pilisuk & Parks, 1986) and a sense of belonging is invaluable to those who have lost much and are often facing the challenges of feeling alone and disoriented. The impact extends beyond those in the choir as audience members have the opportunity to join in sharing our message by singing along during our interactive concerts and participating in a community of diverse voices for the purpose of creating something beautiful.

This chapter will address some of the lessons learned thus far and how we work to overcome the hurdles unique to this model. Although, as of this writing, we are now three years old, we certainly do not have all the answers and feel there is still much we are learning. For those who would embark on this kind of work, it must be remembered that there is more than one way to do things and every situation will require immense flexibility to adapt to the needs and desires of a particular gathering of people.

Foundations: How We Started

The most difficult challenge has been recruiting members for the choir. While Tacoma is officially designated as a Welcoming City, and the State of Washington accepted the fourth highest number of refugees in the nation in 2017, most are settled 30 minutes north of Tacoma, leaving a fairly small refugee population in the city itself. Resettlement agencies are increasingly sending refugees to Tacoma due to lower housing costs, but refugees in this area tend to be scattered and are focused on simply surviving and adapting to life in their new home.

We began in 2016 with a partnership with Tacoma Community House, an organization serving local refugees and immigrants since 1910. They agreed to a pilot project that allowed us to recruit in their English as a Second Language (ESL) classes. Even with this partnership, recruitment was slow. The relationships formed, however, were powerful and we performed six weeks later with

22 singers representing six countries (seven of whom were designated by the United Nations High Commission for Refugees (UNHCR) as refugees). An additional nine refugees joined us for at least one rehearsal during those six weeks. By the end of the pilot project, a strong sense of community among members and a desire to continue singing together had been developed.

Everyone Must Have a Compelling Reason to Be There

As a music-lover, I had thought making music would be incentive enough to join our ensemble, but that alone was not sufficient reason for those struggling with survival. Participation in a choir requires a sacrifice of precious time, stepping outside one's comfort zone to meet new people, and a willingness to be vulnerable within a community. The benefits of participating must outweigh the "cost" of participation. While singing and a concern for a more equitable society is adequate motivation for some, many refugees have very real needs for practical support as they navigate their new lives. When possible, we have tried to connect our choir members to resources and made time to tell them where to turn for the support they need. Many crave familial relationships to compensate for those they lost or are separated from. We initially expected the opportunity to practice English to be the most significant draw for refugees, but this need has not been expressed by most of the refugees.

While there is value in experiencing the love and welcoming in the choir for one night, we have been eager to establish a more consistent group to allow development of deeper and more meaningful relationships. Despite our efforts, attendance by choir members often has been inconsistent and irregular. We have experimented with monetary incentives, including providing food and stipends to offset the cost of gas and their time, as well as additional English practice before rehearsals. While these efforts had some positive impact, the most successful strategy has been making phone calls to check in and express that we care, reminding members of rehearsals, or letting them know they were missed. Regardless of the reasons someone initially attends the choir, retention has been most effective when a member feels deeply needed and appreciated.

Connecting with Prospective Members

The Tacoma Refugee Choir has usually recruited through existing members of the choir and trusted members of the community. While posters around the city are translated into several languages, there is no substitute for person-ally asking someone if they like to sing and inviting them to experience this loving community. A majority of new members report being invited person-ally by a member of the choir who told them how this community had helped them. Worthy of note is that membership in the Tacoma Refugee Choir is not limited to refugees; it includes diverse members of the community united in support for one another regardless of background. Our outreach focuses on refugees and immigrants, but choir membership includes adults aged 18–92 who might wear a number of varying identities including student, father, sin-gle grandmother, wheelchair-bound, gay, politician, nun, Republican, little person, Black Lives Matter activist, uninsured, chaplain, and eternal optimist. We emphasize that we are more than a label and that everyone has a voice that can be used to make a difference

Partnerships Are Golden

Partnerships are invaluable for learning the unique needs of each cultural community, establishing credibility, and connecting with members. We have consciously cultivated relationships with community leaders and attended their gatherings where refugees and immigrants are likely to congregate (ESL classes, cultural festivals, and churches). Through being present at these events and in follow-up meetings, we have been able to earn some level of trust from these community leaders and begin to address concerns. Developing trust is not a quick process. Immigrants and people of color are frequently tokenized, and it takes consistently showing up, being fully present, and truly listening to build trust.

We have developed partnerships with refugee resettlement agencies, orga-nizations serving immigrants and refugees, colleges with music students inter-ested in service, international students studying English, other nonprofit and service organizations, musicians and major recording artists, lawyers, and our city government. Partnerships have allowed us to contribute in practical ways such as serving at refugee volunteer training sessions, attending citizenship ceremonies, and raising money for non-English speaking communities. Being a part of these activities has helped us expand the reach of our message to new audiences, and opened up access to funding sources.

Our partnership with the City of Tacoma was particularly beneficial as it provided significant financial and marketing support resources to advance our efforts and formally recognize our work through a proclamation on pub-lic record. This partnership of government and the arts resulted in the mayor performing with us on one of our concerts, and we reciprocated with a televised performance at the State of the City address.

Recruit Leadership from the Population Served

It is imperative to include diverse voices at the decision-making level of our organization. As a white woman born in America helming a nonprofit celebrating diversity, attempting to lead the organization with limited input from the community would be a disservice to the ensemble's mission and members. Certain perspectives can only be offered by the experiences of the community served, and including these perspectives in all stages of operation can help avoid major pitfalls and encourage positive growth. We make an effort to seek out former refugees to serve on our board (two of eight 2019 board members arrived as UNHCR refugees, another fled war in Ukraine through alternate legal paths, and three more were foreign-born), meet with refugees and immigrants who may not be interested in singing but understand the needs of the community, seek feedback from refugee choir members and people who did not return to rehearsals, and work to develop musical and organizational leadership by refugees and immigrants in the choir.

A turning point for us came when we were able to hire a refugee member part-time to recruit choir members and musicians. This young go-getter was a vocal advocate for us within the refugee community and helped us better understand our shortfalls and the hurdles we face. Her thoughts have been invaluable, as she put challenges in perspective and reminded us to keep going when resources were limited. She has served as a bridge of trust for new members, translated for people with limited English language skills, taught us new songs from her home country, made introductions to other leaders in her community, and enthusiastically expressed how this work made a difference for her. Moving forward, our goal is to obtain paid cultural ambassadors from at least five refugee communities to cultivate relationships, communicate directly with their communities, and translate when necessary.

The Space Matters

Our first rehearsal was in a community center, and when we began not a single refugee showed up despite all the recruiting work done by our partner organization in recruiting attendees. By the end, two Sudanese women arrived and participated in a beautiful sharing experience but they reported feeling uncertain about entering an unfamiliar location. The next week we moved to within the Tacoma Community House location that many refugees visit. This made a big difference. Space became an issue at the overcrowded facility, however, and, regrettably, we had to move to another location.

Buildings have a way of defining who is welcome in that space. Ideally, our rehearsals would be held in tandem with English classes or cultural orientation programs in buildings familiar to new arrivals. Because this has not yet been realized, we considered a number of factors when choosing our location including accessibility, religious affiliation, familiarity, parking lot lighting and other safety concerns, community partnerships, and proximity to public transportation.

The Power (and Danger) of a Name

The name of our ensemble, Tacoma Refugee Choir, has been both an asset and obstacle. When I began the choir, I felt a need to convey that we were united around the circumstances of refugees in order to differentiate it from the typical community choir. The name chosen has helped us connect with community members who are passionate about supporting refugees and with some refugees who might not have found us without the boldness of the name. One choir member exclaimed with delight at her first rehearsal, "When I heard there was a choir for refugees, I was so happy. Someone is actually thinking of us!"

At the same time, the name has set up challenges and expectations that are hard to meet. In particular, the choir has been criticized for not achieving an even balance of refugees and friends at performances. We performed 15 times in 2018 and participation by refugees ranged from 10% to 38% at public events. Our percentage in rehearsal varied even more widely in 2019 with a few discouraging weeks without any refugees, most weeks at about 25% and three times with refugees and other foreign-born participants exceeding 60%. Not all refugees are people of color; the largest number of recent refugees in Tacoma are from Ukraine.

During the course of one conversation about our name, a board member who fled Uganda as a refugee almost 40 years ago was asked, "When does one stop being a refugee?" to which he replied, "When you feel like you belong." He continued, "Perhaps the goal of the choir is to have no refugees because this is a place where everyone belongs."

At this stage, we have determined that we do not want to veer from our mission despite the steepness of the climb and the challenges of connecting with refugees, and amplifying their story. Billie Holiday, in her song *Crazy He Calls Me* (1949), includes the lyrics, "The difficult I'll do right now. The impossible will take a little while." This has inspired me to remember that our choir seeks to accomplish what society so often fails at and that conquering the seemingly impossible task of bringing together "refugees, immigrants and friends to sing together to extend love, hope and unconditional belonging"[4] and represent those aims in every performance is going to take a little while.[5]

The Process: What Do We Sing?

The second most common question we receive is about what we sing. This approach, too, has evolved. Initially, I selected songs in English and largely from the American pop and choral repertoire. The songs were hopeful and intended to build a spirit of unity and offer an opportunity for ESL learners to practice English skills. The feelings during rehearsals seemed positive, but we were not retaining our refugee members, and it took a while to realize that the music itself was part of the problem.

A conversation with my friend and colleague André de Quadros helped me to understand that teaching music from sheet music was not common in those parts of the world most affected by refugee crises. It became obvious that the traditional methods in which I had been trained to teach were a major hurdle that disadvantaged the very people we wanted to build up and support. If we really believed in making our community more welcoming, we had to make the choir more welcoming and that would require ending our reliance on sheet music, which privileges singers trained in Euro-American musics.

Now came the hard part: What would we sing without sheet music and how would we learn it? I struggled to figure out how to teach without the safety of a precise road map, but beautiful things happened as we all adapted to this change. Our first concert under this approach was a community sing-along, a format that offered some cover under which we could experiment and try new things. We taught songs by rote and encouraged harmonies, but singers typically blended together into unison. Because of the nature of this first concert, the unison singing was not problematic, and it probably helped our audiences feel courageous about singing with us. I missed the harmonies, but sought to discourage musical homogeneity. With time, we utilized several strategies that have made a huge difference.

Encourage Choir Members to Share Their Songs

On one occasion when a refugee member led a rehearsal, she shared a song she had written while in a Kenyan orphanage. Her poignantly hopeful ballad moved us all deeply, and we instantly felt a deep kinship with this woman as she talked about her longing for home. It was important to recognize that hearing and singing each others' songs helps us to know each other more intimately and to engage in solidarity with one another. This began a regular practice of sharing songs in rehearsals. We have learned traditional favorites and originals by both refugees and long-time community members. One young man shared an alternative rock song that I initially was uncertain about, which has now become a favorite of the choir. We now share simple songs by rote in the native tongues of our members, which has created a deeper appreciation of the challenges faced by refugees and new English speakers and has cultivated an environment of mutual exchange and appreciation.

Music Selection Is a Team Effort

We have attempted to program music that reflects those who are singing with us, and we encourage members to suggest songs for consideration. Occasionally a song will be selected that someone might find problematic and we make time to discuss together the meanings of texts and any concerns. For example, we sang Michael Bussewitz-Quarm's "Lamiya's Song" after a discussion about the name of our choir and what constitutes a refugee and when one ceases to be a refugee. The poem, written by a then nine-year old Azeri refugee named Lamiya, included the lyrics, "I beg of you, Please, don't call me 'refugee.'" This song led to a powerful conversation about labels and what our role is as a community to empathize and support those who have been displaced.[6] This discussion ultimately affirmed the name of our choir by all members and gave us greater clarity about our mission.

Creating Songs Together

Original songs are increasingly becoming an important part of our repertoire. We began this process when several members shared poems about their refugee experience and we subsequently set the poems to music. Another song developed after a few members wanted lyrics that were more hopeful and affirmed that their past traumas do not define their future. "Everyone Can Love Someone" has become our favorite anthem with lyrics that include "Sad stories can be rewritten where fear ends and hope begins. Everyone can love someone and everyone needs love. It doesn't matter where you're from. We all need love."

Recognizing that creating our own songs is empowering for our members, we spent time in rehearsal each month to brainstorm and write together. One woman wept with pride when we sang the words that she helped write, and our relationship deepened with her as we express her words of hope.

A challenging aspect of improvisation is pitching, and, because many of our choir members are not experienced performers, finding harmonies is not necessarily intuitive. It can be a challenge to break patterns of homogeneity and accept differences as a positive trait. I often remind them that there is no wrong in singing except to not sing, for it is by singing that we improve and find the best sounds. Breaking down the process by starting with rhythms has improved the texture of our songs and given members the courage to be even more adventurous. Some strategies include repeating words on a single note under the melody, basic vocal percussion (making rhythms with percussive consonants p, k, t, s, and sh), holding drone notes, and combining rhythms with a musical motif. After singing the melody of a simple song together, we repeat the chorus a number of times with half the group trying one variation after another and singing it a final time with their favorite choices. Choir members are encouraged to acknowledge someone when they like a sound they have added to the texture. The repetition of this kind of activity has emboldened members to take greater risks and to find more joy in the creative process.

Movement, as well, can be a valuable part of our musical practice[10] and often provides levity and connection in the ensemble. Dancing and singing are inextricably connected, and introducing simple steps with repetition offers the opportunity to feel empowered in our bodies and break down walls of insecurity. We also encourage freestyle movement with some of our favorite songs.

Sing-alongs Invite Our Audiences to Join with Our Mission

At every performance, we invite the audience to join our community and sing with us. Our objective is not only to inspire people with our music but also to move people to act and be changed by our message. Some of our most successful events have been our community sing-alongs. These high-energy interactive concerts engage a large audience in every song and include repetition, movement and popular musical favorites. One attendee at our first Community Sing-Along described the event as "music, community building, social activism, and entertainment all in one."[7] Guest artists such as Grammy winner Wanz and The Voice's Stephanie Anne Johnson and Nalini Krishnan joined us, and we were supported with professional lighting and sound. We projected lyrics on a large screen and encouraged the audience to connect in a celebration of community. One of my favorite moments was seeing an older man with a walker struggling to do the steps and an unrelated young girl helping him. The song and dance helped the years melt between them; they were simply two humans having fun together. At that event, we sang an original song that asserts that everyone has a song to share and that we are better together as we sing together.[8] My favorite line states, "It's hard not to love people when we sing together."

Subsequent events have been smaller in scale but continue to emphasize the value all members have in creating a welcoming and supportive community. An attendee wrote, "I came to the sing-along last month after visiting my son [in prison] and the songs brought me to tears. One song with lyrics about stopping the violence affected me deeply. This time we came with my 92-year old grandmother from El Salvador, and she loved it! It couldn't have been more perfect."[9]

Western music-making focusses on preparing for a culminating concert. Music for some people, however, is entirely about the enjoyment of the process and may not include performance. While many of the refugees in our choir are open about sharing their stories in a smaller setting, they do not always show up for performances, and some have expressed their discomfort with singing on stage. We have tried to emphasize that this is only one part of the choir and that their participation in the choir does not require performance. As a result, our performances do not always reflect the diversity attained in rehearsals, and this has caused us to reevaluate the role concerts play with this vulnerable population.

Sometimes People Need a Break from the Music

Singing is not the only part of rehearsal. Breaks are a critical component. Not singing at rehearsal was initially counterintuitive to me, but if the central goal is to build community and change lives, the entire rehearsal time cannot consist of singing. Singing connects us and brings us together, but individual relationships provide the foundation for unity. People need time to connect with one another on a personal level, and this will most likely happen during non-singing exercises, games, and conversational breaks.[10] At the heart of our mission is creating a welcoming and supportive community, so relationship building must be a top priority. Making time to enjoy each other's company is important, and, while it takes time away from the musical preparation, this social time actually advances our musical goals. We all perform better when unified in sharing the experience with friends.

Where Do We Go from Here?

In 2019, we are a small nonprofit organization, but we are gaining momentum and are eager to make a greater impact locally and share our message more broadly without diluting our impact on individuals in the choir. What began as a small effort to support local refugees has turned into a platform to contribute to the larger conversation about how we treat refugees in the United States. Our future plans include expanding our programs and partnerships to work directly with more refugees in our region, build outreach programs in schools, record an album of original songs, create videos to share online, and produce concerts that bring people together from all walks of life to sing for our community. While our work remains focused locally, we see the opportunity to impact the dialogue nationally and globally.

Does This Really Make a Difference?

The impact of a vibrant and supportive community can be hard to measure. Anecdotal evidence from members, however, suggests that powerful changes are happening in the lives of individuals. A Congolese choir member said, "If I miss it, I'm not OK. It's a home. I feel like I have people there who care, who know what's going on" (Driscoll, 2018, para. 11). A refugee from Chad added, "Having the connection with the choir, it was like a place for love, it's like a home for love, where love is being expressed unconditionally. You come here, and you go home having a smile on your face" (Driscoll, 2018, para. 16). He later said, "The choir healed my mistrust."[11]

On one particularly discouraging day, I made calls to members we had not seen at rehearsal in a while. A Kurdish refugee explained that he missed rehearsals because he was so distraught about the violence his family and friends faced back home. He proceeded to share heartbreaking and disturbing stories and a video of the warring chaos in his home city. For a moment, I thought that the choir was insignificant compared with the heavy problems he was facing. As I was ending the phone call more discouraged than before, he thanked me for *listening and being his friend.* I was struck with the clear realization that the music we had made together had created an intimacy of trust that allowed us to develop a deep friendship. I still could not do anything about the violence and suffering, but I could sit with him to lift him up while his heart was breaking. When we feel powerless to help those we care about, our friendship and support is sometimes the only resource we have to give and perhaps the most valuable. He and I would never have developed this powerful relationship if we had not first sung together.[12]

Martin Luther King, Jr. famously said, "Darkness cannot drive out darkness; only light can do that. Hate cannot drive out hate; only love can do that." At this time in history, when there is so much hate and suffering, this work is really about affirming the power of love and relationships as a precious balm for healing hearts and changing lives. Singing itself does not necessarily change someone's life but if accompanied by love and compassion, it can be a vehicle for building relationships that can rewrite a sad story and bring hope for a brighter future. Ultimately, "singing doesn't change the world but singing changes people, and people change the world."[13]

 VIDEO 10.1 TEDx talk and performance of Everyone Has a Song: Welcoming Refugees through Music.
The video accompanying this chapter is freely available online at https://doi.org/10.6084/m9.figshare.12445826

 VIDEO 10.2 The People Have the Power is performed by the Tacoma Refugee Choir.
The video accompanying this chapter is freely available online at https://doi.org/10.6084/m9.figshare.12445883

 VIDEO 10.3 Everyone Can Love Someone by Trésor John, Erin Guinup, and Nathalie Bajinya (© 2018 Tacoma Refugee Choir).
The video accompanying this chapter is freely available online at https://doi.org/10.6084/m9.figshare.12445895

Notes

1 For more information on Linda K. Burton's speech *I Was a Stranger*, see https://www.churchofjesuschrist.org/study/general-conference/2016/04/i-was-a-stranger?lang=eng

2 To learn more about the founding of the Tacoma Refugee Choir, please visit their website at www.refugeechoir.org

3 Refugee Choir Project's Mission Statement is "We are a welcoming community of refugees, immigrants, and friends who sing together to extend love, hope, and unconditional belonging."

4 Tacoma Refugee Choir mission statement.

5 Tacoma Refugee Choir blog post on October 12, 2019. https://www.refugeechoir.org/post/the-difficult-i-ll-do-right-now

6 "Lamiya's Song (Please Don't Call me Refugee)" by Michael Bussewitz-Quarm, lyrics by Lamiya Safarova. Published by MBArts https://www.jwpepper.com/Lamiya%27s-Song/10867598.item#/submit

7 Gregory Youtz, personal communication.

8 "Everyone Has a Song" by Erin Guinup and Stephanie Anne Johnson. © 2017 Tacoma Refugee Choir https://tacomarefugeechoir.bandcamp.com/releases

9 Facebook message on October 18, 2019.

10 The value of coffee breaks and time to converse is well documented as having value in Swedish refugee choirs; see de Quadros and Vu (2017).

11 Abou Saleh, personal communication.

12 Guinup letter to Tacoma Refugee Choir donors, April 2019.

13 Guinup in speech to Northwest Region American Choral Directors Assocation in March 2018.

References

Crazy he calls me [Recorded by B. Holiday]. (1949). On *You're my thrill/Crazy he calls me* [Shellac, 10"]. Kensington: Decca.

de Quadros, A., & Vu, K. T. (2017). At home, song, and fika: Portraits of Swedish choral initiatives amidst the refugee crisis. *International Journal of Inclusive Education, 21*(11), 1113–1127. doi:10.1080/13603116.2017.1350319

Driscoll, M. (2018, May). Woman who fled atrocities in Congo finds 'home' in Tacoma choir. The News Tribune. Retrieved from https://www.thenewstribune.com/news/local/news-columns-blogs/matt-driscoll/article210781889.html

Pilisuk, M., & Parks, S. H. (1986). *The healing web: Social networks and human survival.* Hanover, NH: University Press of New England.

Reblin, M., & Uchino, B. N. (2008). Social and emotional support and its implications for health. *Current Opinion in Psychiatry, 21*(2), 201–205. doi:10.1097/YCO.ob013e3282f3ad89

CHAPTER 11

Street Stops and Mountain Tops: The Voice of Hip-Hop

Tou SaiKo Lee, Mai Yang Xiong and Keng Chris Yang

Rhythm and poetry are the voice of hip-hop that inspires, moves, and provokes change. Hip-hop has significant impact on our generation. As Hmong youth try to find their own cultural identity in a society that has not yet embraced community, young people find refuge in hip-hop and can communicate about their own struggles and perspectives.

In this chapter, we tell the story of a music education project in which we, as teaching artists, are connected to students of Piyawat Orphan House[1] in Thailand. This orphanage houses 35 young people from ages five to 20. Most of the children have either been abandoned or their parents are in prison due to drug-related activities. The lack of opportunities and pressure to provide for family have created an environment that forces some people to be involved with the drug trade by trafficking amphetamines. There is concern about young people who are involved in activities that do not lead to educational or occupational goals. Many of the young people were born in various villages around the Chiang Mai area of northern Thailand. Hmong, like other refugees, are at risk of gradually being disconnected from their cultural identity when they live away from villages. For example, the children often lose their Hmong language while attending school in the city.

The orphanage's founders, a husband and wife team named Vang Pao Yang and Yeng Cho, created Piyawat Orphan House to honor their late son by the same name of Piyawat. The founders encourage the youth to immerse themselves in the arts as extracurricular activities. Regardless of what the children express in their art, these young people make time to sing, write songs and poetry, and play drums, keyboards, and guitar. All of the students are self-taught either by sharing knowledge with each other or learning how to create music by watching YouTube videos. No music classes are offered in schools in Thailand. These children cannot afford to attend the private music schools that do exist. At the orphanage, some donated instruments include guitars, drums, and a keyboard; however, no music teachers are available to show the young people how to play.

Street Stops and Mountain Tops (SSMT),[2] a Minnesota-based international project, strives to create self-expression within Hmong communities that will empower students in both the United States and Southeast Asia. Teaching artists support students as active learners and artists. SSMT seeks opportunities for students and teaching artists to share art as a way to imagine how identity exists within the Hmong diaspora. Children and youth actively engage, reflect, and learn with one another in a variety of spaces as a way to bridge communities through arts.

This chapter recounts our trip to Thailand from December 2016 until January 2017 in which we had a team of six volunteer teaching artists, including musicians and dancers. Our journey, called Unify Trip, took 14 days in total. We interacted with the young people of Piyawat Orphan House for ten days to teach guitar and songwriting that would culminate in a final showcase. The Hmong students did not have the resources to learn how to read or write in the Hmong language. The young people no longer resided in their villages. The orphanage where they live today is in the city of Chiang Mai. Hence, children were more at risk of assimilating to Thai culture and losing their Hmong culture, especially its language.

Throughout the songwriting process, the teaching artists encouraged students to write about their lives, struggles, and ambitions. They either wrote in Thai or orally told their stories so that the teaching artists could translate and write in the Hmong language. After the stories were collected, the teaching artists taught how to shape their ideas into a song form. The guitar teacher, Keng Chris Yang, helped students to develop the instrumental riffs for the songs, and the voice teacher Mai Yang Xiong mentored students to apply melodies to their music. After the main group song was completed, the teaching artists had the students practice and rehearse their music that also included individual songs. At the final showcase the Hmong founders of Piyawat Orphan House seemed surprised that the young people were able to read, write, and speak more fluently in Hmong language.

Our Hmong on the Move

Hmong are an ethnic group[3] comprised of 18 clans from parts of Southeast Asia, including Vietnam, Laos, Thailand, and Myanmar (Burma), as well as southern regions of China. The construction of an expanded Hmong diaspora resulted from those who fled following the Lao Civil War, often referred to as the US Secret War in Laos.[4] The Secret War separated the Hmong, a nationless people and threatened their survival in the mountains; hence, many Hmong fled Laos. Those who embarked on treacherous journeys down the mountains and across the Mekong River to refugee camps in Thailand, for example, were eventually resettled in countries such as Argentina, Australia, Canada, France, Germany, and the United States, while some remained in Thailand.

We Hmong people are without a homeland, and refugee camps became our foster parents until we were adopted by new countries. In the United States, for example, Hmong refugees were assisted by agencies such as Minnesota's International Institute, Catholic Conference, and Lutheran Immigration and Refugee Services (Hillmer, 2010; Vang, 2008). Hmong refugees moved to the Twin Cities (Minneapolis and St. Paul) in large numbers where social services were readily available. According to Hillmer (2010), Minnesota's Twin Cities became "the epicenter of the Hmong community in the United States" (p. 286). Yang (2015) reported for Minnesota Public Radio News that the Hmong population in the state reached the second largest in the nation and numbered more than 66,000.[5]

Hip-Hop as an Educational Process

In Vu's (2013) dissertation that focused on Hmong youth artists in the Twin Cities, Chili, a Hmong hip-hop artist from St. Paul, noted the importance of hip-hop as an educational tool:

> I think that this kind of education that's been done underground, like much of what hip-hop has always been—I think its ability to inspire, to empower youths has not been present in the education system. I think that music education has become, has been Westernized. (p. 135)

Part of the inspiration for hip-hop as education in the Hmong community arose from youth development initiatives in St. Paul. Hmong organizations, such as the Center for Hmong Arts and Talent, United Prodigies, In Progress, and East Side Rising, planted the seeds for Street Stops and Mountain Tops. In a 2012 pamphlet about the organization East Side Rising, Tou SaiKo Lee wrote, "Hip-hop musicians are encouraged to share their voices with one another in their neighborhoods to confront issues centering on stories of home and social justice."[6]

When writing and teaching lyrics for hip-hop songs, Tou Saiko is influenced by masterful rappers who pushed the boundaries of rhyming with dynamic styles outside of traditional poetic structures like endrhymes.[7]

Teaching and Creating Rhyming Poetry

In teaching hip-hop within Hmong villages in Thailand, I usually reference a type of Hmong rhyming poetry called *Paj Huam*. I say that hip-hop is like *Paj Huam Hmoob Meskas,* which means Hmong American poetry. The way *Paj Huam* works is the final word of the first line rhymes with an internal word of the next line (usually the third word). That rhyme scheme repeats throughout the Hmong poem. Hmong does not have ending consonant sounds; the last letter of a word is a tone indicator. As a Hmong hip-hop teacher who is developing a unique style, I utilize a multi-rhyme scheme that is not as structured as *Paj Huam* in which words could rhyme anywhere in a line (beginning, middle, or end). For instance, I might use two different words that do not rhyme in one line that continue to rhyme in the next line. Below are examples of a *Paj Huam* written by my cousin Phas from Thailand and an excerpt of my first Hmong language hip-hop song titled "Ntiaj Teb Koom Tes," which means "Unified Worldwide." I boldfaced the rhyme words of the *Paj Huam*. For the hip-hop lyrics I boldfaced rhymes and italicized and boldfaced second rhymes within the schemes to identify the style of rhyming.

Excerpt from "***Paj Huam***" of Toj Siab by Phas Vwj

Kuv nrhias txog Hmoob txoj kev **qub**/Ua thaum **ub**, cov laus tso **tseg**/
Txhob sib **ceg**, peb pab tiv **thaiv**/Yuav Tsum **Saib** peb yawg thiaj **pog**/
Kuv pom **txog** Hmoob muaj zog **kawg**/Peb Tsis **tawg** ntxiv yav tom **ntej**/
Qhia rau **nej** ua ntej paub **txog**/Peb lub **zog** tsis yog tas li no

Excerpt from Lyrics of "***Ntiaj Teb Koom Tes***" (Unified Worldwide), by Tou SaiKo

cov paub kev **cai**, kawm ntawv siab, menyuam **laib**/
cov paub **hais** lub dawb, ntsuab, los **txaij**/
tsis ua li **cas**, txhua **yam** teb chaws, sib *paub*, sib *qhaub*, sawv **daws**/

ib pab, ib **pawg**, ib *hnub*, ib *hlub* nrhiav tau **peb** txoj kev vam meej tom **ntej**/
thiaj li cuag tau *ntiaj* **teb** koom tes ua **ke**, *ntiaj* **teb** koom tes.

Teaching Musicians in Piyawat

In the following segments, each of us teaching artists shares a story about music education in Piyawat Orphan House.

Tou SaiKo Lee, Spoken Word Poet and Rapper

I started writing hip-hop lyrics when I was 16 years old. I was living in a juvenile institution in Minnesota called Boys Totem Town. I was inspired by songs by Tupac Shakur such as "Unconditional Love" and "Life Goes On" because I can relate to his expression of vulnerability in a violent and masculine environment. A close friend and I wrote lyrics as letters that we mailed to each other. He was locked up in a juvenile institution in Clarinda, Iowa. After I got out, I continued working on writing poetry and lyrics as a way to keep myself positive and productive. Then my younger brother Vong and I started a hip-hop duo called Delicious Venom (see Video 11.1).

FIGURE 11.1   Tou SaiKo Lee leads a spoken word poetry workshop at Boston University.
PHOTOGRAPH: KÍNH T. VŨ

While taking classes at Century College in St. Paul, Minnesota, I was inspired to get into spoken word poetry by the works of poets such as Saul Williams, Beau Sia, Bao Phi, and Ed Bok Lee. I had the idea of collaborating with my grandma Youa Chang after realizing that what I do in spoken word is a continuation of an oral tradition that she performed called *kwv txhiaj*, a traditional form of Hmong poetry-chanting. Our intergenerational collaboration was called Fresh Traditions (see Video 11.1).

As I learned more from my grandma about Hmong arts that people call *Txuj Ci*, I discovered that these forms of creativity were our everyday ways of survival. For example, when I was staying in a Hmong village in Thailand, I saw a Hmong elder chanting *kwv txhiaj* next to a garden. She told me that she was chanting for therapeutic reasons to heal a past trauma. There is also *paj huam*, a type of Hmong poetry that can teach about culture and history.

I have struggled to speak the Hmong language because I grew up in the United States. It was not until my grandma came into my life when I was a teenager that I started to speak Hmong more often to communicate with her and listen to her storytelling. For the first ten years of writing hip-hop lyrics, I only wrote in English. In 2011, I traveled to Thailand and stayed in a Hmong village for one month. That experience pushed me to write songs in the Hmong language. This is when I thought about creating Street Stops and Mountain Tops. I wanted to bring our knowledge and resources from the United States to Southeast Asia, starting in Thailand.

As an introduction to the songwriting process, we introduced Piyawat Orphan House children to two Hmong language hip-hop songs. The first song was by Bao Xiong, a rapper from St. Paul, Minnesota; her song "Tsis Hnov Kuv" means "You don't hear me." The second song was by TL (Thao Lor), a Detroit, Michigan-based artist. His song "Txog Nej Thib" means "It's your turn." I asked the children to listen to the songs and to remember specific words. The students shouted words such as *txom nyem* (struggle), *ib pab ib pawg* (a group of people coming together), *poob kua muag* (tears falling). For the musical bridge, we emulated a DJ scratching with repetition.

> Peb, Peb, Peb Yog Hmoob. We, We, We are Hmong.
> Peb, Peb, Peb Yog Piyawat. We, We, We are Piyawat.

One experience of some of the students was that when they attend school in Chiang Mai, the other students looked down on them because they were Hmong and were also orphans. These students who now live at Piyawat Orphan House grew up in mountaintop villages, and they came down to live in the big city. I responded by letting them know that even if they are looked down on, they have each other. One of the boys started singing enthusiastically:

Tsis muaj peb,[8] ces muaj plaub,	Without us (without three), there is four,
Tsis muaj tsib, ces muaj rau,	Without five, there is six,
Tsis muaj xya, ces muaj yim,	Without seven, there is eight
Tsis muaj cuaj, ces luag ntxi	Without nine then smile.

A week after the final performance, I returned to Piyawat with my wife Dao Xiong. We worked with Tsuv Vaaj, a local videographer, to create a video testimony in which we interviewed the orphanage parents Vang Pao Yang and Yeng Cho. When the students rehearsed and performed this song for the orphanage showcase, the founders told us that they were surprised that the younger children (5–8 years old), could pronounce Hmong since they have been more exposed to the Thai language while living in Chiang Mai and away from Hmong villages.

Mai Yang Xiong, Singer-Songwriter

I traveled with five other artists, mentors, and teachers to Chiang Mai to work with the youth on music and songwriting. I had no idea what to expect since this was my very first time teaching abroad and teaching in the Hmong language. A regular day for us consisted of traveling to a Hmong village two to three hours away in the morning to hold two-hour music and dance sessions for Hmong students. We tried our best to reach a different village each day. The second part of the day was dedicated to teaching the Piyawat students dance and music in Chiang Mai.

What I first I noticed about the Hmong-Thai students was their respect toward strangers, teachers, elders, and each other. Each day we were greeted with a *wai* (Buddhist praying hands) to welcome us and show respect, and

FIGURE 11.2   Mai Yang Xiong sings songs with Piyawat children.
PHOTOGRAPH: TOU SAIKO LEE

we were offered lunch and dinner with joyful conversations. The children of Piyawat wrote a chorus that they felt true to them and their experience in Thailand. I felt this was also applicable to myself as a Hmong woman living in the United States.

"Children of Piyawat"
By the Hmong students in Chiang Mai, Thailand

Txawm peb yug saum roob	Even though we were born in the mountains
Los peb tseem muaj peev xwm	We still do have courage
Peb yog Hmoob	We are Hmong
Mus kawm ntawv siab siab	Going to get a higher education
Peb yuav ua tiag tiag	We will do our best
Peb yog Hmoob	We are Hmong

We taught a songwriting session in each village we visited. The sessions were accompanied by discussions about what *Kaj Siab* (free of stress) meant to the students. We then created verses to go with a song that I co-wrote with my sister MaiThao called "Kaj Siab." The song attempts to turn the unfair and darker experiences of the Hmong into something more positive and hopeful. Our hope for students was that they would be able to reflect on and cope with stresses through positive forms such as music or dance.

Overall, the experience was impactful. It inspired me to become a teacher back in the United States and to bring awareness to our students in Minnesota so that they can reflect upon the privilege that some of us Hmong in America have experienced, such as public education and non-profit support groups. In turn, I hope to inspire students in the US to love learning and open up to public services while integrating the arts.

Keng Chris Yang, Guitar Teacher
In 2016, I graduated from McNally Smith College of Music with a degree in guitar performance and music business. Following graduation, I worked with Street Stops and Mountain Tops for almost six months and was invited by Tou SaiKo to work alongside him and several other artists in Thailand as a guitar teacher. Much of the way I teach and the music I use is American- and Hmong-based, like the work of multi-genre guitar player John Mayer and Hmong bands like Paradise. The students at Piyawat, however, had their own amazing taste in music. They were more interested in Thai Pop and new generation Hmong music such as Sudden Rush and David Yang.

FIGURE 11.3   Keng Chris Yang performs for children at the orphanage.
PHOTOGRAPH: TOU SAIKO LEE

My ten-day lesson plan consisted of teaching anatomy of the guitar, theory, guitar chords, song building, and playing music with others. While teaching the basics of guitar is not a revolutionary idea and may even be viewed as a colonial music education practice, guitar was embraced by the youth at Piyawat as an exciting and fun way to make music.[9] As we got to know the students, it became apparent that I had prepared lessons for beginning guitar players only, not for experienced ones. Some of the students had more skills than we had anticipated; therefore, we had to modify plans almost every day in order to keep up. This first-time experience kept all the teaching artists on their toes.

The first few days passed and I split my guitar lessons into two groups. One group consisted of the more experienced students while the other had beginners. Although the beginners were young, they really loved playing guitar and singing. Some students stuck around just to sing with the guitar players. I passed out several sheets that had music notation, beginner guitar chords, the circle of fifths, and guitar scales. The younger ones dived into practicing the beginner material while the older, more experienced students asked to be pushed to play guitar solos and to play together rather than by themselves (see Figure 10.4).

I wished we had more time to teach the children; I wanted to pass so much knowledge to them before leaving Thailand. This is one of the main reasons why I keep in contact with several students. Near the end of the visit, several guitar students wrote songs with the singing students and started making

FIGURE 11.4   Learning songwriting with Keng.
PHOTOGRAPH: TOU SAIKO LEE

music together. One of my guitar students named Yeem Xyooj—Yeng Xiong, came up with a guitar part to go with his lyrics in which he sang about the struggles of his father's passing and his mother's drug addiction that made it quite hard for him to get either a proper education or money. He is in college now and, with the support of the Piyawat Orphan House, he is working to become a pastor.

Fostering Cultural Identity through Hip-Hop

With an emphasis on lyrical content and poetry, Street Stops and Mountain Tops workshops engaged Piyawat Orphan House children in hip-hop culture through movement activities, songwriting, and spoken word poetry with Hmong cultural references and energetic hip-hop music. These artistic forms conveyed messages of cultural identity, human rights, racism, and the power of the arts. Our arts residencies explored and expanded ways in which we can make a positive impact on social issues through our words.

We encountered teaching and learning challenges while working with Hmong Thai youth. Chief among those challenges was the language barrier. Some of the youngest students (ages 5–11) were so immersed in Thai language and culture that they did not understand us when we gave instructions in Hmong to them. The teenagers would translate our instructions into Thai language. The process was discouraging for us not to be able to communicate to a few of the students. This is also true of some Hmong children in the United States who have assimilated to the extent where they are unable to speak or understand Hmong language.

Mindful of these challenges, we observed how Hmong language hip-hop empowered youth in a diaspora of displaced Hmong; it is freedom of voice in a land where our ancestors have migrated due to persecution, war, and survival in the mountains. A sense of worldwide identity might be elevated through maintaining creative networks on social media. Music videos on YouTube, for instance, might call for disenfranchised Hmong populations to advocate collectively for basic human rights. The Hmong narrative of surviving oppressive societies has a strong connection not only to the music but also to the hip-hop movement of achieving something from nothing in which disadvantaged communities might persevere and rise from poverty.

Displaced Hmong have utilized hip-hop as an effective way to revitalize language and embrace cultural pride. Hip-hop is also a social and cultural movement which emphasized the Each One, Teach One philosophy of learning, mastering, and teaching the next generation. Through this process of rapping in our own language, we can teach each other about our particular experiences growing up in different parts of the world and how we might continue to bond through the similarities of our cultural kinship in a diasporic community that has always lived without a homeland and without borders.

VIDEO 11.1 Delicious Venom performs 30 Year Secret.
The video accompanying this chapter is freely available online at
https://doi.org/10.6084/m9.figshare.12445901

VIDEO 11.2 Fresh Traditions performs Hmong chant.
The video accompanying this chapter is freely available online at
https://doi.org/10.6084/m9.figshare.12445937

Notes

1 For further information on the Piyawat Orphan House, see
https://unboundedlife.com/piyawat-orphan-house/

2 For further information on Street Stops and Mountain Tops, see https://streetstops.org

3 The phrase "Our Hmong people," rather than "The Hmong people," is used here as a way to lay claim to a personal and/or cultural identity. To illustrate the point, Vu (2013) found that Hmong youth in St. Paul, Minnesota make music for "special purposes including social justice, youth development, Hmong identity (or "Hmong-ness"), and art for the sake of art" (p. 135).

4 The Secret War, according to Hmong historian Paul Hillmer (2010), is a colloquial term for the Lao Civil War (1961–1973). During this period, Hmong people (i.e., ethnic minorities) were victims of systematic eradication by the Pathet Lao (communist guerillas) as a way to punish the Hmong for assisting the Royal Lao Government that had sided with the United States and the CIA to defeat communism on the Indochinese Peninsula. The Lao Civil War and the accompanying killings were *secret* because they were overshadowed by the Vietnam War (1955–1975) (see Vu, 2013).

5 The US Census Bureau reported more recent figures for Hmong in Minnesota in the 2017 American Community Survey 1-Year Estimates indicating that the state is home to a total population of 85,263 Hmong people (+/- 7,239). See the full report titled "2017 American Community Survey Data (Minnesota Hmong Profile)" at https://www.hmongstudiesjournal.org/hmong-census-data.html

6 Unpublished East Side Rising pamphlet, August 2, 2012.

7 My rhyming style is influenced by legendary artists such as Big Daddy Kane, Rakim, and Inspectah Deck; and my rhymes resemble more contemporary MCs like J. Cole and Kendrick Lamar.

8 The word "peb" has two meanings: the number three and *we* or *us*.

9 In conversations with Kính Vu who musicks with orphan children in Vietnam, we realize that any musical interactions, whether Eastern or Western, are in some ways enjoyable to our participants. In some cases, music teaching of any kind might be subversive in contexts such as orphanages where basic human interactions might be limited.

References

Hillmer, P. (2010). *A people's history of the Hmong.* St. Paul, MN: Minnesota Historical Society.

Vang, C. Y. (2008). *Hmong in Minnesota.* St. Paul, MN: Minnesota Historical Society Press.

Vu, K. T. (2013). *Hmong youth arts culture: Music teaching and learning in community settings* (Doctoral dissertation) University of Minnesota, Minneapolis, MN. Retrieved from https://conservancy.umn.edu/handle/11299/154928

Yang, N. (2015). 10 things about Hmong culture, food and language you probably didn't know. *MPR News*. Retrieved from https://www.mprnews.org/story/2015/03/01/10-things-hmong

"You Play Me Your Music and I'll Play You Mine": Munich's First Smart (Phone) Party

Ulrike Präger

Heterogeneous groups, youth culture, nightlife spaces, and mobile phones are often perceived as socially disruptive forces. And yet, in Munich's "Smart (Phone) Parties" a dance party concept developed by community musician, DJ, and cultural pedagogue Thomas Lechner—they combine to become tools with which, according to Lechner, "translational spaces for participation, visible alterity, and lived democracy" according to Lechner (2018), can be created.[1]

Driven to act by the refugee camp built in 2015 next to Thomas's everyday workspace, where he witnessed firsthand both the refugees' burdensome life circumstances and their vigor to start anew and undergo the draining asylum-seeking process after their treacherous journey to Germany, Thomas strove to create an easily accessible and interactive musical event that channeled the refugees' energy in a constructive way. With the support of the city's Feierwerk[2] venue—a cultural institution that encourages and assists people who engage with social issues—Thomas established a musical space in which asylum-seekers, refugees, and migrants[3] found a relaxed and safe opportunity to listen and dance to music, meet other asylum-seekers, participate in the building of a communal space, and musically interact with members of the host society (see Figure 12.1).

As Thomas puts it, at the core of the events lies the engagement with questions of cultural prejudice, gender equality, and youth culture. "For example, we encourage the permanent merging of different seemingly homogeneous groups (as in punks, queers, hip-hoppers, etc.) and thus allow potential disturbances" (TL). And within this mixing of groups is, according to Thomas, where immediate learning takes place.

> Our work is based on processes shaped by the protagonists of our institution: youth cultures, and the fact that they are invited to create their events on their terms. We only intervene where our help is needed; for example, when we experience homophobic, sexist, racist, or otherwise

discriminating situations. Otherwise, provocation and arguments are fine and important for intercultural learning.

Advertising the so-called Handyparties[4] as a space in which "we don't talk about refugees, but celebrate together with refugees," Thomas stresses that this event is not a refugee party, but a participatory event, which invites all partygoers to contribute to the night's musical and cultural output. Firmly committed to advocating for heterogeneity as a prerequisite for fostering equality, the Handyparties are also Thomas's response to a campaign set up by the Munich municipal government to tackle the ongoing social issues in the city (such as violence, sexual harassment, and noise). Since these issues are frequently associated with foreigners, specifically refugees, and are perceived as mostly caused by heterogeneous youth groups in unsafe nightlife spaces, one way to resolve the problem, according to city officials, is the monitoring and elimination of heterogeneous spaces, such as large party venues. Thomas—a firm advocate of diversity who also openly embraces his queer identity and thus acts as a role model in heterogeneous spaces—counters such an approach with his dance party concept. He stresses that the more

FIGURE 12.1
Poster Plug in Beats.
SOURCE: FEIERWERK

heterogeneity one nurtures in problematic nightlife spaces, the more chances for success (TL).

Three questions guided his reasoning: (a) Under which circumstances and with what kind of communal action can prejudice and violence be anticipated and eliminated, or at least reduced? (b) What are the musical ways to utilize diversity as a starting point for interaction and the appreciation of others? (c) What are the musical ways to empower the momentarily powerless?

Based on ethnographic research methods, such as interviews with Thomas and Abolfazl Niknami, his friend and party collaborator, participation in and observation of the dance party, and conversations with other regular party attendees, I describe and analyze in this chapter what Thomas sees as an event "oriented around the musical vocabulary of the party guests." Based on the multiple occasions in which Thomas and I discussed and analyzed the party concept, I suggest that the heterogeneity and cordiality created by the participatory dance party concept is one productive way of generating spaces for cross-cultural contact and communication in environments marked by disruption and outsiderness. As an accessible and inclusive insider space in an outsider context, the dance party is a celebratory shelter allowing for the interplay between belonging, otherness, cultural persistence, and curiosity—all prerequisites for genuine experiences of transcultural processes in a culturally diverse society.

Applying analytical frames pertaining to participation as community-building strategy, distinctive inclusion[5] practices via the use of mobile phones, and heterogeneity created by nightlife contexts, I ask why this event—as one of many artistic projects that have emerged in recent years in response to the European "refugee crisis" in Germany—might have a "built-in sustainability" (Stein, 2018)[6] that is more effective in the long term than other projects addressing questions of diversity and inclusion. More broadly, this party concept shows that employing a musical approach to reinforce heterogeneity not only opens up unexpected places of enrichment, but also provides a model for refugee advocacy within the media-driven discussion of the assumed threat posed by immigration. This chapter, however, is not a plea for music practices and repertoire as tools for the creation of sociality and belonging. As Thomas puts it, "sometimes music can do something for people, but there is a lot that music can't provide"; for example, the party also creates disintegration, and excludes and separates individuals and collectives as much as it invites them to dance and celebrate the moment together.

Orangehouse, *Feierwerk*, Munich, January 2018

The picture seems familiar at first. In the dimly lit dance hall of the Munich Orangehouse, about twenty-five women and men dance *dabke*, an energetic Arab circle and line dance composed of steps, stomps, jumps, and rhythmic bends of the upper body. The dancers are mainly German women (about 18 to 45 years old) and young men mainly from Syria, Afghanistan, and Iran (about 15 to 25 years old). Most of the women also regularly engage with migrants and refugees outside the party. Most of the men fled within the past five years from their home countries to Germany because of war, political pressure, and persecution. The men visibly enjoy the opportunity not only to dance with fellow nationals and other refugees, but also to teach this energetic folk dance to members of the German host society. *Dabke* dancing seems rather straightforward, but the dance scene at the Orangehouse demonstrates the challenge of expressing the energized spirit inherent to this joyous dance. Particularly when watching a group of Syrian men immerse themselves in the dancing, onlookers come to appreciate the powerful and captivating vitality the dance generates. That night in Munich, the dancing has a more easy-going vibe allowing for the mixing of ages and sexes, something rarely seen in *dabke* dancing.

At the beginning of the party, the organizers frequently provide opportunities for migrants and refugees to share—as with today's *dabke*—their boundless passion with the German hosts, showcasing their homelands' cultural gems. The communal interactions provoked by the dancing are a sign of the respect and appreciation for the other that permeates the event. Many of the Syrian *dabke* dancers have discovered this folk dance as an expressive tool only since their arrival in Germany, employing these practices as an icebreaker, a cultural glue among Syrian migrants, and an interactive practice. Drawing on Maurice Merleau-Ponty's (1945/2012) phenomenological reasoning—stating that any human socio-cultural understanding occurs through the body and thus all bodily expressions are always interactions with the world—experiences such as the collective folk dancing, as well as the moving with others in time during the party, has the potential to provide common ground for collective thinking and the creation of sociality (Albright, 2013; Merleau-Ponty, 1945/2012). At the dance party, such non-verbal and verbal sociality was visible and audible in moments such as holding hands while dancing *dabke*, exchanging joyous glances, and later dance moves conveying kind-hearted intentions towards strangers, as well as in conversations between two or more people who had not met prior to the party. Thus, movement and music visibly functioned as communicative tools allowing for interactions between partygoers. And perhaps such interactions might generate more spaces for discourse in the future that address not only personal experiences but also far-reaching issues of power and inequality (Präger, 2018)—as has happened in the relationship established between Thomas and Abi.

Based on the principle "you play me your music and I'll play you mine," the dancing leads to what is titled Plug in Beats, where participants are invited to share a track from their homeland (or music otherwise important to them), which they play for everybody through the venue's sound system directly from their smartphone. These tracks shape the dance party's musical progression. "Pakistani Bhangra pop is followed by Senegalese reggae; after Syrian oriental rock, one might hear German hip-hop. One can expect anything and everything" (TL). As acts of invitation, unconditional welcoming, and hospitality (Higgins, 2012), the participatory practice constitutes the core of the event. It allows individuals and groups to musically denote national belonging and to showcase parts of their rich and diverse backgrounds, aspects that generally interest only a minority of the host society.

The participatory element differentiates Thomas's party concept from other parties in town. The DJs do not determine the music; the partygoers do. "We ask the people, 'Which music do you like?' And I think this is crucial because it does not matter if someone is a refugee or not. We encourage individuals to be active, and this prompts appreciation by others" (TL). Consequently, the musical choices articulate a wide variety of experiences of mobility and locality, home and homelessness, as well as of the past, the present, and the future. As such, the democratic and invitational offer is extended to anyone interested, which results in the attendance of groups of traveling American students, Munich youth cliques who enjoy music not played in their favorite discotheques, as well as refugees from Pakistan who perhaps only ever danced at a wedding and use the party as a safe space to develop listening habits and individual dance styles (TL).

Despite the party's openness in terms of musical repertoire, songs with misogynistic, racist or homophobic themes, or containing lyrics glorifying violence, are prohibited at the event. Although several individuals collaborate as translators at the party, it can be challenging to identify problematic lyrical content. Furthermore, to ensure that everyone adheres to the party's rules, guidelines are explained in various languages (see Figures 12.2 and 12.3).

اطلاعيه مهم

به اولين جشن تلفن هوشمند پلاگ-این بیترمونیخ هوش آمدید.

اگر دوست داری در آن شرکت کنی لطفاً به دکات زیر دقت کن

یک-یک شماره یکش وخوب از آن نگهداری کن

بو-خر نزدیکی جایگاه دی جی (کسی که موسیقی پخش میکد) بمان تا نوبت را از نست نذهی .اگر نبر بوسی باید یک شماره جدید بکنی

سام-وقتی شماره هل از شماره ات نشان داده شد برو پیش میر دی جی و گوشبت را بده به او (بطور مثال : اگر شماره ات سی باشنپس بایین شماره بیست و نه برو پیش دی جی

چهار-توجهاگوشبت باید حتماً شارژ داشنه باشد(اگر شارژ گوشبت ضعیف است میتونی فبلاً توسط ایستگاه شارژ بمان گوشبت را شارژ کنی

پنج-لطفاً رمز گوشبت رباز و تصویر صفحه در حال انتظار را خاموش کن

شش-آهنگت را انتخاب کن وصدای گوشبت را تا حداکثر بلند کن

هفت-بخاطر نوبت رسبن به مهمانان دیگر آهنگی را انتخاب کن که حد اکثر هشت دقبقه زمان ببرد

هشتما همه آهنگهارا تا اخر پخش میکبیم و آنها را قطع نمبکبیم

ده-لطفاً از انتخاب آهنگی که دیگران را آزرده حاطر کند اجتناب کن قایرورک محلبست که باید همه افراد بتون در نظر گرفتن ملبت، جنسبت و سلبقه جنسی بهشان هوش بگذر در صورتی که آهنگ انتخاب شده بیان نگریم از زور و تجاوز،توهین به خانمها ، نژادپرستی و یا هر اس جنسی کند،بلافاصله آهنگ را قطع خواهبم کرد،ما مترجمی در محل داریم که به محص بروز خطایی ما را مطلّع خواهدکرد

FIGURE 12.2   Guidelines in Arabic

Plug-In Beats – Läuft bei dir! - A SMART PARTY – HOW TO…?

START Neben dem DJ stehen nette Menschen bei denen du eine Nummer ziehen kannst

VIEW Damit du weißt wann du dran bist werden die laufenden und kommenden Nummern projiziert (wenn du deinen Einsatz verpennst, musst du dir eine neue Nummer holen).

CHECK Damit wir vorhören und einpegeln können, komme bitte schon spätestens zum DJ wenn die Nummer vor deiner eigenen angezeigt wird.

PLUG Wichtig! Dein Handy muss aufgeladen sein! (Falls dein Akku schwach ist, kannst du ihn vorher an unsere Ladestation – bei der Nummernausgabe - anschließen)

SWIPE Wir kennen deine Pin nicht (und wollen sie auch nicht wissen), also mach bitte vorübergehend deine Tastensperre und den Bildschirmschoner aus.

CHOOSE Wähle den Song aus und dreh die Lautstärke auf deinem Handy auf Maximum

PLAY In der Regel spielen wir alle Songs aus, außer dein Lied hat mehr als 8 Minuten, dann ist's aber auch echt mal gut und wir blenden aus.

RESPECT Bitte verzichte auf Musik die andere verletzen könnte. Das Feierwerk ist ein Ort an dem sich jeder, unabhängig von Herkunft, Geschlecht oder sexueller Orientierung wohl fühlen soll. Bei gewaltverherrlichenden, frauenfeindlichen, rassistischen oder homophoben Texten brechen wir den Song sofort ab. Wir haben Dolmetscher vor Ort die uns auf Verstöße hinweisen.

….HAVE FUN AND ENJOY THE PARTY!

FIGURE 12.3   Guidelines in German

Plug in Beats—A Smart Party—this is how we do it!

START Close to the DJ booth there are friendly people who provide number cards for you

VIEW You'll know it's your turn when we project your number on a screen (if you miss your turn, you'll have to pick a new number)

CHECK Please show up at the DJ booth *one number* BEFORE *your own* because we need to give your track a listen and level out the volume

PLUG It's very important that your phone is fully charged! (If you have a weak battery, you can charge your phone at our charging station. Please do this before it's your turn!)

SWIPE We don't know your pin (and don't want to know it), so please switch it temporarily off and unlock your screensaver

CHOOSE your song and turn the volume up to maximum

PLAY Usually we play the tracks to the end, but after 8 minutes we will fade out your song.

RESPECT Please respect other people's feelings when choosing your track. Feierwerk is a place for everybody, regardless of gender, nationality, or sexual orientation. We want everybody to enjoy the evening. If your track has racist, sexist, or homophobic lyrics, we will stop it immediately. We have interpreters on site who will indicate violations.

...HAVE FUN AND ENJOY THE PARTY!

It is striking to consider the amount of randomness permeating each migration story. A case in point would be Abolfazl's (nickname Abi, 22 years old) displacement experience. Abi, now one of the main party organizers, fled in 2015 from Iran to Germany. He was assigned to live in the refugee camp next to the Feierwerk and thus, by chance, went to one of the newly initiated parties, where he also helped out as a translator. Since early 2016 to the writing of this text he has not missed a single event and has joined Thomas in planning and conducting the parties. Abi describes Thomas and other Feierwerk employees as his friends and supporters in the exasperatingly protracted asylum-seeking process. In our conversation, he specified that he attends every Handy party because he does not want to miss an opportunity to deepen his relationships with other Iranians, other asylum-seekers, as well as with Germans attending the party. Furthermore, he, as well as many other regular attendees, cited the lack of racial profiling as an important reason why a core group of about 30 partygoers, as well as a few new people, show up each time (Abi Niknami, personal communication). In other Munich clubs, their identity cards are checked at the door and they are questioned about their reasons for entering. Although the Orangehouse's employees do keep an eye on who is entering the space, according to Niknami and Thomas,

everyone can enter because the party's motto is that you may and can—
and not that you should not. It does not matter where you are from, who
you are, or what your story is. If things go wrong, we immediately start a
conversation. The atmosphere is very kind and friendly, and this is different from outside the party space. Also, this is a no-cost event, which
matters.

Furthermore, the opportunity to experience both familiar and unfamiliar kinds
of music, which Abi Niknami says he has learned to appreciate, is what makes
him keep coming back. He describes the various kinds of music played at the
party as a way to understand other participants' backgrounds and contexts.

I did not know African or even Arabic music at all, but now I find this
music fascinating because of the event. And I learned more about the
people. I was perhaps also one of the first to play German hip-hop here.
I wanted to get to know German music and also encourage others not to
play only music from their home country. For example, I wanted to show
that we as foreigners can play German music here as well.

Music and mobility scholars have established that music is an immaterial and
mobile culture: it travels and alters during these travels, no longer "belonging"
to specific places. Remarkably, in the context of the Handy parties, participants use musical practices and repertoire as place-making tools for establishing nationalities, as well as for forming (insider) communities, potentially
constituting moments of belonging.

Regarding place-making concepts, Thomas describes how the party space is
usually marked by the various groups attending the party.

At the beginning, one specific group of people always plays their music.
Most often first the people from Afghanistan and then the Syrians. And
then people from African countries. This means that we also need to
organize the space to accommodate these groups. If a group of Senegalese arrive, and Syrian music is being played, we need to make sure they
have a space to arrive so that they don't turn around immediately. They
need a space where they feel comfortable waiting until we play their
music, which is queued up in the line of smartphones.

Thomas stresses that this event could not be held in "just any old space."
Divided by a couple of columns, the Orangehouse comprises a dance floor and
a rather spacious community area with benches and tables. Furthermore, the
space features a stage where the DJs operate, as well as a bar with barstools.

The configuration of the space facilitates party guests to gather in various seated areas and watch the party unfold, until they feel comfortable to enter the dance floor and meet other party attendees. Thomas observed that this initial spatial negotiation is usually replicated in the music played at the event.

> On most nights, the party starts slowly, and people only dance to the music they know well or to the music from their country, but because the songs change quickly, eventually people dance to each other's music. You suddenly see the laughing faces of individuals who, for a moment, forget their dire everyday lives. They begin to unwind and are joyful, and that positively influences your mood as well. (See Figure 12.4)

FIGURE 12.4   Plug in Beats Party 2018.
PHOTOGRAPH: MARKUS RUCH, © RUCH-PHOTOGRAPHY

The fact that several party attendees might never before have encountered a woman at a party, or danced with a woman, or interacted with a queer person, clarifies why the party space's layout is crucial. It comprises areas from which one can watch, observe, learn, wonder, accept, and try out. In these ways, many party guests describe the Handyparties as an event that both transcends and reinforces cultural differences by creating "contact zones" (Pratt, 2008) between partygoers.

Plug in Beats: Challenges and Chances

Although Plug in Beats was initially planned as a target group-specific event, the organizers' main aim is to draw in a diverse crowd, specifically, to attract more Germans to attend the party. Furthermore, because the party claims to encourage cross-cultural interaction and the bi-directional exchange of values (JLS), it is essential to interest not only those individuals who already regularly engage with refugees outside the event. As a model event to address inhibitions when it comes to interactions with refugees, having more Germans attend would make interactions—which many Munich inhabitants might appreciate but do not (know how to) seek out—more tangible and less theoretical (JLS). Thomas hypothesizes that the reason young people would rather visit other parties in town is their practice of going out in groups of four or five. Plug in Beats offers a space to meet new people, which is not a major concern for many young people in Munich.

> I think that some are curious about our event because it is not a mainstream party. But groups need consensus; it can be too risky for individuals to convince the group to go to an event that initially arouses so many extra associations and prejudices and where you don't know what to expect. (TL)

Nevertheless, Thomas is constantly thinking of ways to interest more Germans. He suggests that a larger group of "insiders" might assist other attendees in getting over their homophobic behavior, which Thomas experiences from time to time. Such behavior consists of arguments between partygoers of different backgrounds, as well as a reluctance to engage with refugees at the party. Thomas perceives it as his duty to immediately verbally address such issues. This is also the case with any gender-related matters. Although I experienced the party as remarkably deferential, unavoidable tensions as well as awkward moments of gender negotiations—resulting from cultural differences—constitute another challenge of Plug in Beats. Both Thomas and Abi recall such tense moments, concluding that all were solved via conversation.

Thomas and Abi are frequently discussing how to reach out to female refugees and migrants who might be interested in participating in Plug in Beats, and how to create opportunities for their inclusion. Although they deem it presumptuous to assume that a party can overcome the barriers that exclude women with specific cultural and religious backgrounds from public events such as Plug in Beats—specifically women who might have been sexually molested during or after their flight—they recently discussed the possibility of launching a smartphone party in one of Munich's refugee camps. As gender issues of accessibility are critical for the Plug in Beats concept, Thomas and Abi are searching for migrant women as vital collaborators in order to establish trust and reach out to other females.

Musical Participation as Community-Building and Isolating Practice

When listening and dancing to the tracks played at the party, sonic and corporeal elements such as rhythm, timbre, performance practice, lyrics, genre, style, dance steps, and choreography establish "audible [and felt] entanglements," (Guilbault, 2005), solidifying sound and dance worlds (or scapes)[7] that potentially function as community-building forces. Acting as signifiers that migrants bring from their homelands—inscribed into their minds and bodies—these sonic and corporeal elements create opportunities for individuals and collectives not only to renegotiate ties to both their old and new homes, but also to share with others the stories and emotions these signifiers carry (Präger, 2018). This kind of "corporeal mediation" allows everyone present at musical events "to engage in the behavioral [and bodily] resonance with music, so that personal subjective feelings, moods, flow experiences, and feelings of social bonding can be activated and exchanged" (Leman, 2010, p. 48). Thus, specific sonic and corporeal elements, familiar or appealing to the partygoers, have the potential to generate shared audible, visible, and felt moments accompanied by imaginary and even temporal experiences of belonging (Shelemay, 2011, p. 363), at times even allowing for experiences of "poly-belonging" (Unseld, 2018), moments of belonging felt in the place left behind and also experienced in the new environment.

For some migrants, however, musical experiences at the party do not always give rise to exclusively pleasing reactions and emotions. Different kinds of music evoke in listeners a variety of memories, interactions, behaviors, and bodily reactions. Feelings and memories of pain, loss, violence, unpleasant relations to places and people, and political pressures are also conjured up and communicated in and through specific musical and dance practices. At a more abstract level, embodied musical metaphors move players and listeners physically and emotionally between mental places and physical spaces that they create and inhabit. When the sonic or corporeal codes permeating the room are not understood or decoded by participants, music and dance can cause them to feel separated or isolated. Sometimes, such elements can be used deliberately to discourage the presence or participation of specific groups (Frith, 2003). Thomas aims to eliminate such feelings of separation by creating an appreciation of the normality of heterogeneity, thus enabling the overcoming of its divisive elements. To achieve this, he added the inclusion of partygoers' smartphones to this list of community-building party strategies.

"Immobile Mobility"

As a technological, mobile, and musical force, smartphones "produce" and determine the party's development in the music consumed by the people listening and dancing to it. In this way, participants are momentarily put in a position of responsibility for the party's progression. This socio-technological and participatory leading approach is one aspect that distinguishes Thomas's party concept from other musical collaborations involving migrants and members of the host society that have developed since 2015 in Germany. In recent years, I collaborated with a variety of such projects to observe how the voices of refugees and migrants—which sound migration narratives, for example, in adapted operas, mixed ensemble performances, and plays on the streets and the web—enable individuals and collectives to situate themselves in their worlds as well as to understand how they embody and enact their biographies. Most of these initiatives, however, place migrants into musical projects planned and led by members of the host society. Moreover, events that utilize explorative pedagogical approaches such as improvisation are most often attended only by Germans. Migrants have told me that such approaches are too closely related to how they experience much of their lives since their migration, constantly needing to improvise and react to their changing and provisional life circumstances.

Guarded by a code, swipe pattern, or some other protective feature, the mobile phone is an extremely private tool. Since the smartphones are unlocked while waiting in line, individual phones temporarily become devices that soften, mediate, and translate between the private and public, openly displaying a part of their owner's musical identity for everyone at the party to experience (see Figure 12.5). Although most of the time a track cannot be paired with a specific individual in the room, the smartphone simultaneously acts as an object and a subject, creating digital public spaces where one allows information about oneself to be made publicly available. Partygoer Jessie Lauren Stein describes this process as making people tangible through bodies, voices, and taste. "This creates a humanizing quality, and a softening happens between people with different musical vocabularies when they confront each other with their differing tastes."

The tangibility this process generates is the reason why the musical selections significantly vary during the event. Some choose to play more crowd-pleasing music, such as the popular *Macarena* accompanied by a choreography well-known to everyone at the event. Others choose music displaying cultural qualities not understood or appreciated by some of those present. Thomas craves exactly these musical moments as they advance the knowledge created about the people attending the party and potentially serve as a bridge between

FIGURE 12.5   Plug in Beats—Mobile phones waiting in line.
            PHOTOGRAPH: ULRIKE PRÄGER

people, places, and times. Community-building processes built on musical preferences, such as specific music or dance styles, or the shared enthusiasm for a particular artist, are sometimes also driven by shared cultural heritage, which then functions as the community-building element (Shelemay, 2011).

Much has been written about how the smartphone shapes and represents cultural behaviors and processes while operating "neither as a value-neutral nor as an autonomous force" (Wallis, 2005, p. 5). As one of the few material items brought from the homeland, the smartphone is often the only device enabling the holder to connect to family members and friends. Today, most smartphones allow their users to travel to known and unknown places, connect with families, friends, and strangers at any moment, and thus constitute a place of comfort, and even of virtual belonging. In these processes, the smartphone transforms into an invaluable friend, comforter, and endless storage space for old and new experiences. The smartphone grants refugees, who most often are proscribed from moving across borders during asylum-seeking processes, what Cara Wallis (2005, p. 6) calls "immobile mobility."[8] Constituting freedom, self-determination, and a connection to faraway people and places, this immobile mobility generates communicative spaces created by the interplay of insider- and outsiderness.

In these musical, virtual, community-building, celebratory, and communicative ways, "Plug-in-Beats" functions as music education. Recognizing the party's inclusive educational approach, negotiating and even temporarily overcoming outsiderness, the Bavarian state recently awarded Thomas the

Popkulturpreis (popular culture prize) in the Inclusion category.[9] Thomas and Abi together went to the award ceremony, celebrating a successful collaboration as well as a friendship grown out of the concept "you play me your music and I'll play you mine."

Notes

1   All subsequent references to personal communications with Thomas Lechner are indicated by the initials TL.

2   For information on Das Handy als "Inklusions-Tool" – drei Jahre "Plug-in Beats"-Party, see https://blog.feierwerk.de/das-handy-als-inklusions-tool-3-jahre-plug-in-beats-party/

3   Although terms such as "refugee," "migrant," *Flüchtling*, and "*Geflüchtete*" are problematic when dealing with the refugee condition, because for lack of a better term, I still use the labels migrant and refugee to generally refer to people who, based on war and persecution in their homelands, recently made their way to Europe.

4   Germans generally use the term "Handy" for the mobile phone.

5   Thomas Lechner stressed in our collaboration that his focus lies on inclusion rather than on integration strategies. He defines inclusion as a process that views all individuals as equal—being part of a whole despite specific individual characteristics. Integration strategies, however, are purely built on the needs and interests of a homogeneous majority group into which the minority group has to integrate (understanding that the majority group also is not a homogeneous entity). Therefore, integration requires individuals to assimilate into the majority group. Strategies of inclusion consider participation as a given prerequisite, while participation is more of an abstract possibility in integrational contexts. Integration further relies on concepts such as "Leitkultur": core and mainstream cultural characteristics of the majority group, which need to be adopted by the newcomers. Inclusion, on the other hand, uses cultural diversity as a guiding principle for cultural communication and interaction.

6   All subsequent references to personal communications with Jessie Lauren Stein are indicated by the initials JLS.

7   In *Modernity at Large* (2005, p. 33), Arjun Appadurai designates ethnoscapes, mediascapes, technoscapes, financescapes, and ideoscapes, which deterritorialize culture, space, place, and time as constitutive of mass migrations and the pervasiveness of electronic media.

8 Wallis explains that she heard the term "immobile mobility" for the first time in a talk by Sebastian Ureta (2005). Her use and understanding of the term is, however, different from Ureta's.

9 For information on Das Handy als "Inklusions-Tools," see https://blog.feierwerk.de/das-handy-als-inklusions-tool-3-jahre-plug-in-beats-party/

References

Albright, A. C. (2013). *Engaging bodies: The politics and poetics of corporeality*. Middletown, CT: Wesleyan University Press.

Frith, S. (2003). Music in everyday life. In M. Clayton, T. Herbert, & R. Middleton (Eds.), *The cultural study of music: A critical introduction* (pp. 92–101). New York, NY: Routledge.

Foucault, M. (1988). In L. H. Martin, H. Gutman, & P. Hutton (Eds.), *Technologies of the self: A seminar with Michel Foucault*. Amherst, MA: The University of Massachusetts Press.

Hahn, T. (2007). *Sensational knowledge: Embodying culture through Japanese dance*. Middletown, CT: Wesleyan University Press.

Higgins, L. (2012). *Community music: In theory and in practice*. Oxford: Oxford University Press.

Leman, M. (2007). *Embodied music cognition and mediation technology*. Cambridge, MA: MIT Press.

Low, S. (2017). *Spatializing culture: The ethnography of space and place*. London: Routledge.

Merleau-Ponty, M. (1945/2012). *Phenomenology of perception*. New York, NY: Routledge.

Präger, U. (2018). Musically negotiating difference: Cross-cultural sounds of empathy in contemporary Germany. In W. Gratzer & N. Grosch (Eds.), *Musik und migration* (pp. 67–76). Münster: Waxmann.

Pratt, M. L. (2008). *Imperial eyes: Travel writing and transculturation* (2nd ed.). London: Routledge.

Shelemay, K. (2011). Musical communities: Rethinking the collective in music. *Journal of the American Musicological Society, 64*(2), 349–390.

Turino, T. (2008). *Music as social life: The politics of participation*. Chicago, IL: University of Chicago Press.

Wallis, C. (2005). *Technomobility in China: Young migrant woman and mobile phones*. New York, NY: New York University Press.

CHAPTER 13

Music in the Margins of America: Black Marching Bands in Post-Katrina New Orleans

Matt Sakakeeny

From the perspective of those in the United States, displacement is often imagined as a problem for others, happening elsewhere. This most powerful and wealthiest of nations has for a century or more represented the pinnacle of global stability and security. But the ongoing debate about immigration to the US, reaching fever pitch under the leadership of President Trump, is one indication that displacement has been central to American identity. The country was founded on displacement, voluntary and forced, and from its earliest days there has been disagreement over who belongs and what paths to citizenship are available to them. The problem of displacement is not confined to those relocating to the US but also marks those within the nation who have not been granted the full rights of citizenship. Undocumented immigrants, Native Americans, and black Americans are among those who have faced internal displacement, with differing experiences of forced relocation as well as metaphorical abandonment to the margins of American society.

The most visible example of internal displacement in recent US history is Hurricane Katrina, which struck the Gulf Coast on August 29, 2005, and wreaked particular havoc on the lives of black New Orleanians. When the levees broke, floodwaters blanketed the cityscape and paradoxically uncovered the nation's open secret: that to be black in America is to live with the eternal threat of risk and insecurity. Multiple cases of innocent black residents killed or injured by gunfire, by both police and civilians, came to light after the floodwaters receded ("Law and Order," n.d.; Solnit, 2007). Meanwhile, viral reports from the front lines—of hundreds of armed gang members, of children and even babies being raped, of murder victims stacked in piles in the Superdome—all turned out to be unfounded (Thevenot & Russell, 2005). In temporary shelters set up throughout the South, evacuees were repeatedly referred to as "refugees," as if they had been displaced from another nation. There was a Katrina "diaspora" to every part of the country—concentrated in Houston, Dallas, Atlanta, and other southern cities—and an estimated 100,000 people of color never returned (Bliss, 2015).

In a critical study of race and racism in New Orleans, Clyde Woods situated Katrina within an unbroken history of "planned abandonment" (Woods, 2017). So while physical displacement due to a singular catastrophe was highly visible, other patterns of social dislocation have been more submerged, pervasive, and persistent. Take public education. Starting in 1960, school desegregation caused a massive "white flight" of families to suburban areas, leaving behind a chronically underfunded and mismanaged system. New Orleans was effectively re-segregated into what education activist Jonathan Kozol calls "apartheid schools" (Kozol, 2005, p. 19). Before Katrina, the city's public school population was 94% African American, far less than the overall African American population of 66%. Seventy-three percent of students qualified for the free and reduced lunch program (Perry et al., 2015). There was a robust teachers' union, made up primarily of black New Orleanians, but they were not empowered to redress the administrative neglect that trickled down to their classrooms. The district ranked among the lowest in the state in test scores and graduation rates, which state politicians used as ammunition to justify the most sweeping educational "reforms" in the country.

In November 2005, while over 90% of New Orleanians were still living in exile, the Louisiana State Legislature passed Act 35, firing 7,000 veteran teachers, dissolving the regional school district, and replacing it with an "all-choice" system of independently operated charter schools. The rates of uncertified teachers, Teach for America recruits, and other transplants rose to dramatic heights. School names with deep attachments for generations of New Orleanians were changed. Frederick Douglass became KIPP Renaissance. John McDonogh is now Bricolage Academy. Neighborhood schools became a relic of the past because parents enroll in a citywide lottery and their child is assigned a school regardless of proximity to home. Oversight is divided up among clusters of independent Charter Management Organizations like KIPP, Choice Foundation, or Inspire NOLA. Student experience varies widely across what critics have referred to as a "non-system." Kids bounce between schools. Teachers come and go. Underperforming schools close. Inconsistency has become the new normal.

In this shifting landscape, one social and cultural anchor that has remained is marching band. Throughout the Southeastern US, in highly segregated school systems, black marching bands have flourished since the mid-twentieth century. Generations of New Orleans jazz, blues, soul, and funk musicians got their start in band. The city is in the middle of a "marching band belt" that stretches from Florida to Texas, where middle schools serve as "feeder schools" for high schools, and high school as a training ground for Historically Black

Colleges and Universities (HBCUs) such as Southern University, Grambling State University, and Florida Agricultural and Mechanical University (FAMU). In New Orleans, football games are overshadowed by halftime shows and drum majors receive more notoriety than quarterbacks. Post-Katrina, the return of band signaled the possibility of coming home and reestablishing social and familial ties to place. In a crisis of upheaval, students, parents, and alumni demanded that this culturally relevant tradition be included in the radically altered system of education. This very specific cultural practice, in a particular place, at a precise historical moment, tells a larger story about the intersection of race and displacement, music and education, in the US.

The significance of band was made evident just months after the storm, when mayor Ray Nagin decided to go forward with the city's annual Mardi Gras festivities even though New Orleans remained virtually uninhabited. The Mardi Gras organizations that sponsor the parades, known as "Krewes," faced many obstacles to mounting a successful season. Krewe members were displaced around the country, the massive floats that carry them were destroyed by flood waters, and there was no guarantee that spectators would travel to New Orleans to marvel at their costumes and beg for their beads. Another problem loomed: only a handful of schools had reopened, which meant there were no marching bands to fill the stately boulevards of St. Charles Avenue and Canal Street with sound.

For many parade-goers, school marching bands are the highlight of the Mardi Gras season, the two weeks leading up to Mardi Gras day when there is at least one parade per night and at least ten bands in each parade. The most impressive bands stretch for a full block, with the color guard, drum majors and majorettes, flag team, and cheerleaders, followed by the musicians (trombones, mellophones, trumpets, woodwinds, tubas, and drums), and finally the dance team marching under the streetlights. Without the bands, one music educator joked, a Mardi Gras parade was "all floats, dune buggies, and cotton-candy vendors." For this Mardi Gras, Krewes had to scramble to find bands at schools unaffected by the storm, and ultimately a composite band was formed with students from three Catholic schools with predominantly black students: St. Mary's Academy, Xavier University Preparatory School, and St. Augustine High School. The Max Band, as they were called, marched in all the parades and quickly became a symbol of recovery on the local news and in multiple articles in the *Times-Picayune* newspaper. For many spectators, including myself and a few friends attending a parade a few nights before Mardi Gras, just seeing and hearing the bands pass us by was enough to bring tears to our eyes.

I moved to New Orleans in 1997, having trained at Peabody Conservatory in Baltimore as a guitarist and audio engineer. As a producer for the public radio program *American Routes* I became immersed in the local traditions of the jazz funeral and the second line parade, musical processions that wound through the city streets. I moved to New York in 2003 to enter the PhD program in ethnomusicology at Columbia University, returning to New Orleans in 2006 to research the brass bands that provided the music for funerals and parades. These ensembles of eight to twelve instrumentalists operated with an entirely different set of principles than the musical styles I had studied in conservatory. Methods of improvisation were valued over composition; audience participation was expected through dance and other forms of bodily engagement; songs were generally learned by ear rather than from musical notation.

It's not as though I was unfamiliar with these approaches to music-making. Like most Americans I grew up surrounded by black popular music. In graduate school, I read studies of black musicians' socialization into culturally-specific musical practices. What did surprise me, and what was largely missing from popular and scholarly discourses of black popular music, was the role of formal education in the development of performing artists. When I spoke with brass band musicians nearly all of them told me their first encounter with an instrument was in school, specifically in marching band.

The depth of significance of band was evident at an event I organized in Fall 2007 called "Brass Band Music Across the Generations." I had invited members of the world-renowned Rebirth Brass Band to introduce students from John McDonogh, Joseph S. Clark, and St. Augustine high schools to brass band performance practices. The excitement in the room was palpable. Here was a group of adults who had gotten their start in schools much like the kids were now attending, playing the same kind of music they were now studying, and had gone on to receive international adulation. The familiar sounds of brass band music provided everyone in the room with a sense of rootedness in place and the possibility of continuity after the displacement caused by the flood two years earlier. The night ended with dozens of musicians young and old playing through Rebirth's most popular song "Do Whatcha Wanna" in a joyous clash of brass and drums.

On my way out, Rebirth drummer Derrick Tabb approached me about a music education program that he was trying to launch. Derrick had been a member of the celebrated Andrew J. Bell Junior High School marching band in the late 1980s. He had begun experimenting with drugs when band director Donald Richardson intervened and helped redirect him toward a career in music. In the 1990s, after Derrick graduated, budget cuts in arts education had eliminated many middle school band programs, including Bell. The restructuring of the school system after Katrina hit exacerbated an already deteriorating situation. In the changeover, high school bands would return while only one or two middle schools would offer band. Derrick handed me a proposal outlining the social, educational, and economic benefits of band and asked for help in securing donations to implement a program for middle-school students. His program would teach kids ages nine to fourteen the fundamentals of music and marching, preparing them for high school and offering a safe and productive afterschool environment.

On May 22, 2008, Roots of Music launched with Derrick, Lawrence Rawlins, Allen Dejan, Shoan Ruffin, and Edward Lee teaching about 40 kids the fundamentals of music. Our talks with the school district had gone nowhere but Tipitina's offered up their nightclub as a rehearsal space, so every weekday, all summer long, the teachers and students piled into the hot, dark, musty bar, beaming with enthusiastic smiles. I was able to get a few instruments and some money donated. In these negotiations, I learned that many granting institutions would only place instruments in pre-existing schools or support programs run by teachers during normal school hours. "They never received a situation like this" Derrick observed of the new education landscape. In an "all-choice" network of charter schools, not all principals and administrators saw the value of arts education. Schools are assessed solely on standardized test scores and the arts are not tested. Students of color in urban charter schools have been relegated to the margins of American educational policy.

But as Derrick's example shows, there are tangible social and cultural benefits to participating in the arts and band directors have potential to influence the lives of young people. I was initially drawn to marching band as pre-professional training for musicians in New Orleans but when I began attending rehearsals I was made aware of what participation offers all students, whether or not they wind up pursuing a career in music. In the band room, every child is taught aesthetic expression through performance, social bonding through ensemble teamwork, the discipline necessary for group collaboration, and the long-term payoffs of practice. My own awakening to these lessons came about as I witnessed two neighbors join Roots of Music and then follow very different life paths that were both fulfilling, in part, because of their formative experiences there.

Reginald and Jaron Williams were looking for something, anything, to do that summer. While many residents remained displaced and much of the city was still rebuilding, there were few programs for kids. The brothers were first in line on the day Roots of Music opened. Reginald, like a lot of big kids, wound up on the tuba, while Jaron, younger and more compact, went for the trumpet. As students and teachers unpacked the shiny new horns, I was taking photographs to send back to the donors in hopes of getting more instruments, and I snapped a picture of Reginald cradling a tuba for the first time, fingering the valves and adjusting the mouthpiece, a look of wonder in his eyes. Before Katrina, Jaron had played cornerback in an afterschool football league, and he liked the competition but sports never gave the sensation that music did. "It just sends chills through your body," he told me later. Each afternoon, Jaron would head to the upper brass sectional led by Lawrence Rawlins while Reginald studied lower brass with Edward Lee. After a break for dinner, rehearsal would end with the whole band bringing their parts together and learning to step in time.

One evening I saw Reginald standing and waiting in the rain so with Derrick's permission I offered him a ride. At first he politely declined, saying he was waiting for his brother to finish practicing, but then Jaron appeared, trumpet case in hand, and we all climbed into the car. I asked where I should take them and we were surprised to find that we lived a few blocks from each other. Their grandfather Rowan Williams Jr. owned a modest home in the Uptown district that had been spared the worst of the flooding, and they stayed there with younger brother Derrick and mother Melody. The oldest, Darrell, had died at 19 years old after being shot in broad daylight the previous summer. Melody went looking for a safe place for her younger sons to spend their out-of-school time and heard about Roots of Music through a family friend. The brothers were so eager for the program to kick off that Derrick Tabb would sometimes stop by the house and direct them to practice marching around the block. On opening day Reginald and Jaron were first in line.

Once he was up and running, Jaron immersed himself in music. I could hear him practicing his scales day and night down the street. Lawrence noticed his talent right away: "I said, 'Nobody has a sound like this boy.' The tone was just there. I said, 'Man he's going to be off the chain [fantastic].'" One afternoon an older student was leading the trumpeters through warm-up exercises when Lawrence came up from behind. Jaron tells me: "He heard me playing, and he said. 'Bear, that was you?'" Jaron is known to all by the nickname Bear. "He said, 'Play that again.' I played it for him again. And he asked the guys on first trumpet to play it and they couldn't play it so he put me on first trumpet and one of them on second."

Roots of Music became a gateway for Bear to channel his competitiveness along with that creative energy he first felt playing music. "Before I did music I wasn't really doing anything," he says. "I had started being bad in school." Katrina sent the family to Texas and when they returned home the football league was in disarray and there were few other activities to take up. Darrell had been his closest friend and the loss sent him adrift in fourth grade. "You go in class, you're not really feeling anything. You don't want to be there, so you're not doing anything. You're just sitting there." Playing with Roots of Music that summer helped him reset his equilibrium. "I believe if you have something that you want to get good at in your life, if you do good at that then you're going to start doing good at everything else." Music helped Bear navigate the many challenges he faced.

Bear's older brother Reginald goes by the nickname Diggy (see Figure 13.1). He's less interested in competition than socializing and collaborating with family and friends. When Diggy introduces me to people he says, "that's my partner, Mr. Matt," and everyone he likes becomes his partner. He values those relationships and the moments of sociability and intimacy they come with over excelling in narrowly focused tasks. He switched to trombone after starting out on tuba, and while he came to rehearsal every day and practiced at home most days he was not particularly interested in mastery of technique. For Diggy, band was an opportunity to take up an activity he enjoyed more than school, to strengthen relationships with peers, and to perform in front of an audience. Unlike Bear, he was more concerned with being connected with others than being the best.

FIGURE 13.1   Members of the roots of music in the author's yard, including Reginald "Diggy"
              Williams (far left) and Jaron "Bear" Williams (to right of Reginald), 2009.
              PHOTOGRAPH: MATT SAKAKEENY

A musical ensemble is at once a hierarchy that rewards leadership while also a collaborative endeavor that requires teamwork. Participation differs markedly from core curriculum subjects that stress individual expertise and measurable outcomes. In the model classroom, the dialectic is one between individual autonomy (of the student) and sovereign authority (of the teacher). As Paul Willis has argued, arts education in the US traditionally extends

Eurocentric values as it "connives to keep alive the myth of the special, creative individual" (Willis, 1990, p. 1). Band, like orchestra and chorus, is an inherently participatory art form in which members must abandon attachments to full autonomy and individual expertise for the sake of collaboration. Sovereignty is largely maintained, through the figure of the conductor or director, but they reign over a more dispersed hierarchy that might include assistant directors, section leaders, first and second "chairs," and all others. The dialectic in participatory arts is one between competition and peer-to-peer learning, individual development, and social bonding.

In an ethnographic study of George Washington High School in Chicago, Carlos Abril analyzes several factors that contribute to students' experiences with band. As a creative activity, music-making cultivates emotional awareness and facilitates a degree of individual expression within the limits of the ensemble, and the shared time and interests allow for the formation of social bonds. The participatory experience of the ensemble is derived from specific musical practices that alert individuals to their role within the larger collective. Moving together in rhythm creates an experience of group solidarity through embodied and temporal synchronization. The ensemble brings together distinct sections—upper brass, lower brass, woodwinds, and percussion—that rehearse separately, and provide opportunities for the cultivation of leadership roles within each section (Abril, 2012). Peer socialization, leadership cultivation, and social bonding and bridging are inherent to band instruction regardless of students' particular social identities or life experiences.

In predominantly white institutions, or racially diverse schools like George Washington, members often constitute a unique social structure, a subculture of so-called "band geeks" that is distinct from the larger school culture and other subcultures. This contrasts with the status of students of color in schools located in the marching band belt. These "show-style" marching bands, now highly imitated at historically white colleges, were pioneered by legendary band director William Foster, who led the FAMU band from 1946 to 1998. It was Foster who developed the marching band into a black music ensemble, writing band arrangements of popular songs and introducing dance routines into the drill maneuvers, such as "barrel turns, backbends, hitchkicks, swivel turns, pelvic thrusts, [and] pelvic rotations" (Malone, 1990, pp. 1–2). The drum section plays syncopated rhythms and stacks parts into dense layers of polyrhythm. The winds produce a loud, strident tone, and pile on multiple melodies into rich polyphonic textures. These musical practices expand the collaborative elements of any marching band while fortifying the specific cultural relevance of black music (Sakakeeny, 2015). In New Orleans charter schools, being part of a collective based around the musical inheritance of black people amplifies the shared sense of belonging that is inherent to band.

Band takes on added local significance through the spectacle of Mardi Gras. From the first day of rehearsal at Roots of Music up through the Mardi Gras parade season in February 2009, the excitement of growing the program was compounded by the rush leading up to their official debut on the streets. Word of mouth and a few local media stories had drawn attention to the band, named the Crusaders, and their ranks had swelled to over 100 members. As the organization scrambled to setup its 501(c)3 status, there was a relentless hustle to get teachers paid, expenses for busing and meals covered, and instruments donated. Lawrence, Derrick, and his wife Keisha cobbled together the Crusaders' uniforms, stitching patches with the Roots of Music logo on used jackets (see Figure 13.2). They collected parts discarded by other bands, like the "spats" worn over boots to protect from mud, and spray-painting them to match the black and gold color scheme. Without a permanent facility, the band had relocated four times but Mardi Gras gave everyone an incentive to keep moving forward.

FIGURE 13.2   The Roots of Music, New Orleans, Louisiana, 2009.
PHOTOGRAPH: MATT SAKAKEENY

Nerves were running high when we loaded into yellow school buses and headed to the first parade. Jaron wondered aloud if he had the endurance to walk six miles in the cold and blow his horn for hours without a break. Derrick and Lawrence, who had marched in hundreds of parades since entering junior high in the 1980s, were nonetheless anxious to see the public's reaction to the new band they had built up from nothing. The buses dropped us on a side street where the bands waited for their cue to join the parade, one by one, in between the floats carrying Krewe members dressed in gaudy costumes. The Crusaders watched wide-eyed as high school bands faced off against each other, trading songs to see who sounded fullest, ramping up the spirit of competition. A procession of band directors came over to congratulate Derrick and Lawrence and admire the uniforms and shiny gold helmets. The buzz in the air that accompanies any Mardi Gras parade was amplified by the arrival of a band of young upstarts. A space between floats opened up and it was our turn to go.

"Band!" Derrick called out. "Hey!" they shouted in response. "We ready?" "Born ready!" The drum major gave four chirps of his whistle, the entire band counted "1-2-3-4-5-6-7-8" in tempo, and the drummers started their cadence on the downbeat. Marching off the median and into the street, the Crusaders got in formation, five astride, in straight lines, high stepping to the beat. The wind players pumped their forearms in alternation, cradling their instruments, then lifting them to play. The blast of sound was met with cheers and squeals of excitement from the crowds lined up along each side of Napoleon Avenue. Derrick and Lawrence were in the lead in their black suits, followed by the auxiliary team carrying the banner, then the drum major moving his baton in time with the instrumentalists lined up behind him: trombones, baritones, mellophones, trumpets, clarinets, saxophones, flutes, sousaphones, cymbals, snare drums, and bass drums. As I kept apace along the side with some parent volunteers, curious spectators kept stopping us to ask who we were, and we handed them a flyer and kept marching.

Jaron, who had been named co-section leader, marched at the end of the first trumpet row, signaling the start of each song with his hand in the air. Reginald was several rows back where the sousaphones peaked up above everyone's heads, the shiny brass reflecting off the street lights. When we reached the spot along St. Charles Avenue parallel to grandpa Rowan's house, the whole Williams clan was there, screaming and waving, and Melody came over to hug her sons. All along the parade route, as we wound toward the downtown tourist district, I could hear occasional shouts of "Diggy!" and "Bear!" from friends and classmates. We passed the mayor's viewing stand, turned onto Canal Street along the edge of the French Quarter, and finally finished at the convention center where the buses were waiting. As we drove off, the staff congratulated each other while the kids recounted musical highlights and traded stories of their encounters along the way. Just eight months earlier, at the start of the program, no one could have imagined a stronger debut.

My experience volunteering with Roots of Music, learning from teachers and students, transformed my life and work. I not only realized that formal education is an underappreciated aspect of musical socialization in the lives of black New Orleanians but that culturally relevant pedagogy is critical to making music education accessible and inclusive. I came to see the possibility of arts education as a form of social justice, leading me to seek out progressive education researchers who have been arguing this for decades (Hess, 2018). When I started teaching at Tulane University, I set up a service learning class for Tulane students to tutor Roots students. I am currently collaborating with Roots to write a book about the musical and social benefits of participation in bands.

Since 2008 Roots of Music has become a critical institution for arts education in New Orleans, directly impacting the lives of hundreds of middle school kids and seeding talent for dozens of high school bands. Reginald "Diggy" Williams went on to O. Perry Walker High School, where Lawrence's brother Wilbert Rawlins directs the most celebrated band of the post-Katrina era. Diggy continued on the trombone and enrolled in Southern University, but he couldn't afford tuition and had to return to New Orleans. He took a job at a restaurant, working his way up from dishwasher to line cook to sous chef. Diggy is a dependable team member with the kitchen staff, reliably doing his part, collaborating with others, a quality that was fortified in band. The death of his older brother saddled him with the responsibility of being "the man of the house," as Bear describes him, and he stepped up. "He's my number one supporter, I could tell you that," says Bear. Diggy, now 25, is the father of a son, Royal, and picks up his trombone only occasionally.

By the time Bear followed his brother to high school, Walker had merged with another school to become Landry-Walker College and Career Preparatory High School. There, under Wilbert Rawlins' guidance, Bear rose up to become section leader by his junior year. The brothers were featured in the documentary *The Whole Gritty City* (2016), and Bear was chosen as a featured charter in the HBO series *Treme*. Now in his twenties, standing over six feet tall, Bear is section leader at Southern University, consistently ranked the top HBCU band by ESPN and the NCAA. "The story was supposed to happen that way," says Lawrence, who beams with pride as he shows me pictures of Bear in uniform before a Southern football game. Starting with those earliest rehearsals in the dimly lit Tipitina's nightclub, Lawrence, Derrick, and the other teachers at Roots of Music cultivated the potential for students like Bear to excel in music.

With every passing year since Katrina, more charter schools have integrated band into their elementary and middle schools, partly as a recruitment tool to entice parents to enroll their children. Students who have received this training go on to high schools like Landry-Walker with higher performance scores and a stronger investment in band. But at less desirable high schools, like McDonogh 35 where Lawrence teaches, band directors face many obstacles in recruiting top students. An all-choice system is essentially a market-based system with winners and losers. Once a public right for all, arts education has become a privilege for those who wind up in schools that see value in it.

This "access gap" is one of many examples of planned abandonment that Clyde Woods argues has maintained inequality along the lines of race and class. He cites local business entrepreneurs who saw a silver-lining in the mandatory evacuation of black New Orleanians, in the shuttering of public housing projects to stem the return of the poor, and in the forced transformation of public schools into an education marketplace. Within an all-choice charter network, the fate of arts education and culturally relevant pedagogy is in the hands of stakeholders with very different assessments of value. Band has survived in the education marketplace because students and parents demand it, and this demand gives some administrators an incentive to invest in arts education. Whether or not charter schools see the educational value, some have recognized the financial value of attracting students and their state vouchers, currently $5,441 per pupil (Charter Per Pupil).[1]

In an interim period during the tumultuous decade after Katrina, an opportunity of sorts was created for Roots of Music to emerge as an out-of-school program to address an access gap in middle school marching band. The sights and sounds of the band provided New Orleanians returning home with a shared sense of belonging, and in the everchanging education landscape Roots of Music continues to provide young people with a safe and nurturing environment to learn the fundaments of music. The life experiences of two "graduates," Reginald and Jaron Williams, demonstrate the significance of the program in training a new generation of professional musicians and instilling in everyone the importance of creativity and collaboration, practice and discipline. The unprecedented event of Katrina, and the aftermath of the flood in a unique city, nonetheless offer broader insight into the role of music education for the displaced.

Note

1   "Charter Per Pupil Amounts," https://www.louisianabelieves.com/funding/charter-per-pupil-funding

References

Abril, C. R. (2012). Perspectives on the school band from hardcore American band kids. In P. Shehan Campbell & T. Wiggins (Eds.), *The Oxford handbook of children's musical cultures* (Vol. 2, pp. 434–448). New York, NY: Oxford University Press.

Barber, R. (Producer), & Barber, R., & Lambertson, A. (Directors). (2016). *The whole gritty city* [Documentary]. United States: Band Room Productions.

Bliss, L. (2015, August 25). 10 years later, there's so much we don't know about where Katrina survivors ended up. *CityLab*. Retrieved from https://www.citylab.com/equity/2015/08/10-years-later-theres-still-a-lot-we-dont-know-about-where-katrina-survivors-ended-up/401216/

Hess, J. (2018). Revolutionary activism in striated spaces? Considering an activist music education in K–12 schooling. *Action, Criticism, and Theory for Music Education, 17*(2), 22–49.

Kozol, J. (2005). *The shame of the nation: The restoration of apartheid schooling in America*. New York, NY: Crown Publishers.

Law and Disorder: New Orleans Police under Scrutiny. (n.d.). *ProPublica*. Retrieved from https://www.propublica.org/series/law-and-disorder/p2

Malone, J. (1990). The FAMU marching 100. *The Black Perspective in Music, 18*, 1–2.

Perry, A., Harris, D. N., Buerger, C., & Mack, V. (2005). The transformation of New Orleans public schools: Addressing system-level problems without a system. *The Data Enter*. Retrieved from https://www.datacenterresearch.org/reports_analysis/school-transformation/

Sakakeeny, M. (2015). Music lessons as life lessons in New Orleans marching bands. *Souls: A Critical Journal of Black Politics, Culture, and Society, 17*(3–4), 279–302.

Solnit, R. (2007, March 15). Unstable foundations: Letter from New Orleans. *TomDispatch*. Retrieved from http://www.tomdispatch.com/post/174800/rebecca_solnit_on_not_forgetting_new_orleans

Thevenot, B., & Russell, G. (2005, September 26). Rape. Murder. Gunfights. *Times Picayune*. Retrieved from https://www.nola.com/katrina/index.ssf/2005/09/rape_murder_gunfights.html

Willis, P. (1990). *Common culture: Symbolic work at play in the everyday cultures of the young*. Milton Keynes: Open University Press.

Woods, C. (2017). *Development drowned and reborn: The blues and bourbon restoration in Post-Katrina New Orleans* (J. T. Camp & L. Pulido, Eds.). Athens, GA: University of Georgia Press.

PART 3

Belonging

∴

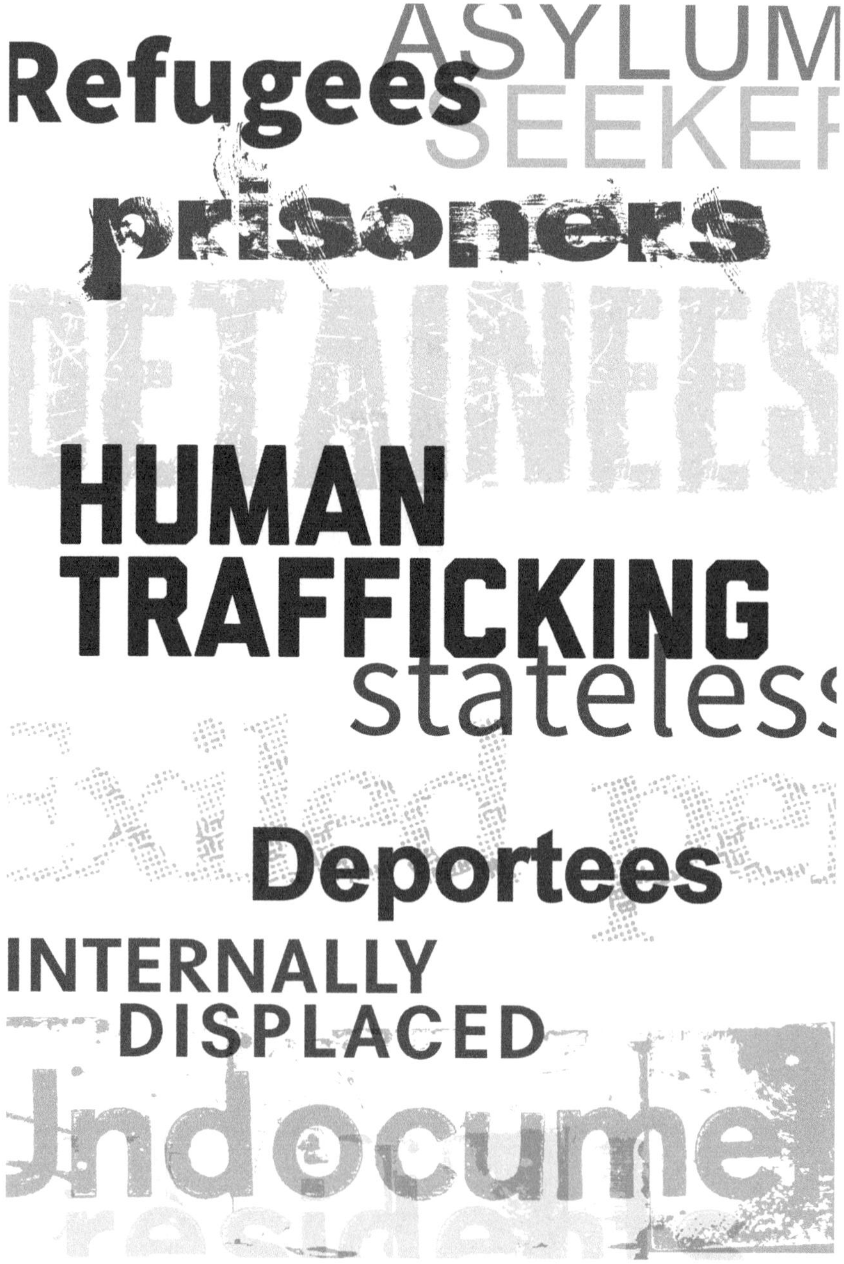

Refugees ASYLUM SEEKER

prisoners

DETAINEES

HUMAN TRAFFICKING stateless

Exiled

Deportees

INTERNALLY DISPLACED

Undocume

resident

Key terms 2.

GRAPHIC DESIGNER: ANISSA MARTÍNEZ LOZANO

CHAPTER 14

¡Qué Linda!

Kate Richards Geller and Kat Bawden

> People who are new to the choir always say how nervous they are to perform. I tell them, "You're in a group, we're not gonna let you fall. We hold each other up."
>
> LINDA

∴

Co-founded in 2013 by music educator/performing artist Leeav Sofer and community outreach coordinator Christopher Mack, joined in 2015 by music therapist Kate Richards Geller, Urban Voices Project (UVP) uses music to create supportive community spaces that create a sense of purpose and improved health for vulnerable individuals. Our music workshops engage men, women and families across the greater Los Angeles area in partnership with social, civic and healthcare organizations. Urban Voices Project's outreach ensemble performs inspirational songs and shares personal stories that shift the narrative and perception of homelessness in today's society. The epicenter of homelessness in the US is located in downtown Los Angeles. The Skid Row neighborhood is a vibrant community of remarkable human beings most of whom live in abject poverty.

UVP Choir is composed of artists from the Skid Row neighborhood of Los Angeles, currently or formerly coping with the condition of homelessness. Community outreach shifts the narrative and perception of homelessness in today's society.

Linda enters the choir room with a calm, curious, caring presence that ripples over us:

> When I was first "living in the elements" (I don't say "homeless" because I didn't feel homeless), I was staying at the Union Rescue Mission.
>
> In the summer of 2014, my friends and I were on our way back from dinner. There was a group of people across the street playing music, and there was a man singing along to Smokey Robinson. Me and my two

friends joined him, pretending to be the back-up singers. Then we started dancing with him.

I realized in that moment, that being in Skid Row didn't mean you had to be unhappy. And that night, singing with people I didn't even know, just being able to be that open in that moment, allowed me to have the feeling I've now felt for the rest of my time here. Not closed off, or fearful...None of the preconceived notions of Skid Row apply any more. In that moment, my notion was that I could be happy here. It was just a moment's realization of, "I'm OK." I knew I landed on my feet. I felt as though I fell into grace inside of myself.

Joining Urban Voices Project continued this. It allows me to find my voice and have peace with myself.

In the photo essay below, Linda describes each moment. The images are by Kat Bawden.

FIGURE 14.1   After Linda's first performance with UVP, when they sang to a group of Skid Row residents at a health fair: "Here I'm enjoying the moment after singing. That peaceful moment. I felt like we had touched people with our performance."

FIGURE 14.2   Linda sings with UVP at the Messiah Project, the choir's flagship holiday performance every year: "We sang the Hallelujah chorus and it was something I had
always wanted to do. Once when I was a sophomore in high school in New York,
I went to the beach with my sister. There at the beach was a group of high school
students singing the Hallelujah chorus together. And I said, 'Oh my God, they're
so awesome. One day I want to perform that.' So at 70 years old I finally got to do
what I wanted to do when I was 17."

FIGURE 14.3   Linda at UVP's weekly choir rehearsal: "I'm holding hands with Rosa, another
performer in Urban Voices Project, while we sing to each other."

FIGURE 14.4
Linda at UVP's music wellness lab: "Here I was telling a story about an experience I had at the post office. As I was waiting in line, a little boy was singing. His mom was trying to get him to be quiet. In this picture, I was talking about how important it is not to discourage kids from singing. We can find freedom in our voices."

FIGURE 14.5　UVP performs for Voices of Our City, a choir addressing homelessness in San Diego: "I'm singing for joy with the visiting San Diego choir."

FIGURE 14.6   Linda sings with UVP at the Skid Row farmers' market: "People who are new to
the choir always say how nervous they are to perform. I tell them, 'You're in a
group, we're not gonna let you fall. We hold each other up.'"

CHAPTER 15

A Citizen without a Home

Ismael "Q" Garcia-Vega

Believe it or not, I love this professor.[1] I've done multiple times of incarceration. I can explain it. Like many minorities I was born in the South Bronx to a very poor family. My mom was a heroin addict and my father was never there. By the time I was nine, my mom gave me away to one of her dealers so that I can be molested while she gets high. By the time I was 10 I tried killing myself. By the time I was 14 I had already been shot at, stabbed, run over by a truck and was the founding member of a gang in my own city, because I finally reached the point in my life where in order to stop being the victim I became the predator. And that started my criminal career. At juvie[2] I did three years. The day I turned 18, I was arrested in Florida. I did two years down there and a little bit after my 21st birthday, I was incarcerated up here in Massachusetts and recently released from serving 13 years straight. I'm not an angel, but the system is so flawed and so broken that my experience in there transformed me and a lot of it is due to this class,[3] is due to the work that this gentleman does. Because he created a safe zone in that prison where we were allowed to be something other than what we've known our whole lives.

I mean, the very first day I walked into that class I'm sitting across from another rival gang member whom one of my brothers had just recently attacked one of his and put him in the hospital, and this gentleman comes in and he tells us we're going to sit in a big circle, hold hands and close our eyes. Which is something you don't do in grown prison, especially when your rival enemy is sitting right across from you. It was the experience of doing that as well as watching the other individual do it that began the transformation in both of us. 'Cuz I'm actually friends with that dude to this day. And it was through that process in the class when he would have us acting. I mean, the correctional officers think he's crazy because they would come by doing rounds and some of us would be on the tables or on top of the cabinets. It was going through that that my own walls and shells began to crack, because I had grown into a state where I had gone indifferent. I didn't want to feel nothing. And he brought me back into a state where he made me realize that it's in those moments when we are vulnerable and when we are feeling especially uncomfortable emotions that we are most human.

I don't know what much more to say other than I really do value what this gentleman does. I value what his choir[4] does because they speak for individuals who don't normally have a voice and I am completely transformed as well as mesmerized by the way that they integrate all aspects of artistic expression...

#W88570

Refrain
I'm sorry my people not evil inside
I'm sorry you people are quick to imply
It could be contagious don't look in the eyes
It could be the reason the reaper decides
To show you his face no longer disguise
Don't need you to lie, don't need you to cry
But look deep inside beneath all the pride
'Cuz either you eatin' or either you die

I'm sorry my hitta but who gone acquit us
If they getting paid every time they convict us
They getting paid every time they oppress us
And they getting paid every time they forget us
'Cuz people forget that we equal to lessen
People forget that we break under pressure

People forget all the shit that we weather
So thick and their shit that we should stick together
Instead what we do is grow more indifferent
I'm trying to be me but nobody will listen
If you was like me would you ask for permission
Or ask to be given the face of religion then face the division
The state that we live in is not a conclusion
not a decision to die up in prison
Especially when money can talk to the system
and buy us our freedom.

Refrain

I'm sorry my people not evil inside
I'm sorry you people are quick to imply
It could be contagious don't look in the eyes
It could be the reason the reaper decides
To show you his face no longer disguise
Don't need you to lie, don't need you to cry
But look deep inside beneath all the pride
'Cuz either you eatin' or either you die

I'm sorry these people don't do what they say
They say that is love but we know that is hate
Know the mistake and the guilt don't erase
Know that the shame go beyond any cage
Beyond any pain in the bottle of rage
Mix with the deuce and the sour we chase
Like fuck it my worth is an hourly rate
Watching awake every hour they take
Emancipated or be the slave
Tripped on a case and be next to decay
Next to convey every dollar they make
Lost and always if we trust what they say
Lost in our ways like the sun in the shade
Either behave or get whooped in your place
Or you choose to rebel and live free in your grave.

Refrain

I'm sorry my people not evil inside
I'm sorry you people are quick to imply
It could be contagious don't look in the eyes
It could be the reason the reaper decides
To show you his face no longer disguise
Don't need you to lie, don't need you to cry
But look deep inside beneath all the pride
Cuz either you eatin' or either you die

First and foremost, thank you for the experience that we shared. Like always I find myself motivated, and inspired by the work that we encountered in our classroom. Not only do I discover pieces of myself I was not aware existed (like my humanity), but I also take pride in maintaining or rather continuing to walk in my new growth. For it will be an injustice to forget, ignore. and/or return to my old sheltered, and indifferent nature.

I know that at times it's difficult to believe that someone could be so distant from the love, and beauty that exist in our world. However, anyone who knows my artistic voice acknowledges that my experience has been painful, lonely, violent and oppressive.

Thus, it's moments like when we embrace each other that teach me how I'm capable of both receiving and reciprocating love. It's moments like when we express our vonerability that has helped me understand, connect, and even respect a total stranger; and it's moments like when we all surrender to the concept, as well as, the experience before us that has not only begun my transformation but will also serve as a reminder of the importance of unity amongst our diversity.

In fact, when the world you know opperates completely in solitude it is only the love precipitated in our classroom that validates the power of community; not to mention, it's necessity. The beauty in ___ life is not based on any achievements,

nor the perception of perfection, but rather in the act of selfishly committing yourself to the total experience life is offering you.

As I am now afraid that our journey is coming to an end this semester; I am also hopeful of what the future will possess. I am confident that the man you've helped mode or even slightly impacted will not return to this savage, humiliating, and oppressive setting. However, I am not naive to the fact that my new walk and perception of life will be an everyday struggle especially, when everyone I encounter will not be as kind, caring or open minded as you are.

Still, I take with me the many faces, that smiled, sang, rollplayed, painted, danced, and/or expressed an authentic concern for the healing and development of someone like myself. I take with me the courage and the pride of doing the work that you've shared with us; plus the desire to travel down a similar path. So in the event that we never get the oppertunity to meet and/or speak again; I would like everyone whose ever walked through these doors to know that I keep them tattooed on my mind, my spirit, my soul, and more effectively, my heart.

So Again,

Thank You!

For everything.

P.S.

Here's a song (poem) inspired by this years theme.

FIGURE 15.1 Thank you letter to the Empowering Song instructors.

A Citizen Without A Home

        The following is a trilogy of poems that depict the manner
in which someone can be displaced within their own country.
For as a citizen of the United States I've always been faced
with the simbolism, the legislation, and the presence of a deep
rooted culture that constantly reminds people like myself of
the fact that the U.S. is not our home, nor were we (minorities)
ever intended to be included in its creed: "We the people."
In fact, my treatment of a second-class citizen began before
my conviction of any crime, and due to the indoctrination of
this country I am left to struggle with an identity crisis.
belonging to a nation that does not see my face, embrace my
being, or hear my voice. Thereby, forcing me to be its breathern
As if the migration of my people were by choice instead of
circumstances and brute force. After all, I had no say in what
race, place, and/or what lessons, in addition to what history
my person would belong to. Yet as a direct result of these social
concepts I and many more like myself, remain as the tital
suggest, a Citizen Without A Home.

By: Ismael Garcia-Vega

FIGURE 15.2   A citizen without a home.

                            I Am, Who I Am

        I am,
The micro aggression of a C/O
The shit inside your water
The white painted on your walls
The decaying in your Quota
The condescending tone in Authority
The slop inside your Stew
The whistle when it's count time
The trash you are; --It's you--
The path you walk; --It's true--
The ending in your calls
The deterrence every visit
The man whom you've conned
The man whom you've wronged
The one in Charge of who you are
And thus, the hate you face to learn.

By: Ismael Garcia-Vega

FIGURE 15.3   I am, who I am.

FLAG

It hangs there on its pole
Just as it has for years.
Flapping in the breeze, waving in the wind,
And standing guard over a nation.
Fifty white stars,
Red and white stripes.
Whoes blood is represented in that red?
Whose face is in those stars?
Why is it unpatriotic to
Kneel during the National Anthem?
We stand for our troops--is what they say--
Yet during both World Wars, my face and
Service were never respected.
During the Vietnam War, I was a "Spic"
Or a "Nigger"-- a "savage" or a "Kook"--
Was it okay for me to kneel then?
What oath can be made to undo
Hate and pain?
How dare women protes for their right to vote.
How dare any American refuse to stand for a
Symbol of opperssion.
Would it be fair to ask the Jews to stand for the
German National Anthem?
Sure, their flag is not Hitler's flag anymore
Than this one is a Confederate flag.
But is this home not "Brave" and built on the same
Foundation?
So while it hangs there on its pole
As it has for years
Flapping in the breeze, and waving in the wind
Standing guard over a nation.
Should I stand with it?

By: Ishmael Garcia-Vega

FIGURE 15.4   Flag.

TRAPPED!

Trapped in my own skin;
My hair,
My weight,
My color,
My face.

Trapped in my own mind;
My ideas,
My influence,
My intellect,
My ignorance.

Trapped in my own space;
My car,
my house,
My fashion,
My Doubt.

Trapped in my own time;
My age,
my memory,
My sight,
My odyssey.

By: Ismael Garcia-Vega

FIGURE 15.5   Trapped!

Notes

1   André de Quadros.
2   A juvenile detention center.
3   The class led by André de Quadros and his colleagues.
4   VOICES 21C.
5   "Q," as he is known among his friends, provided the editors with a series of prose and poetry that he typed on an electric typewriter while incarcerated. They are presented here in their original format inclusive of Q's handwritten corrections and without revision by the editors of this volume (see Figures 15.1–15.5).

CHAPTER 16

Voices of Peace: Ancient Queens Bringing Peace in a New World

Sarah Mandie

Meeting weekly in Craigieburn (Melbourne, Australia), the Assyrian Chaldean Syriac Women's community group was established in 2012 with the support of Foundation House, an organization that provides services to advance the health, well-being, and human rights of those who have experienced torture or other traumatic events in their country of origin or while fleeing those countries.

The majority of the refugees are from Iraq and have been arriving in Australia over the last 20 years. The group's focus is to build friendships and create a social support network in their new country. The women maintain strong links to their country of origin; they commence each meeting with a prayer remembering all the killed, sick, and missing people. They pray for peace all over the world and collect donations for families or individuals in need back at home. The women love to sing and aspire to sing together as a choir. As untrained singers with little experience playing music, they sought guidance and leadership. The group speaks Arabic and is facilitated by Foundation House's Salam Dankha, who also speaks the Assyrian and Chaldean languages with the women.

Community Music Victoria (CMVic) aims to achieve high quality participatory music-making experiences available to people across the state of Victoria in Australia. The aims are to develop music leadership skills, networking, skills-sharing, mentoring for emerging community music leaders, and to support them in starting new music groups. In line with their shared belief in the community-strengthening effects of singing in a group, CMVic connected with Foundation House, and the choir project Voices of Peace was born. As a mentor, singing leader, songwriter, and CMVic's Diversity Coordinator, I was to collaborate with the group to help them find and reveal their collective voice.

The First Meeting

I came to meet the group for our first session. The women exuded the joy of their close bonds, and they revealed their generosity by sharing their world of

© KONINKLIJKE BRILL NV, LEIDEN, 2020 | DOI: 10.1163/9789004430464_016

song, rhythm, and dance with me, an outsider. They shared their lunch too. It was Lent and, as soon as I arrived, I was offered a plate of homemade lentil soup with flatbread. Food, that other great connector!

My knowledge of the linguistic roots of the Hebrew language and my smattering of Hindi and Urdu vocabulary helped me to remember crucial Assyrian and Arabic words such as *listen, start,* and *quiet*. Because I grew up uttering the guttural 'ch' sound so unfamiliar to many English speakers, I was equipped with the ear and the tongue to learn and copy their Arabic and Assyrian song lyrics.

The Process of Becoming One

Warming up, they follow me. I stretch and they stretch. I draw a circle with my hand and hum from low to high and back again. They copy. Our voices make circles. The voice can become disconnected from the ear and from the body. How to gently introduce the idea of tuning, to bring the voice out of the body to meet a note that sits in the center of the group? I ask everyone to sing the same note. I repeat that note; I play it on the keyboard, and I sing it. I am using that one note to draw the group of women together and toward an awareness of sound, to develop listening skills and awareness. Turn to your friend and sing your note, now, listen to theirs. Are you singing the same note? Can you meet their note with yours? The notes and sound waves vary. Each woman's voice has a unique timbre and tone. They listen to each other's voices, each other's differences. The sound waves beat against each other highlighting the vocal diversity in the group. Some voices are low, coming from the depths of the chest, heavy with experience. Other voices are lighter and brighter, smaller and sweeter, louder and more confident, rough and weary. The notes and the waves begin a great distance apart, but slowly, as awareness grows, they come closer and closer together. This vocal syncing is a restorative experience, bringing a sense of healing to all of us. Each individual voice remains unique in itself as it merges into the group.

Finding an Anthem

The women want to write an anthem, a theme song from the heart. I ask them to bring in a meaningful object. A young woman in the group, Nagham Al Samak, brings dates and homemade Klecha, a pastry they bake and serve in their homes especially during Iyad (Easter and Christmas). I taste the dates and the Klecha. The other women don't need to taste. "You have it," they say. They know it too well. Each writes a few words in response to the dates: "The sweetness of life." "I make the Klecha and eat it all myself." "The strong palm tree, the pride of Iraq, it can live for hundreds of years." "The date grows on palm trees in the south of Iraq and is a symbol of pride and patience." "Everyone is proud of their culture."

An older woman brings her traditional silver headdress, worn by the bride at weddings and reminiscent of Iraqi queens and ancient goddesses. The women admire it as they pass it around the room: "It is bright and shining and a sign of luck." "It is a custom to wear it at weddings and celebrations in North of Iraq." "Ancient traditions that make me happy when I see it." "Olden day queens, connection to our ancestors." Resonant themes are emerging; dates, palm trees, and ancient queens and goddesses.

In another session, I ask the women for themes they want to include in their song. The short list of words is *Motherland, peace, forgiveness, contentment, love,* and *pride*. Groups use these words to create short poetic contributions. Salam takes their writings, and we sit together as she translates and I transcribe. The next week I come to the group with a selection of lyrics and an idea for a slow, lilting tune. Their words are haunting and seem to express the depth of their experiences.

Lost country, my love

Whoever has lost their gold, they can find it in the market, in the market
but whoever has lost their country,
where can they find it, where can they find it?
[This text comes from an unidentified existing song.]

Chorus
Lost country, my love: Where can I find you?
In the eyes of my mother, in the eyes of my mother.
My mother is the light of my eyes, and the candle of my way.

Chorus
Umi, umi, noo iyuni wo shemat darbi.
Ama, ama, my angel and my protector.

They listen, some are visibly moved as they hear their words sung in English, and they show appreciation for my effort, however, the tone of sadness and longing is not what they really want to express. "It's too sad and slow, we want something upbeat and inspiring!" one woman unashamedly asserts. I am not offended. My role is to initiate the songwriting process in order to activate the members of the group to make their own lyrical and musical choices. Nagham, who brought in the dates, offers a musical idea with a lyrical phrase. It has energy and spirit. I ask for more. We record it into my phone. I send it to her and she runs with it.

Week by week and with every word of encouragement Nagham develops her new-found creative confidence and she works on the group's anthem. Nagham emerges as a poet having taken the group's sentiments and shaped them into the song, *Aswat Al Salam* (Voices of Peace). In the song she connects their femininity as mothers and grandmothers to Ashtar, the goddess of fertility, and as resilient survivors of war and displacement she likens herself and her group to the exceptional first Queen of Babylon, Semiramis. The references in the anthem embody a pride in their historical past and culture, a strong identification as powerful women with their ancient feminist figure and a resounding message of peace.

Aswat Al Salam (Voices of Peace)

Lyrics by Nagham Al Samak and Voices of Peace. Music by Afram Suleiman and Nagham Al Samak and Voices of Peace. A song of Assyrian migrant women.

> Verse
> *We are the women from Voices of Peace*
> *from a country named Iraq*
> *from our beloved Baghdad.*
> *Our fragrance is of the blossoms*
> *from the lap of Hor*
> *from the palm*
> *and from our history.*
>
> Chorus
> *Our steadfastness comes from the palm tree,*
> *Our patience comes from the date,*
> *Our pride from the mountains,*
> *Our giving from the Spring,*
> *And our beauty from the shining sun.*

Verse
We are Semiramis and Queen Ashtar.
Not forgetting
Nineveh, Babel and Akad.
Not forgetting
the mountain and valley,
the beauty of the Shenashil,
and our most elegant art.

Chorus
Our steadfastness comes from the palm tree.
Our patience comes from the date.
Our pride from the mountains.
Our giving from the Spring.
And our beauty from the shining sun.

Verse
Come, homing pigeon, white dove.
Come from Baghdad.
We will give you an olive branch.
Spread the peace! Send love, care and happiness! [1]

Leaving Space

As a member of culturally diverse Melbourne, Australia, I believe I represent the same openness to and interest in different cultures that many people feel. My regular appearance at their meetings and my continuing belief in their musical path has developed a connection between the women as a minority community and the audiences they are yet to meet. I have encouraged them and enabled performances by giving them first-hand experience of the value of what they have to share. I have also inhabited a temporary space as a leader, always preparing to be replaced. Helping to set up a choir with the aim of providing the group with the skills and resources to ultimately lead themselves is also a particular challenge. How can I be present and yet invisible? How can I be a leader from behind, to reveal the way, while leaving open space for emerging leaders to step into. I decided to learn where they have come from and not to control the process. My role is to enable them to choose their repertoire and to create their own group identity. As an outsider and a product of my specific cultural background I know I cannot erase my unconscious bias but in order to counter this I consciously focus on allowing, listening and adjusting to who they are and what they want.

Their first public performance as Voices of Peace at the community music fundraiser was a highlight. Just as they were about to start, I experienced a moment of uncertainty: What do I do? I am not part of the group, and I do not want to stand in front of them conducting. I quietly left the stage and took a seat in the front row. The energy and palpable joy in the room was spectacular as they accompanied their traditional songs with regal and sensual dance moves and electrifying ululations. They shared their identities and made genuine connections in their new world while strengthening their ties with the old.

One often refrains from singing while in mourning, and when a community has suffered great loss and grief, singing can feel like the last thing one should be doing. In the case of the Voices of Peace, the women are singing for their health, for their healing, and to bring joy back into their lives. I asked the women what Voices of Peace means to them. They responded:

> I am proud to be member of my community, and this singing group represents my community!

> I feel, when I sing in the choir, my mood lift up and happier; also I forget the difficulties I have in my life.

> Singing will [fill] my chest with oxygen, and I feel happier and heavy load came off my shoulders.

With a songbook, a rehearsal, performance backing CD, and crisp blue and white chorus gowns we have made it to the choir's official launch (see Figure 16.1). In a run through before the guests arrive I am at the front supporting Nagham as the leader, reminding them not to push their voices and using images they relate to—"voices like honey." It's time. I sit in the center front like an anchor. By now I have learnt the lyrics to their songs and I sing along in Arabic and Assyrian. They have pulled me in with their warmth, trust and joy. Each individual character with her unique voice and expression shares the strong message of peace as they wave their olive branches to their anthem. Holding their hearts as they sing the impact of this project is clear. They share this with their families and dance with their supporters until the end of the night.

FIGURE 16.1   Voices of Peace Launch June 2019.
                       PHOTOGRAPH: DEBORAH CARVETH

The women have found their way as a choir and plan to embrace more opportunities to share their music with new audiences. They *are* the ancient queens of Mesopotamia, powerful survivors and the mothers and daughters of Australia, blessing their journey between the old and new worlds with a message of peace and forgiveness.

Note

1   *Hor*, region in the south of Iraq. *Semiramis, Shamiram* (Assyrian) the Lydian Babylonian legendary wife of Onnus and Ninus and the only woman ever to have ruled the mighty Assyrian Empire. *Ashtar*, the Babylonian goddess of fertility and war, Ishtar, Innana, Astarte. *Shenashil*, stained glass. Basra was the City of Shenasheel and is crumbling from neglect.

CHAPTER 17

KörKraft: The Power of Choral Singing as a Way towards Inclusion and Integration

Marie Bejstam and Charlotte Rider

Choral singing is an integral part of the Swedish folk soul. About 10% of residents in Sweden sing in an organized choir. Therefore, it is one key way to integrate into Swedish society. As such, the goals of KörKraft are learning Swedish and realizing integration through singing. Specifically, the project works with language choirs, friendship choirs, integration choirs, and provides competence development for choir leaders and language teachers through networking meetings.

KörKraft is a national project financed by the Swedish Inheritance Fund, run by Kulturfyren in collaboration with the Eric Ericson International Choral Centre, working together with the Swedish Choral Society, the study association Bilda, the Salvation Army, and Folkuniversitetets Internationella Gymnasiet in Uppsala. We lead two language choirs. The specific purpose of a language choir is to use singing as a tool for learning Swedish. The young people in the pictures are predominantly asylum-seekers who have lived in Sweden just a few months to a couple of years. They go to the International Gymnasium in Uppsala, Sweden, and have choir two hours a week. During each choral session, the young people work on language skills (vowel sounds are an integral part of correct Swedish pronunciation and understanding), Swedish pop songs, as well as some traditional Swedish songs.

The majority of the singers have no experience with choirs or choral music. The concept of singing together with others can be completely new. We have discovered amongst other things that singing can: (1) create a moment of well-being for the otherwise quite distressed young people waiting to find out if they will be allowed to stay in Sweden or not; (2) be a great tool in pronunciation and language intonation; (3) give the students a richer understanding of the language as songs are often poetic and descriptive, using synonyms, complete phrases, etc.; and (4) create an atmosphere of community, collaborating with others.

In the photographs singers are preparing for their concert together with their friendship choir from Lilla Akademien, a highly skilled chamber ensemble.

FIGURE 17.1 Ram from Syria showed himself to be quite musical. During the project, he joined a community youth choir with other Swedish teenagers.
PHOTOGRAPH: CHRISTJAN WEGNER

FIGURE 17.2 Dante, aka Razak, from Ghana, loved both singing and dancing. When we saw his dance skills, we helped him find a Swedish dance company for further training.
PHOTOGRAPH: CHRISTJAN WEGNER

FIGURE 17.3   The choir sessions empowered all, especially women, to use their voices and
                body language in front of others. Top: Rufta (left), Raina (middle), Shad (right).
                Bottom: Mujtaba (left), Fati (right).
                PHOTOGRAPH: CHRISTJAN WEGNER

FIGURE 17.4   Students from Stockholm's Lilla Akademien's chamber choir in concert at the
                Eric Ericson Hall together with the choir from Uppsala.
                PHOTOGRAPH: CHRISTJAN WEGNER

FIGURE 17.5   The final rehearsal at the Lilla Akademien in Stockholm one week prior to
the concert in the Eric Ericson Hall. The students in the picture are from the
language choir in Uppsala.
PHOTOGRAPH: CHRISTJAN WEGNER

CHAPTER 18

Navigating the Borderline: An Exploration inside a Community Music Workshop

Hala Jaber

This is a story of a group of migrants, with a special focus on two Syrian women and the changing nature of their music-making. The events of this story take place in Limerick City in Ireland. The people in the story are refugees and asylum-seekers who reside in the suburb of Limerick. The journey starts with an exploration of the research, the connection to making music, explaining my usage of the metaphor of borderline, and exploring the musical workshops where I met the women.

Before commencing our journey, it is important to be aware of two matters. First, I am Palestinian, meaning I have experienced conflict. Although I currently live in Ireland, I have faced issues similar to those faced by incoming migrants and refugees. Having this background and being able to speak Arabic allowed me to connect with the participants and prompted them to feel understood and safe to express their feelings. Secondly, to protect the privacy of the participants, not all details of their stories are shared.

This chapter is based on my PhD research in structured arts practice. The data presented in this chapter emerged from preparing, performing, and documenting the first performance titled *The Journey from Within*. This research aims to recognize the best suitable approach to the community music workshop when working in the context of post-conflict migration.

Bergh and Sloboda (2010) and Urbain et al. (2008) explain that music in its nature is neither peaceful nor hostile. It can be negative or positive depending on the intended use and agenda. In addition, the way participants perceive and feel the music used in the workshop may determine their experience of the workshop. In this research, I make the argument that engaging with music-making can be a negative experience. As an example, music can stir emotions and bring forth memories that may overwhelm the participant. Thus, the musical space needs to be safe and the facilitator must be able to deal with these experiences and make sure the participant is in good form before heading home. This is an especially delicate issue when working with refugees who have survived traumatic events.

Community Music

When fleeing, refugees leave behind their possessions, taking with them the most essential items. Music and dance are embodied knowledge that can travel with the person anywhere, transforming them into resources for individuals to dip in when needed (Phelan, 2012). For that reason, refugees hold on to some of their musical and cultural practices.

Numerous musical programs are offered for refugees in Limerick City. They take place in schools, hostels for asylum-seekers, and community projects. Younger children have access to musical programs in schools through various organizations such as Music Generation,[1] and families are invited to participate in the Health Hub initiative run by the University of Limerick through its sanctuary program.[2] These music programs, however, often do not address the needs of young adult refugees. After resettlement, they attend adult education institutions restricting their time and chances to engage in music-making activities. It was important for me to create a community music space that provided the chance for these young adults to engage with music-making, to challenge the language barrier, to help them find their voice, to encourage them to express how they feel, and to share their stories.

My expertise in community music falls under the paradigm of intervention, which can come as facilitating workshops, negotiating with groups and providing them with support to pursue their musical adventures (Bartleet & Higgins, 2018). The community music workshop I lead operates in the post-conflict framework. Howell (2018) argues that even though working in the context of post-conflict may differ, it shares similar characteristics with other community music activities.

The Borderline Metaphor

In this chapter, the metaphor *borderline* represents the uncomfortable space of negotiation, hesitation, and decision-making when someone faces sensitive moments related to the past experience of conflict, in which participants either chose to push the borderline and open up about their struggle in conflict or not. These moments emerged during the music-making moments. Working with people affected by conflict, I found that traditional and popular music may be situated within a *borderline*. It is important to note that each participant engages with music within the perimeters of their boundaries. A traditional piece of music may be a positive memory to a participant yet be traumatic to another. These reactions produce sensitive moments that need to be handled with care.

The Community Music Workshop

The story begins when I was volunteering in Doras Luimni, a non-governmental organization that promotes refugees' and asylum-seekers' rights.[3] These workshops took place in the Central Buildings community project (CB1) in Christ Church, Limerick City.[4] The aim was to create a space that welcomes and celebrates everyone regardless of their background, a space where young adults could meet, make music together, and share their stories. I sent invitations to asylum-seekers' hostels and to the Syrian families in Limerick City and put up flyers and posters as an invitation for the local community. I volunteered to run the sessions, and CB1 provided us with a hall free of charge. Since the workshops were not constrained by funding, I was determined to keep running them until they ended organically. The workshops did end about a year after we started due to issues such as conflicting timetables.

CB1 and Doras Luimni warned me prior to the first session not to feel disappointed if only a small number of people (or none) showed up. At first, the number of participants fluctuated; at times there would be twelve participants and on other days one or two would show up. Slowly, a core group of five young adults and a mother emerged. The participants were mainly from Zimbabwe and Syria. The workshops were a combination of sharing traditional songs, writing original music, playing percussion instruments, and socializing over a cup of tea.

After a few sessions and some negotiations we named our group Afrostinians. This name is a mix of African, Syrian, and Palestinian, representing all the nationalities in the group. We saw ourselves as one community that united and supported each other. Our experiences of conflict and being migrants brought the group together. Each member of the group approached music differently; for some, music represented hope and new beginnings; for others it was a reminder of a long-gone life.

During sessions we often found ourselves navigating borderlines. Every member of the group wanted to offer support to the others by sharing their stories and listening to the stories of others. Nevertheless, the gray area in which we constantly found ourselves was holding us back. This gray area was our first borderline to cross, which was trust. Each person questioned whether they could trust the others, and each negotiated crossing the invisible border between fully trusting the group or not. As the facilitator I needed to be patient and to give the group the space and time needed for trust to be built.

This border was crossed during a non-musical moment when participants' need to have a conversation overpowered the need to make music. On that day we all sat down and as we were chatting, the talk was slowly moving from general conversation to more personal. At that moment the atmosphere in the room was changing, and it became warmer, open, and trusting. This was the day the group crossed that border to fully trust each other.

During our time together, we composed many musical pieces; each had a special meaning to us as a group. It is not possible to explore all of them in the scope of this chapter. I will present one of the earliest songs we composed together called "Oh, Night." Here is an excerpt from the lyrics:

> *Oh, night!*
> *The stars are shining*
> *The witch is flying*
> *Owl watching from the tree,*
> *Wishing it was free*
> *Happy me, I want to be free*
> *High in the sky*
> *Spread my wings and fly.*

This song started as a story we wrote together. The personas in the song were the owl, witch, and thief (the thief was eliminated when the story became a song). The events of the story took place at night. The owl represented the participants, the witch was war and conflict, and the thief was the henchman of the witch and referred to all parties that contribute to war.

An owl is a bird that can fly, yet in the song, it cannot fly and longs for freedom. In the original story and the song, there was no indication that the bird was injured or chained; it simply could not fly. I wondered why the participants chose the owl to represent them? Could it be simply because the story took place at night and the owl is a night bird, or does it have a deeper meaning? We all come from different cultures, thus, the owl may represent different meanings for each of us. For example, in the Arabic culture, owls are considered as an omen for bad luck, and when people see one, they tend to shoo it away.

In this song, the participants used the owl to convey their feelings without having to directly face the omens. Thus, the borderline is the emotions that needed to be expressed. It is that moment of transition between feeling something and talking about it, the moment where you make peace with your emotions and share them with the world. How do you explain what you feel? And how do you express it through music-making?

These questions constituted a large grey area in which the group found itself. Within this area were smaller borderlines to overcome. The text below is an exploration of two borders we negotiated as a group.

Who We Are

The participants know who they are within their own community. Their old selves, however, did not match the new landscape in which they were living. In their homeland, they belonged to the community, built their identity to suit that community, and knew how to negotiate relationships. In the new community, they faced a change in their social status, a new language to learn, new culture, and new rules on acceptable behavior.

Returning to the song, this can be observed in the owl feeling trapped without actually being chained, and wishing to be free. This was a shared border within the group; we do not know who we are, where we belong, and how to act according to Irish society's rules. These sentiments were shared within the group through our many informal conversations during teatime.

Which Language and Which Music Style

Four languages were spoken within the group; English, Arabic, Ndebele, and Zulu. The group members argued over which language was more suitable to use in our songs; some preferred using English to allow other people to understand the songs, while others argued that using the native language was more important. Exploring this debate, it was clear that the border was between exploring the new culture versus holding onto traditions and native culture. Perhaps the participants wanted to hold onto their language as a representation of their culture.

The members of Afrostinians were outspoken about their preferred musical styles. All members had been heavily engaged with music-making in their home countries prior to being displaced. They developed a musical style linked to their culture that they were reluctant to relinquish. The borderline here was the transition between one's own musical style and creating a collective style that represented all the group's members. Transferred to real life, the question became: What is the balance between holding on to one's original culture and adapting to the new culture? Participants used the community music workshop as a safe space to express and negotiate these borderlines. It is important to note that music-making does not magically make these issues disappear. It makes participants face questions and consider the answers.

In the next section, I explore the story of two members of the group more closely. Other members are in the group, but for this chapter I explored the journey of two Syrian women.

The Tale of Two Syrian Women

The group and I were in the middle of a discussion when two women walked into the musical space. One was clearly much older than the other. They were told of my Arab background and that I speak Arabic, so they approached me and asked if this was the music workshop. I answered in the affirmative and welcomed them. After a small chat, it became clear that the older woman was the mother of the younger one.

The mother's name is Ghada, a woman in her late thirties, although one can easily mistake her for being well into her forties. She asked me questions about the nature of the workshops, who can join, and what kind of music was played. Hanin, Ghada's daughter, is in her early twenties. She was attending a community college to make up for the years she missed in school due to displacement. Hanin was enthusiastic and interested in joining the workshops (see Figures 18.1 and 18.2).

FIGURE 18.1   Ghada Al Khous reciting the poem she wrote.
PHOTOGRAPH: LUCY DAWSON

FIGURE 18.2   Hanin Friha performing.
PHOTOGRAPH: LUCY DAWSON

During the first workshop, Ghada excused herself and found a seat in the corner of the room explaining she was only accompanying her daughter. At first, I did not give it much thought; I believed she was making sure her daughter was safe. But as Ghada continued to attend most of the musical workshops, I noticed that she was attentive to what we were doing, yet she was in her own little world.

Ghada and Hanin had had a life in Syria that was disrupted by war. They had no choice but to flee for their lives from accidents and near-death incidents. These experiences changed the women in various ways. Each week Ghada and I chatted a little longer. When I invited her to join the music-making, she apologized and informed me that music has no place in her life right now. She had stopped listening to music and singing after the war had started in Syria. Ghada later explained:

دائماً عم بسمع موسيقا و ارتاح، انو كنت حبها بس المشكلة وين صارت اكتر الأغاني لما اسمعها منت اسمعها مع اخي، بس اخي مات بالاحداث تقوس براسه، وين وقتها كنت حبيت اسمع موسيقا لأنو كل ما بسمع الأغاني تاخدني الذاكرة لعندو او بتحبطني

[I used to listen to music and feel relaxed, I used to love music. But the problem is most of the songs I listen to, I heard them with my brother. My brother died in the war; he was shot in his head. After that, I no longer liked to listen to music. Every time I listen to songs, I remember him and become depressed.]

If interactions with music were so emotionally challenging to her, why did Ghada come to the musical workshops?

After a month or two, Ghada invited me to her house for dinner and tea. I had the privilege of meeting the family. I was informed that her husband was killed in the Syrian conflict. The family did not learn of this dreadful news until three years later, when they were refugees in Lebanon. I noticed that Ghada's children—especially Hanin—engaged with music and they sang frequently when at home. When I asked her about how that made her feel, she responded:

بنبسط. فيهم انو هنّ بيحبو الموسيقا و بسمع ا موسيقابس ما بعطي انتباه ما بحب تأكد بالأغنية.

[It makes me happy that they love music and they sing, I hear the music, but I never give my attention to what song it is, I don't like to know what song it is.]

I noticed that the more I accepted invitations to visit the family, the less frequently Ghada was coming to the musical workshops. It took me a while to understand that this woman was seeking human connection beyond her children. Ghada wanted to have a conversation in Arabic and a cup of coffee. She was not interested in the musical aspect of the workshop but rather the social one.

My relationship with Ghada grew outside the musical workshops. We met for coffee, she invited me to her house a couple of times during which she told me she wrote poems to express how she feels. I invited Ghada to take part in my first PhD performance, *The Journey from Within*. Ghada agreed and performed a very moving poem titled "My Life":

"يا حياتي أخبريهم
اخبريهم ماذا حدث
انت وحدك تعلمين
انت رأيت ما حدث
أروي لهم و قُصي عليهم
ربما فيأخذ الأيام سمعوكي
عذروني و عذروك
يا حياتي احكي لهم

عني و عنك
ربما رحموني ورحموكي
قولي لهم ماذا جرى بروحي و قلبي
قولي لهم كيف حطمو تلك الروح
قولي لهم كيف كسروا ذلك القلب
قولي لهم كيف قهروا تلك النفس
قولي و قولي
كيف دمروكي و جرحوكي و اتعبوكي
قولي لهم و اساليهم لماذا فعلو هذا بك
هل انا استحق ذلك و خلقت من اجل ذلك
او ربما ظنوا انك معتادة على ذلك
او حب الحياة و التماس الحنان
و الشعور بالعطف خطيئة لاتغتفر
اساليهم يا حياتي وان رفضوا رد الجواب
قولي لهم بان ما حدث قضاء و قدر
أجيبهم كما يحيبون بأنهم دائماً هاربون
هاربون، وتأسفت منهم لانك أضعت من وقتهم
و هي بِنَا نرحل و نرحل كما وحلمت قبلنا الكثيرون
فهي بِنَا نرحل بكل بؤس و حزنت أسف نرحل
مثل تلك الأيام التي رحلت و اعتدنا بها عل كل الاسى
وضعنا بها و تهنا قبلها و رحلت و تركت كل شيء خلفها فهي بِنَا نرحل
نرحل بدون تردد و خوف نرحل
فكل الدقائق دقيقة
و كل الساعات ساعة
و كل الأيام يوم واحد‟

Tell them my life

Tell them what happened

You alone know

You saw what happened

Say and express to them

Maybe one day they will hear you

Excuse me and excuse you

Tell them my life

About me and about you

Maybe they will have mercy on me and you

Tell them what happened to my soul and heart

Tell them how they crushed that soul

Tell them how they broke that heart

Tell them how they killed that sprit

Tell and tell how they destroyed you, injured you, fatigued you

Tell them and ask them why they have done this to you
Do I deserve this or was I born for this?
Maybe they thought you are used to this
Or your love for life and seeking compassion
Is an unforgivable sin
Ask them my life even if they refuse to answer
Tell them what had happened was meant to be
Answer them and tell them they are always running
Running, and apologies for wasting their time
And let us leave, leave, as many have left before us
Let us leave in all our misery, sadness and sorrow
Leave as all those days have left, where we got used to their sadness
The days that we lost before they arrived and departed leaving everything behind
Let us leave, leave without hesitation, without fear
For all the minutes are one minute
All the hours are one hour
And all the days are one day[5]

When I asked her about the reason for choosing that poem, she answered:

لانها بتعبر عني و عن اخي انا اخترتها لاهي القصيدة مشان اقرأها لانها بتعبر عني و عن اخي و عن حياتي و حياة اخي

[Because it represents me and my brother; it represents our lives, mine and my brother's.]

Ghada expressed her feelings during and after the performance:

كنت حاسة حالي عم بعمل شي منيح انو هادا الشيء الي كنت عم بحلم في أي أكون شاعرة و اني روجي شعري للناس بس لظروف ما شاءت اني اكمل دراست... كتير كتير كنت مبسوطة كنت فرحانة خاصة اني هيك عملتولي حفلة عيد ميلاد صغيرة و قتها كنت مبسوطة فرحانة بحس انو هادا العالم الي كنت لازم عيش في انا و مو العالم الي عشت في.

[I felt that I was doing something good. It is something I dreamt about, to be a poet and show my poems to people. However, circumstances didn't allow me to finish my education...I was very very happy especially because you celebrated my birthday. I was very happy then because I felt that that is the world I want to live in, not the one I used to live in.]

It is interesting to note that my social interaction with Ghada prompted her to take part in the performance. Ghada's poem "My Life" spoke about the pain she experienced after the war had started in Syria. Standing on the stage was a huge leap over a personal boundary for Ghada. She was hesitant at the beginning; then she insisted on doing it. The poem was incredibly personal and revealed raw emotions. Ghada's borderline was the most difficult to face. For her, music is no longer a comfort. Yet, she attended the music workshops, and her children constantly sing and listen to music in the house. She was walking through the borderline between painful memories and a hopeful future. She chose to write "My Life" and perform it without music.

Meanwhile, Hanin was thriving, she was highly engaged with the music-making. She was making friends with the other participants, slowly finding her voice, and making sure it was present within the group. Hanin expressed her desire to improve her vocal abilities. Since I am not a vocal teacher, I connected Hanin with one.

When I asked Hanin why she likes to engage with music-making, she answered:

كنت دائماً حس بكبت جوات قلبي بحس لما بغني بيطلع هذا الكبت و بقدر أتخلص منو بدون ما ابكي

[I always felt there is pressure in my heart; when I sing, this pressure is released without my crying.]

This prompted me to ask her about her experience in leaving Syria and coming to Ireland to live. Hanin explained that she lived in Lebanon for some time before coming to Ireland:

اول فترة وقت نقلنا انا ضليت ٣ أشهر ابكي فيهم و ما كنت نام أبدا، صار نعي توتر عصبي مو طبيعي و طول الوقت كنت عم ابكي ابك

[In the beginning when we moved, I cried for three months. I couldn't sleep at all. I suffered from tension in my nerves. All the time I was crying, crying.]

Now and after moving to Ireland Hanin does not feel completely safe:

انو صرت خاف من الموت، صرت خاف من الرصاصة، و صار عندي خوف انو بيوم من الأيام تيجيني رصاصة يعني لحد الان بخاف انو تيجيني رصاصة و انا ماشية و ماني حاسة فيها و ما اعرف من وين اجتني

[I am now afraid of death, afraid of a bullet. I am afraid that one day I will be hit by a bullet. Until this day, I am afraid to be hit by a bullet, not know where it came from, and not feel it.]

Hanin and I had many conversations and sang many traditional Arabic songs. Through those interactions we created a song titled "In the Middle," written in both Arabic and English. The song presented the dilemma of a young Arab woman who finds herself in the West, with different traditions and expectations. Women's rights and freedom are a major topic in this song. The following text draws attention to prohibitions in parts of Arab society yet is permitted in Ireland. The Arabic words mean "No, that is forbidden":

Can I wear shorts? لا ممنوع ع
Can I go out? لا ممنوع ع
Can I sing? لا ممنوع ع
Can I dance? لا ممنوع ع
Can I smile? لا ممنوع ع
Can I walk in the street? Can I buy myself a treat? لا ممنوع ع

This small excerpt highlights the confusion some Arab women experience when they move to a Western culture. For Hanin and me, everything we have learned, everything we were told about the right way to behave suddenly changed. What was not allowed is suddenly permitted. This conundrum cannot be solved through making a song; however, the process of writing and performing the song allowed Hanin to express her confusion. It is important to note that the Arab culture imposes more restrictions on women than on men. The culture dictates the way they dress, their behavior, and the extent of their engagement with society. This piece of music represented Hanin verbalizing the borderline between what she is experiencing in Ireland and what she was taught in Syria.

For Hanin, the borderline she had to cross was between two different cultures, the Syrian culture she was raised in and the Irish culture she found herself living in. On one hand, she wants to imitate the norms of the new culture; on the other, she wants to hold on to her traditions. This drastic change caused Hanin to question elements of both cultures. Engaging with the process of songwriting helped her to reposition herself away from the personal confusion.

In this chapter, I explored borderlines and how they are navigated throughout the music workshop. The borderlines mentioned in this chapter are not musical; they are a gray area the participants found themselves walking in. Making music highlighted those issues, gently pushing the participants to deal with them. At times, participants chose not to venture across the border-line. It is my hope that readers might acquire an idea of how displacement changes people and the role that music can play in challenging the effects of displacement. When faced with constant uncertainty, people create borders to protect themselves. Extra care is needed when working in the context of conflict. Community musicians could have a conversation with their participants to acknowledge some of their borderlines and perhaps to identify aspects of music that can be harmful to participants.

In the end, how we identify with music is related to the place we are at in life. Experiencing music develops in time with unpredictable changes and transformations (Zbikowski, 2010). As of late 2019, the workshops came to an end, but the friendships were still going strong. Hanin was attending vocal lessons and wanted to write her own music. Ghada was interested in future performances, because she wished to write another poem.

The community music workshops may not have solved the problems or eliminated the borders. They simply gave people space and time to negotiate those borders and the tools to express their feelings and confusions. Music cannot stop displacement or war, but it could empower people to find hope again.

Notes

1   For further information on Music Generation, see https://www.musicgeneration.ie/
2   For further information on the University of Limerick's sanctuary program, see https://www.facebook.com/groups/2120835471279956/?ref=br_rs
3   For further information on Doras Luimni, see http://dorasluimni.org/
4   For further information on Central Buildings Community Project/Christ Church Limerick, see https://www.facebook.com/CentralBuildingsLimerick
5   "My Life" was written by Ghada Al Khouse in 2018 and later translated by Hala Jaber.

References

Baily, J., & Collyer, M. (2006). Introduction: Music and migration. *Journal of Ethnic and Migration Studies, 32*(2), 167–182. doi:10.1080/13691830500487266

Bartleet, B. L., & Higgins, L. (Eds.). (2018). Introduction. An overview of community music in the twenty-first century. In B. L. Bartleet & L. Higgins (Eds.), *The Oxford handbook of community music*. New York, NY: Oxford University Press.

Bergh, A., & Sloboda, J. (2010). Music and art in conflict transformation: A review. *Music and Arts in Action, 2*(2), 2–17.

Goatly, A. (1996). *The language of metaphors*. New York, NY: Routledge.

Howell, G. (2018). Community music interventions in post-conflict contexts. In B. L. Bartleet & L. Higgins (Eds.), *The Oxford handbook of community music*. New York, NY: Oxford University Press.

Lakoff, G., & Johnson, M. (1980). *Metaphors we live by*. Chicago, IL: University of Chicago Press.

Lakoff, G., & Johnson, M. (1999). *Philosophy in the flesh: The embodied mind and its challenge to western thought*. New York, NY: Basic Books.

Nelson, R. (2013). *Practice as research in the arts: Principles, protocols, pedagogies and resistance*. New York, NY: Palgrave MacMillan.

Phelan, H. (2012). Sonic hospitality: Migration, community and music. In G. McPherson & G. Welch (Eds.), *The Oxford handbook of music education* (Vol. II, pp. 168–184). New York, NY: Oxford University Press.

Urbain, O., Lopez Vinader, M. E., Cohen, C., Boyce-Tillman, J., Jordanger, V., & Kent, G. (2008). *Music for conflict transformation: Contributing to sustainable futures*. Retrieved June 6, 2009, from http://soc.kuleuven.be/iieb/ipraweb/papers/Music%20for%20Confl ict%20Transformation.pdf

Xiaomei, Z., & Shimin, W. (2014). Political identity: A perspective from cultural identity. *Social Sciences in China, 35*(2), 155–173. doi:10.1080/02529203.2014.900890

Zbikowski, L. (2010). Music, emotion, analysis. *Music Analysis, 29*(1–3), 37–60. https://doi.org/10.1111/j.1468-2249.2011.00330.x

CHAPTER 19

Pihcintu: Young Women Whose Voices Carry Far

Con Fullam

Welcoming immigrant children from around the globe, the Pihcintu Multicultural Chorus seeks to restart young lives. War-torn villages, bloodshed, refugee camps, famine, and political turmoil were devastating realities for many of these young singers before being embraced by the warmth, companionship and harmony that Pihcintu provides.

FIGURE 19.1   Ana (Democratic Republic of Congo) in a rehearsal for a United Nations
performance in 2018.
PHOTOGRAPH: KEVIN FAHRMAN

The Pihcintu Multicultural Chorus[1] was born on a cold, rainy, windswept November day at the Reiche School in Portland, Maine, where the first audition for the chorus was held. Some four months earlier, I had had lunch with a long-time friend who had taken the job as the executive director of Catholic Charities of Maine. It was at that lunch where I learned of the astounding number of countries from which so many people of refugee backgrounds came and the rich contributions that they were making to their newly adopted community. I also learned of the challenges they faced adjusting to

© KONINKLIJKE BRILL NV, LEIDEN, 2020 | DOI: 10.1163/9789004430464_019

this dramatically different culture, not the least of which was the language barrier.

At Deering High School, one of four high schools in Portland, over 50 languages and dialects are spoken and an equal number of cultures, creeds, and countries are represented. In 2008, only a few students of color attended Deering. The population in 2019 was evenly split between white students and those of color. A great testimony to the faculty and staff at Deering is the fact that, despite continuous clashes, frustrations, and tense moments between students, the school operates as a cohesive institution in which one can recognize a close intermingling of students from many countries.

In thinking about the ways in which I might be helpful to the incoming immigrants and refugees, music immediately came to mind. I am a professional singer-songwriter who has been performing since the age of five, when my father died suddenly, and unexpectedly, of a heart attack. We were close and his passing was difficult for my five-year-old mind to comprehend. I struggled to accept his absence, and my saving grace was his ukulele that he had begun to teach me how to play. I took to the ukulele almost instinctively; its soothing sound made me feel better and gave me a sense of self-worth and meaning. In school, I was the only child without a father, a fact that was often pointed out by the nuns who taught me and by some peers who taunted me. Singing songs and accompanying myself on the uke was something only I could do, and it gave me strength and self-confidence. Knowing that music has potential to create a common bond shared by many, I decided that I would form a chorus that might do for these newly arrived refugees and immigrants[2] what music had done for me— give them opportunities to explore their voices and a platform to use them.

It took the better part of a year to recruit the first 20 singers who, at that time, represented 10 countries. Several more years elapsed before we could establish the chorus as a legitimate entity with a mission and a purpose. In the beginning stages of the choir, transportation for singers and funding posed challenges. Then, there is always the tension caused by new arrivals who must find their way into the hearts and minds of their chorus mates. While occasional confrontations still occur, new arrivals are eventually welcomed into the choir. Despite, or because of, the challenges experienced by singers, every member of Pihcintu, in the 14 years of its existence, has graduated from high school and 85% of all singers who have sung in the chorus for at least two years have pursued post-secondary education. As of late 2019, Pihcintu has grown to 34 singers from 22 countries.[3]

The chorus was mostly unknown at its start, but in 2011 my entertainment attorney in New York, Micky Hyman, was working with an Emmy

Award-winning documentary producer Patrice Samara. Patrice managed a project called Alphabet Kids, a series of children's books by Joyce Kassin, promoting the importance of diversity and understanding among children of all cultures, creeds, and countries. Micky knew about Pihcintu and felt that we were the living embodiment of Joyce's fictional characters, and so he introduced me to Patrice who flew up to Portland from New York City. Upon meeting the chorus members and hearing their stories (see Figures 19.2 and 19.3), Patrice committed to producing a documentary about Pihcintu. For a multitude of reasons, the documentary was never finished. Preliminary footage, however, landed in the hands of a producer at NBC's Today Show and, within hours, reporter Jenna Bush was on her way to Portland to film a segment for the morning program. That five-minute segment, which ran on Christmas Eve, was the greatest single gift that Pihcintu had ever received. The publicity caused the phone to ring for booking concerts and the local media to call for interviews.

FIGURE 19.2   Sandra (Cambodia): "Pihcintu is a place where I can be myself and not be judged."
PHOTOGRAPH: KEVIN FAHRMAN

In terms of the music-making in Pihcintu, the singers curate the content by informing me of their preference for a specific song.[4] When little enthusiasm is aroused for a particular song, we simply move on to other tunes. As what I would call a "message chorus," we work through the challenges presented to us in our repertoire by determining the power of any given song to expand the chorus's mission (see Video 19.1).

Pihcintu's message centers on the cultivation of understanding within diversity and the exploration of solutions to conflict; often these singers come from warring countries and tribes, and from quite different social and cultural backgrounds. Discussions occur about what a given song's inherent message

FIGURE 19.3 Mercia (Gabon): "The world is not really made to be all happy and easy. We have issues and we have problems, but we are able to fix that. I feel like we have a good bond."
PHOTOGRAPH: KEVIN FAHRMAN

is. And, at times, the end result of the discussion is that, although a specific song is not entirely representative of the mission, the singers relate to the song on a personal level and are happy when they rehearse or perform it. When that is the case, the song is added to the repertoire. Singers' ears are perpetually filled with earbuds as they listen to music constantly, in classes or when talking amongst themselves. Their music listening inspires a constant flow of song suggestions. That said, the singers realize that a typical performance set is 45 minutes, and we have a set number of songs as part of our regular repertoire; therefore, it takes a very special song to make it into the concert set. As an example of one of these special songs, the musicians chose to sing "I Was Here" by Beyoncé. This song concerns leaving a mark on the world, touching others' hearts, and succeeding in life; all goals that each singer in this chorus aspires to.

Being part of Pihcintu provides a space for young women to tell their stories through word and song. It may well be that each singer experiences and grows from the sense of confidence they receive from audience reactions to their performances. That confidence carries them through the current challenges they face and into their futures (see Figure 19.5). As an example, a young chorus member from El Salvador came to rehearsal and usually sat alone. She was clearly a bright person, but very shy. Six months into her chorus experience, I asked her to sing a solo; to my surprise she agreed and sang it beautifully. From that moment, she began to come out of her shell, culminating in a speech she gave a year later in front an audience of 5,000 at the Sylvan Theater in Washington, DC. She received a standing ovation and upon exiting the stage she looked at me and said, "I wasn't afraid."

I conclude this story with the words of two singers who describe the impact of the choir:

> Hi, my name is Brenda, and I'm from Kenya. Music means so much to me that I'm able to be myself and able to express who I am into a song. And [I'm] able to share those heavy stories I've been holding for a long [time] to put into a song and share it to the people … And being able to sing it out there just makes me be who I am. I was not comfortable to put it out there—it's kind of like making myself release [a] heavy burden that I've been holding. And that's how [the chorus] brought me to a connection with the music where I can be myself, be who I am. And for me to be in this group, it's like I've found where my second family are now. We just have this bond, this connection that I never really experienced before, and that's what I love about Pihcintu. (Brenda, personal communication)

Fatimah is from Iraq. She described the meaning of music in her life (see Figure 19.4).

> What music means to me it's like an outlet for me to express my anger for anything outside of the chorus, and I can just express it as happy feelings and the audience can see hope in that. For me, the chorus personally is a place where I can go to for support and to have fun. Like all these girls that are from different cultures that can give me insight about their lives and how to make my life better. (Fatimah, personal communication)

FIGURE 19.4   Fatimah (Iraq): "It's like an outlet for me to express my anger for anything outside the chorus, and I can just express it as happy feelings and the audience can
see hope in that."
PHOTOGRAPH: KEVIN FAHRMAN

FIGURE 19.5   Pihcintu Chorus (2019) at University of Southern Maine.
PHOTOGRAPH: SHAWN PATRICK OUELLETTE, PORTLAND PRESS HERALD

   VIDEO 19.1   Con Fullam's Somewhere composed for his choir Pihcintu Multicultural Chorus.
The video accompanying this chapter is freely available online at
https://doi.org/10.6084/m9.figshare.12445961

Notes

1   For further information on the chorus, see http://pihcintu.org/index.html.
2   Of the 34 current singers, 32 are considered either asylum-seekers, refugees, immigrants or first-generation daughters of refugees and immigrants
3   As of early 2019, the countries represented in Pihcintu include Afghanistan, Angola, Burkina Faso, Burundi, Cambodia, Democratic Republic of Congo, El Salvador, Ethiopia, Guatemala, Honduras, Iraq, Ivory Coast, Jamaica, Kenya, Namibia, Rwanda, Somalia, South Sudan, Sudan, Uganda, United States, and Vietnam.
4   I write many of the songs, so the process for selection is simple. I play the song for the singers and they decide whether they like it or not. The melody, beat, and lyrics are the criteria. As for outside material, singers present suggestions to the chorus and the chorus decides.

CHAPTER 20

Polyphonica: Bonding through Music

Efi Averof Michailidou, David Nnadi, Irene (Peace) Ebhohon and Nelly Yurina

Polyphonica was established in 2011 as a non-profit company aiming to host children from underprivileged backgrounds, whether Greeks or foreigners, regardless of their place of origin, their religion or their language. The vision was and is to give these children the opportunity to participate in collective cultural activities and offer them a chance to learn and create through music, dance, and art in general. The fact that for the last few years Greece is undergoing a period of economic and refugee crises makes Polyphonica's task even more challenging.

In 2019, about 200 children from 20 countries participated in Polyphonica's cultural and educational activities. About 40% are of Greek origin, another 40% are second-generation immigrants, and the rest are mostly refugees. Workshops for the period 2018–2019 included five choirs in Athens and in Lesvos,[1] as well as classes for ukulele, contemporary dance, drumming, acting, and African dance and drums. Polyphonica is well established in Greece, and teachers feel honored to work with the program.[2] All teachers employed by Polyphonica are highly experienced professionals and sensitive to community projects. They do not work on a voluntary basis and are paid according to their skills and involvement. The majority have participated in voice, music pedagogy, and music therapy seminars and have worked in community choirs with an intercultural character. Many of our skilled teachers have also worked with children who have special needs and with underprivileged groups. As we keep an eye on our singers' interests, it is not difficult to focus on our vision of community projects.

For Polyphonica, it is important to give every child tools for personal development, for growing, and for acquiring self-esteem. Participation in the choir is free of charge and no child is rejected. It is important that all children participate of their own free will. Our mottos are mutual respect, solidarity with peers, and non-violence.

Healing wounds and emotional injuries of refugee children is a step-by-step process. Their integration into local society is of utmost importance to us. We focus on boosting their self-esteem by bringing out the best in them. Lack of discipline and abundance of energy sometimes disrupt concentration and the cohesion of the classes. We believe, however, that working in teams toward a common goal may eventually help these children understand and appreciate one another, and this result could reduce tensions.

In addition to the the use of many internationally recognized methods, we use non-verbal methods of teaching and take into consideration the fact that refugee children often only speak their native languages. Among non-verbal activities are soundpainting, body percussion, and drumming, to name a few. In our choir, the children are exposed to languages and musical traditions of countries from all over the world; this exposure reinforces the message that they are part of a global community.

To demonstrate how non-verbal activities and methods are important in our context, I shall share more about the soundpainting process. Soundpainting is a kind of sign language,[3] accessible to all students of any age from pre-schoolers to collegians, including immigrants, refugees, or those with special needs. Using this method, the hidden creativity of students is drawn out and developed constructively by way of the gestural signs and symbols created by the soundpainter. Soundpainting enables each individual or group to express his or her own ideas and feelings in an experiential learning process. In closeup, the soundpainter acts like an orchestra conductor and she or he presents the signs that the children have to follow. There is no right or wrong, the soundpainter can continue the open composition by using any sound the recipients make. Soundpainting does not rely on written notation. The vocabulary consists of approximately 1,200 gestures from which about 25 simple symbols are sufficient to teach children. Soundpainting is highly popular among our children. It is fun, and at the same time it boosts creativity, helps children concentrate, become more disciplined, and work together. We believe it is an appropriate educational tool, as it makes it easier for teachers to address all children directly (non-verbally) and involve them in the musical process, regardless of their native language.

On the island of Lesvos, greatly affected by the refugee crisis, Polyphonica runs two choirs. The choirs are led by two music educators and community artist facilitators. The members of the choirs reflect the community structure, thus including children from Greek schools—a majority—and from camps and refugee accommodation centers. Because a number of the refugee children are in transit with their parents to other locations in Greece or abroad, the teachers need to re-adjust their programming quite often. Our intercultural, interactive musical projects on Mytilene in Lesvos are good examples of community spirit and teamwork. Our choirs join forces with other choirs, volunteers from NGOs working in refugee camps, and travelers. Singing, dancing, juggling, doing acrobatics, and enjoying the team spirit clearly show that integration can be achieved and at minimum cost.

One of our daily challenges is racism in our classes, mostly from Greek parents who do not wish their children to mix with refugees when the percentage of refugee children is high. We try to gradually incorporate the refugees into our classes and on one hand to keep the intercultural character, but, on the other hand, to keep the refugees to a number not exceeding 15%. The fact that the schools we have chosen for the rehearsals are Greek makes the Greek parents feel safe. During performances, the children wear colorful T-shirts that help to unify their look. You cannot tell who is who! If some parents insist on having a purely Greek choir, they are free to go somewhere else. They know this!

We have often changed our attitude regarding the difficult issue of integration. What works with us now is a collaboration with Greek schools. The main core of the choirs (Greek children and second-generation immigrants who speak Greek) is stable in its number as well as in attendance. We gradually incorporate refugee children into our classes in a controlled number; this facilitates their integration as they have to follow the others. The games during the breaks do wonders since all the children join in. Also, they love the concerts where one can see that all of them are trying their best for a successful performance. Small excursions and other extras are also helpful. For everyone working in Polyphonica the motivation is the children's smiles. But no assessment would be valid unless it came from the children themselves, who are ultimately the participants and judges.

Polyphonica's practices in music and music education have as its main goal the effort to change disadvantaged children's lives and facilitate their transition to a better and more dignified life. It expresses the experience gained through the eight years of the organization's existence, and it focuses only on its music groups. Are we on a good track? What's next? These are questions we often consider. Our daily concern is to act to the best of our knowledge and abilities for the benefit of vulnerable, underprivileged children. Our work is a never-ending process. The political, social and economic situations are changing so rapidly that we must re-adapt to the new challenges and reconsider our practices accordingly. We believe that the best criteria for determining the next steps come from our children whose feedback is so important. Below, David and Irene share stories about their lives and how participation in Polyphonica is important to them. Nelly's story is told via her folksong about mermaids in the Aegean Sea.

David, Irene, and Nelly: Telling Our Stories

David Nnadi
The benefits this young boy gained are obvious. He mentions freedom of choice, enjoyment of playing the drums, desire to progress and grow, teamwork, feeling

of responsibility towards his team, trust, connecting with peers, building friendships, self-confidence, self-esteem, and pride.

My name is David; I come from Nigeria. I was born in Greece in 2005 and I have lived here since. I feel that Polyphonica is not something I am obliged to do; I feel that it is something I like to do. It is not like a job. I do it freely because I like it. I've been in the world of music for about four or five years. I've been to Polyphonica for three years.

I believe that Polyphonica has helped me a lot with my voice. In the past, I used to have a, how can I say? a higher voice, but this year, I think the teacher called it metaphony. You can now realize that my voice has become deeper. Polyphonica has helped me a lot. For example, with the drums. I must admit that, three to four years ago, I had no idea of how to play the djembe or the drums, but now with Polyphonica I have started to understand. And now I am very good in drums. You must learn so you can grow.

In Polyphonica I met a girl, a friend whom I hadn't seen for quite some time, and I have [made] many other friends. I have another friend whom I know for two or three years. For some reason, I feel that he has a positive impact on me because he tells me things like an older brother. And I know that whatever he tells me *is* helping me growing up. I feel freer in Polyphonica thanks to him. Concerning the other friends, we are having fun during the lesson but we are all committed in becoming better in the world of music.

Polyphonica has helped me a lot to face the outside world because I now have more self-confidence. During my first two years in Polyphonica I was very shy. I didn't know whom to talk to, I was scared to talk. I was scared to sing until this year in September, I started getting used to the fact that I had to sing, because if I don't sing in this song I have the feeling inside of me that something would be missing.

Especially in the concerts that we give, I am very satisfied and I believe that we will do even better in 2020. In Polyphonica we are planning new concerts and there are people who listen to us. Someone stopped me in the street and told me, "Wasn't it you in this concert singing with other kids? You sang well, we took a video of you, we showed it to our friends." They asked me how I felt on stage.

I am not obliged to sing, I only sing if I want to, and this is what I love best about Polyphonica, that you sing with your own free will. If you don't wish to sing that day you are not obliged to. You are asked to sing only if you feel well" (see Figure 20.1 and Video 20.1).

FIGURE 20.1
David.
PHOTOGRAPH:
EFI AVEROF MICHAILIDOU

Irene (Peace) Ebhohon

Irene stresses the importance of music in her life. Furthermore, she expresses the importance of freedom of choice, the need to be accepted for who she is, making friends, and expressing her gratitude.

My name is Irene and I come from Nigeria. I am 15 years old and music has helped me in many occasions. When I went to elementary school, I was bullied and I didn't know how to deal with this situation but at some point, I realized that I can sing. I have the voice and I can give it all.

At some point I heard a song. I might have it here [she looks at her mobile phone]. Wait. It is a song from the past that always moves me. It is called "Scars to your beautiful" by Alessia Cara and I can listen to this song for ten days in a row! I was influenced a lot by this song because when I was being bullied, the words said "You are beautiful no matter what," inside out, and you don't need someone to tell you, you must feel it by yourself. And no matter what they do to you, you will always be the same. [She plays the song and sings along.]

Honestly, I thank God or whoever created music and musical instruments. For me music is part of life, without music I cannot live. Without music, I don't exist! Music has helped me in many ways in my life. When I'm unhappy

I always listen to music. Sometimes songs make me cry, like the previous one and now I am holding my tears.

In my church, in the choir I wasn't accepted as I was. I was expected to change my character, the way I dressed, the way I sang. I was expected to change completely, not to be "Peace" [Irene in Greek] anymore, but to be a completely different person. And this was very difficult; it was a great step. But when I came here, I felt that this was a real family, for example, that we are all brothers and sisters. I was accepted as I was, I was helped in many ways, music was the best possible thing, the children, the teachers, everything! I was treated in a proper way, much better than any other place I've been to. I am very thankful for that (see Figure 20.2 and Video 20.2).

FIGURE 20.2
Irene.
PHOTOGRAPH:
EFI AVEROF MICHAILIDOU

Nelly Yurina

In Video 20.3, readers will hear a song that Nelly (from the Ukraine) created in 2016, when the big flow of refugees crossing the Aegean on boats was underway in Greece. I believe she was influenced by the sinking of boats and the drowning of so many people in the Aegean, as we had talked about it in one of our rehearsals.

Some of the words she uses are present in Greek folksongs. The melody is hers. I believe that her song is related to displacement and immigrants and refugees, in perhaps a symbolic way, but I think that this is the beauty and originality of her work, especially for someone of her age.

The folksong is about a mermaid who lived in the Black Sea and the Aegean Sea. Each time the mermaid encountered a ship, she would immobilize it and ask the sailors, "Does King Alexander live?" If the answer was "Yes," she would let the boat free, singing with her lyra. But if the sailor said that he had died, she would sink the boat. Alexander in the folk stories and songs is Alexander the Great, King of Macedonia (see Figure 20.3 and Video 20.3).

FIGURE 20.3
Nelly.
PHOTOGRAPH: EFI AVEROF MICHAILIDOU

   VIDEO 20.1   David's interview with English subtitles.
                        The video accompanying this chapter is freely available online at
                        https://doi.org/10.6084/m9.figshare.12445991

   VIDEO 20.2   Irene's interview with English subtitles.
                        The video accompanying this chapter is freely available online at
                        https://doi.org/10.6084/m9.figshare.12446006

   VIDEO 20.3   Nelly performing her song Alexander the Great.
                        The video accompanying this chapter is freely available online at
                        https://doi.org/10.6084/m9.figshare.12446036

Notes

1 Lesvos, also called Mytilene, is an island of the eastern Aegean Sea. Because of its closeness to the Turkish shore (6.2 miles), the island suffers greatly from a daily influx of immigrants.

2 Yona Stamatis's presentation for the 2019 Society for Ethnomusicology focused on the Polyphonica-Lesvos project. Her paper was entitled Polyphonica Choir: Singing Communitas with Refugees on Lesvos, Greece.

3 For further information on Soundpainting, see http://www.soundpainting.com/soundpainting/

CHAPTER 21

Coming out Twice, Singing All the Way

Timothy Seelig

It was a hot summer in Texas. I had just graduated from high school and spent the summer getting ready to go off to college. Moving away from home for the first time, I had bought new "college" clothes and everything for my new dorm room. It was an emotional time, full of equal parts excitement and apprehension. It was only a couple weeks until I would be heading to freshman orientation. Then life took an unexpected turn.

Our house burned down. Everything literally went up in smoke; it turned out to be arson. I was devastated on so many levels. Mom and Dad moved into temporary housing, and I headed off to college with my worldly possessions in shopping bags, price tags still attached. It was the first time in my life I felt displaced. But it was not the last.

Rebuilding began immediately. One at a time, I began putting life's building blocks together, creating what the world told me would ultimately result in a "perfect" life. All the while, in the back of my mind I knew that in a twinkling of an eye, it could evaporate as if it never existed. I somehow knew I could find myself displaced and, yes, even out on the street. It is that very fear that causes us to prepare for all the disasters we know about—and even make some up.

The "disaster" that was to befall me had no preparation guides. It had no survival backpacks. There was no storm cellar to run to when Auntie Em hollered out. There were no shelters set up to receive me. There were no first responders to be found. For 35 years, I worried about what might happen should this disaster strike, but had no way to prepare. I just knew that the "life blocks" I had been erecting could fall if someone were to remove one from the bottom row.

As an overachiever, I was busy building. As a perfectionist, I did it well. It was all about music. I had the perfect wife, two beautiful children, new house, great career, and a huge circle of friends. I was the Associate Minister of Music at a mega church, First Baptist Church of Houston. I was an associate professor of music at Houston Baptist University. I was a concert artist as well—both operatic and gospel. All the puzzle pieces had been meticulously gathered and put in place, including four college degrees. The resultant picture was admired by all. Yet, I was miserable: Dr. Miserable. But no one knew.

My perfect life was far from perfect. The entire picture was built on a fundamental lie. The truth was buried so deeply I could not imagine any way it could

© KONINKLIJKE BRILL NV, LEIDEN, 2020 | DOI: 10.1163/9789004430464_021

ever be told. Everyone would be better off without me. Then my "unnatural" disaster struck. It was not war, weather, death, or other acts of god. The ramifications were nonetheless calamitous. I lost almost everything and everyone. I found myself on the street—literally and figuratively. What happened?

I came out.

No one, except me, saw it coming. No one. I suspected when I was a teenager, but was convinced that Jesus could take it away. That very belief and the conflict it brought with it, sent me down a difficult path for the next 16 years. At the age of 19, I went to my first Christian psychiatrist. I walked into his office, gathered up every ounce of courage I had, and blurted out what I feared was wrong with me. "I think I'm a homosexual." He talked me through some Bible verses and gave me a test. The next week, much to my great joy (and surprise), he declared, "The test results are back. You are NOT a homosexual." He then helped me to understand that finding a nice girl from my college, Oklahoma Baptist University, should be the next step. I did what he said. A few years later, I graduated from college at 10:00 a.m. and married at 2:00 p.m. the same day.

Life just swept the young marrieds away and thirteen years passed by quickly with the addition of two children and two relocations to Europe. I continued to struggle. I did not know where to turn or whom I could trust with my secret. I just buried it deeper. While the picture we presented to the public —and at church—was of the perfect family, it was far from that at home. I was unable to give my wife the emotional support she needed, but there was no way to communicate why. We argued. A lot. I was despondent.

I questioned God often as to why this would not go away. My "sexual preference" was heterosexual. It was what I had chosen and it was what I asked God to confirm. I cannot tell you the countless times during the 'invitation' or 'altar call' at the end the services, I would literally weep and ask God to "take this cup from me" and allow me to be straight. I know those around me just thought I was weeping for the lost souls yet to find the light. No, it wasn't about them at all. I was the lost soul for whom I was weeping. I asked God to take this from me. Maybe one more verse of that invitational hymn? He did not remove it. It was years before I finally accepted the fact that He did not change me, because I was already whole and perfect and a homosexual.

One counselor, actually hired by First Baptist Church, advised, "Don't let this small little problem ruin your ministry. Just take care of those urges on the side." The final one blackmailed me into telling my wife that I was "struggling with homosexual tendencies." After 16 years of seeking help from Christian counselors for my own lies, I finally realized they were lying, too. One of us had to tell the truth.

For most, coming out is a personal event and comes in stages. For me, it was sudden and made public almost immediately to my entire family and to the 22,000+ members of the church. And not by me. To them, it was unnatural. For me it was a disaster. My very own personal, unnatural disaster.

The very day I was "outed" to my wife by my last-ever Christian counselor, she shared the information with the pastor of our church who, burdened by my state, shared it with others. Called to the pastor's office, I was given a set of requirements if I wanted to keep my job. A few of those requirements included in-patient reparative therapy or shock treatment in an out-of-state location. I was told to provide a list of other staff members at the church who were also gay, stand before the congregation accused by two clergy, acknowledge my sin, and repent publicly. I chose "none of the above" and walked out. Out of my life as I knew it. It was October 1986.

Displacement happened quickly. I was thrown under the church bus. It then rolled over me, backed up, and rolled over again. My body was left on the street—not by a natural disaster or pestilence, but by the very people who had preached compassion, love, and "Do unto others." No Federal Emergency Management Agency for this disaster. No Red Cross. No safety net. No community. I was displaced. Completely.

The losses were great. I lost my children who were seven and nine years old, family, jobs, house, car, and most (99.9%) of my friends. I was forced to move from my beautiful home, which would soon be foreclosed on, to a Motel 6. I went from a beautiful, supportive nuclear family and countless "friends" and religious fans to no one. I did not know a single out gay person in Houston, Texas. Okay, that's not true. I suspected my hair stylist. My wife took my children to West Texas ten hours away to live with her parents.

As I sat in that Motel 6, that dreary November night, I had a peace of mind no one could ever understand. I had told the whole truth for the first time in my life. The displacement was not just the removal or destruction of physical things or even my occupation. It was a displacement of my center—my being. It was 35 years of living one truth that turned out to be a lie. The building block at the very bottom of the structure was pulled out. The emotional house of cards came tumbling down. I was alone, adrift physically and emotionally.

Many years later, one of my daughter's friends wrote to me as an adult and described what it was like for her at church. "One day, you were gone and no one ever spoke of you again. In my child's mind, I assumed there was something that you could do that was so bad, you would disappear." That's what had happened to me; I had disappeared from my previous life. Displacement is devastating, destructive, and demoralizing at best. At its worst, it leaves despair so great, there was no light until I stopped, rested, and looked inside myself for the light. And there it was.

While in college, I had studied Abraham Maslow's Hierarchy of Needs. The first need is to take care of physical needs. I was never without food, water or warmth, but I couldn't live in a Motel 6 forever. Because I had learned to type through four degrees, I fell back on that skill. I became a temp. I was a "Kelly Girl." (That was Dr. Kelly Girl!) I found a small apartment in Houston and slowly filled it with the few things I needed to get by. I was literally putting one foot in front of the other. It seemed that every single day brought a new twist and new drama. I was a brand new gay—at 35 years old. How could there not be drama?

I think I could have dealt with one single disaster. I could have looked up and seen some hope on the horizon. I could have started to put the blocks back in order. But that is not what happened. Even though the "coming out" happened quickly, the rest unfolded slowly. It would be a long time until I found the home of self.

The second need is safety and security. Unlike many natural disasters, my physical safety was never at risk. It is interesting that once I told the truth, even though I was alone, I never again had thoughts of self-harm. The safety I had lost and I sought was family.

The Seelig name was synonymous with successful Baptists, and it's not a name that is easy to forget. My brother Steve and I were raised in the arms of the Southern Baptist Church. My father was the vice-president of Southwestern Baptist Theological Seminary for 30 years. It is the largest Baptist seminary in the world. My mother was a singer and taught voice at the seminary for 30 years. Mom was a gospel recording artist and traveled the world with Billy Graham. Steve and I both chose careers that were compatible with ministry—and the Southern Baptists—he with youth and I in music. When I came out, there was no way to hide as Smith or Jones.

Steve served some of the great churches of the convention from Second Baptist, Little Rock, to First Southern Baptist Church of Phoenix. That is where he was when his little brother came out. It was not pretty. One of the things I was doing at First Baptist Church (FBC) of Houston was to direct the 200-voice single adult choir. Since my departure was sudden and not knowing what to do with that, FBC hired my brother to take over.

So, there we were, power Baptists completely torn apart with no way of knowing what to do next. We stumbled. A lot. My brother passed away last year after a horrific four-year bout with brain cancer. Did we ever really and truly reconcile? No, we didn't but in the end, he made efforts—in private. He disowned me three times over the early years. He was very kind to my children all along and to my husband in the end.

Sometimes, in moments of weakness, I think maybe it wasn't that bad. Then I am reminded that it was. At my brother's funeral, the pastor used the scripture "In my Father's house are many mansions. I go to prepare a place for you." Steve suffered debilitating and excruciating brain cancer for four years. The explanation of this lengthy suffering was that his mansion just wasn't ready yet. I wanted to jump up and scream out "Of course it wasn't ready. All the interior decorators are in hell. The three straight ones who made it to heaven are busy, busy."

My daughter Corianna never left her Dad's side. She was a huge support and took a great deal of criticism for it. We remained close through all the years. She lives only a few miles from me here in San Francisco. Throughout her teenage years, she watched my singers suffer and ultimately die from complications due to AIDS. She chose her life path to be pediatric oncology, as did her husband. They produced granddaughter #1, Clara Skye.

My son Judson was a different story. He remained much closer to his Mom. When he was a senior in high school, he decided he wanted to go off to college and sever ties with me. He went on to get his MBA and became a CPA. At the age of 21, he was already being recruited by the big accounting firms in Dallas. The possibility of moving there was causing him a lot of stress and anxiety—his Dad was a very well-known LGBT activist. He decided to change his last name to avoid the connection. It was painful for all of us. Once Judson had moved to Dallas with a new name, he joined a large contemporary megachurch. When he joined, he was assigned a spiritual mentor. As Judson began to trust him, he told him about his dad and that he felt he should ask my forgiveness. We met for coffee and that is exactly what he did. I think I was in shock, and I was the one who didn't immediately trust.

After a couple of years, Judson started dating a wonderful young woman who wanted to get to know his biological father. We hit it off famously. In fact, when Judson decided to propose, he asked me and my partner to help him plan it because gay guys are much more creative! Over the ensuing years, my relationship with my son has healed completely. He is still not a Seelig by name, but that is his journey. He and his beautiful wife live in Dallas with granddaughter #2, Eden Mae.

When I came out, Mom and Dad—the super Baptists—asked what they did to make me queer. I told them, "absolutely nothing." What they did was instill a deep sense of telling the truth that would not allow me to live a lie anymore. I am not sure they were happy with that either. But they did what Christians should do: They prayed for me. They knew that it was not their job to convict me of sin. They believed in a God big enough to do that by Him or Herself should the need arise! They simply loved me and encouraged me to be the best person I could be. Thus, it was with my coming out. From that day forward, everything changed. Mom is gone now. Dad is in his 90s, and he and I are best friends. We are all we have left. I know they wished things had been different, but they were not.

When I found myself displaced from all I knew, I looked around to take stock of what I had left. First thing that was strangely intact was my sense of humor. I had music. Music had been my rock in every single moment of my life since standing on a piano bench at three years-old and singing "You Are My Sunshine" for just about anyone who visited our house. Music was at my core.

The third need, according to Maslow, is belonging, relationships and friends. Less than a year after coming out, I heard there was a gay men's chorus in Dallas looking for a conductor. I had no idea there was such a thing as a gay choir, but I needed to pay child support. I took the part-time conducting job with the Turtle Creek Chorale, all 40-some singers, and did temp work as a secretary (Kelly Girl) on the side to make ends meet. I was going to do it for one year and move on. I stayed 20 years.

I had nothing to lose and jumped in with both feet. At my first board meeting, they asked what my vision was. I told them I had come out just nine months earlier, an event witnessed by thousands of people. I did not have the luxury to fail—especially since so many people were expecting just that. What I found provided both comfort and discomfort, ease and dis-ease. I also found love and belonging.

When I began conducting Turtle Creek in 1987, it was in the early days of the AIDS crisis. I knew nothing about HIV and AIDS. It was not a topic in the world from which I had come. At my very first rehearsal, sitting on the front row, was a man literally covered in sores. I had no idea what it was or what he was doing at a rehearsal. One of the singers told me after rehearsal that he had full-blown AIDS and, through great effort, made sure to come to rehearsal each week because it "kept him alive." I was changed. This was church. It also began the next to final step in Maslow's pyramid: esteem and pride in accomplishment.

Among the things that I never could have imagined I would find was the deep passion around social justice. I became an activist through music and in the early years, that was mostly surrounding AIDS and HIV. In my second year, we decided to hold a poinsettia plant for each of the 11 singers we had lost to AIDS. As the years went by, not willing to stop the tradition, we were forced to erect a metal tree to hold the plants. There were just under 200. The chorus was asked by PBS to be the topic of a documentary on grief and recovery and hope with Dr. Elisabeth Kübler-Ross. It went on to win the Emmy for Best Documentary.

Toward the end of my 20 years with the Turtle Creek Chorale, PBS came back and said, "Let's do a follow-up story on what's happening now?" We produced another documentary about how we had risen from the AIDS pandemic to work for gay marriage, adoption, and, of course, continuing relationships with organized religion. It had a theatrical release and was named Best Documentary by the USA Film Festival.

Progress is never a straight line. My chorus was lauded for its work in the fight surrounding the AIDS pandemic. I was a leader in that movement and in 1996, even carried the Olympic torch as a hero in the fight. During a regular doctor's checkup, he came in and said, "In all the years you've been working in the AIDS field, have you ever imagined what it would feel like if you found out you were HIV positive?" The answer was "Yes." He then shared that I was, indeed, positive.

I was not prepared. At all. I had watched my friends die horrible, prolonged deaths. Even more than that, I had walked through the valley with countless friends as they experienced rejection and dealt with the stigma attached. After living a life that was completely transparent, I had a secret again. I was supposed to be the strong one, the activist, the role model. There were many times I just felt I could not go on, could not tell anyone or bear the stigma still attached firmly to those who are HIV+. And, I had to tell my son. That was the hardest thing of all. I didn't want him to think less of me after all the struggles we had been through to get back to where we were.

Just maintaining and letting people wonder was not enough for my daughter. Always one to push the envelope—and her Dad—she decided to participate in the seven-day, 545-mile AIDS/Lifecycle ride from San Francisco to Los Angeles. That was great, but she wanted to do it in my honor. That required me being OK with her putting it out there for the world to see. My Dad is HIV+. Of course, I said "Yes," and was so very proud of her. Incidentally, my husband, Dan, is preparing for his 11th AIDS/Lifecycle ride this year!

At the end of my 19th year conducting the Turtle Creek Chorale, I realized it was time for a change. It was certainly one of those times that reminded me of one of my favorite poems by Patrick Overton:

> When you walk to the edge of all the light you have and take that first step into the darkness of the unknown, you must believe that one of two things will happen. There will be something solid for you to stand upon or you will be taught to fly.[1]

When I took that step—away from my family, which was the Turtle Creek Chorale, there was solid ground to be sure. I was hired by GALA Choruses (Gay and Lesbian Association of Choruses) to start a program as Artistic Director-in-Residence. In a two-year span, I was able to visit almost 40 choruses—gay men's choruses, lesbian choruses, mixed choruses—every size, every shape, from the United States, Canada, and the UK. I could see how, in almost every instance, gay choral music is central to the fabric of the community. The movement is now global.

In summer 2010, the San Francisco Gay Men's Chorus announced it was looking for a new artistic director. What? I had wrapped up my long-term commitments to LGBTQ choruses. I was fine living in Dallas doing my thing — teaching, traveling, guest-conducting. But, it was the SAN FRANCISCO GAY MEN'S CHORUS. It was the first chorus on the planet to proudly proclaim sexual orientation in its very name! It was the Granddaddy of the entire LGBT choral movement. And it was in San Francisco! Let's see, San Francisco, Dallas—the same, but different. Even though I thought I was done with conducting my own gay chorus, I applied for the job, and I got it in January 2011. I was not a young man! But the challenge and the opportunity were just too incredible to pass up.

The San Francisco Gay Men's Chorus was founded in October 1978. In its fourth week, City Supervisor Harvey Milk and Mayor George Moscone were murdered. The chorus sang in public for the very first time on the steps of San Francisco City Hall at the candlelight vigil. This began what is now more than a 40-year legacy of activism through music. Harvey Milk is considered the patron saint of the chorus for his work to promote LGBT rights. "You gotta give 'em hope." I've learned the importance of stepping out and being out. I've learned that normal, everyday people have potential and power. In 2013, the SFGMC, along with five other gay men's choruses, commissioned Broadway composer Andrew Lippa to put those stories to music resulting in an amazing oratorio, "I Am Harvey Milk."

It was time for me to really embrace Maslow's final step of self-actualization: achieving one's full potential including creative activities.

There is no doubt that the creative activities had been going on at a furious pace for a long, long time. But arriving here in San Francisco, knowing it was my last chapter, allowed me to settle in and look inward. Oh, there was and is still so much to learn. But I am finally in a place to welcome all those lessons: Okay, most of them. San Francisco brought a new level of awareness and sensitivity and inclusion. It is truly one of the epicenters of all things LGBTQ. As such, we are called to stay ahead of the curve. It is a challenge and a thrill.

Readers might wonder how a gay chorus is special. Having conducted and performed in countless choruses of every type, I can say with no reservation whatsoever that being in a chorus that proclaims its sexual orientation is like no other experience I have ever had. The San Francisco Gay Men's Chorus was the first on the planet to do that. When a person joins a choir, there is already an affinity with other singers simply because of one's love of music, singing, and the choral art. Singing is an incredibly vulnerable activity. In addition, and considering the fact that most members of the LGBTQ community have to step out of a comfort zone to be who they are, it makes the music-making powerful in so many ways because of what the members have experienced in their lives. There is one guarantee in joining an LGBTQ chorus: they have found a completely safe place. They will not be bullied, ostracized, or made to feel less than. They are home and with their logical family.

SFGMC has performed in many cities where the LGBTQ community is not open and able to be out. It has performed in cities from the most conservative in the central valley of California to the Deep South. There is definitely an unsafe feeling on the part of the singers in some places. That said, our singers are equally passionate about the twins that make up SFGMC: Music and Mission. Having had difficult experiences ourselves, we know how very important it is to stand proud and sing out to encourage those who have been brave enough to come hear the chorus sing in a very conservative area.

What is life like now? I am married to a wonderful husband who sings in the chorus. We could not be a better match. In a very strange twist of fate, his parents introduced us in 2000 at an LGBT choral festival in San Jose. It's a story for another book. We remained friends, living in different cities. In 2013, we found ourselves both in San Francisco and single. Our 13-year friendship turned into romance and ultimately marriage. Dan was also married in his former life, so our daughters gave us away at our wedding. My hobby is named Clara Skye and she is seven years old.

My journey has been filled with the push and pull of organized religion. A couple of days after the election in 2016, SFGMC decided to take its message of love and inclusion and hope to the Deep South. We took nearly 300 singers to Mississippi, Alabama, Tennessee, South and North Carolina. We did 23 appearances in eight days. One of the things we realized from the outset was that if we were to reach some of these communities, it was going to have to be straight through the church (forgive the pun). We sang in many churches as well as high schools, universities, city parks, and Selma's Brown Chapel African Methodist Episcopal Church and reenacted the 1965 march across the Edmund Pettus Bridge. It was life-changing for sure.

During our preparation, we were invited to perform one of our big concerts at First Baptist Church, Greenville, South Carolina. At first, I didn't believe it. But it was true. The huge church was packed to the last seat and then some. As we entered the sanctuary, the congregation stood and applauded until the last singer got to the stage. It had been 32 years since I stood at the pulpit of a Southern Baptist Church and directed a choir. It was an incredible full-circle moment for me and many in the chorus. It was one of the most moving and healing moments I can remember. We sang "Amazing Grace"; there was not a dry eye in the house (see Figure 21.1).

FIGURE 21.1   Members of the chorus comfort each other after an emotional journey
through the Deep South of the United States. Pictured are Frank, Ashlé, Thao,
and Kevin.
PHOTOGRAPH: ADAM HOBBS, TRIBECA FILM FESTIVAL

Some folks asked if I got saved all over again. That is not what happened. I likened it to being estranged from your family because of deep disagreements. After years, they invited you to share Thanksgiving dinner with them with trepidation; you accept. They greet you with open arms at the door and the meal is fabulous! None of the difference of opinion were changed or even addressed. At that moment, it didn't matter. You were home—with Mom's stuffing and Grandma's pumpkin pie. That's the way it felt for me to walk back into church.

In 2013, we performed a concert with Broadway composer Stephen Schwartz. In the planning phase, he mentioned that he had been so very moved by the courage demonstrated by the *It Gets Better* movement. I connected him with founder Dan Savage, and they worked together to create an incredible piece based on the stories of people who had been displaced—people who had found themselves on the street. *Testimony* has been performed all over the world. The first part of the song uses the words of young people who have found themselves on the edge of life, considering taking the final step to ending it all. These are the words Stephen and Dan shared:

> *I was more loved than I dared to know*
> *there were open arms I could not see*
> *And when I die, and when it's my time to go,*
> *I want to come back as me.*

It has taken a long time—half a lifetime—for me to be able to embrace and believe those words for myself. Looking back, there was no one burning bush by the side of the road telling me it would be okay. It was that one step at a time. It was that one person holding out a hand or speaking a kind word. It was the moment I could pay child support and look in the mirror with pride that I had lived to tell my story.

I think every person who recovers from a devastating event looks back with surprise at the resiliency of the human spirit. That's hindsight. It never feels that way while you are in the middle of it. Just know that if you can find the strength to do one thing, take one step, ask for help, that the light at the end of the tunnel will brighten until it literally shines like a spotlight on a fabulous actor at the end of a play. That would be you.

Take a bow.

Note

1 "Faith" by Patrick Overton (1975), *The Leaning Tree.*

PART 4

Land(s) and Culture

∴

Political Conflict

COLONIZATION

COLONIZATION

LGBTQ

Discrimination

CONVERSION

Gender HOMELESSNESS

Persecution

WAR

GENTRIFICATION

HOMELESS WAR

Key terms 3.
GRAPHIC DESIGNER: ANISSA MARTÍNEZ LOZANO

Addressing Tribalism in Displacement: Self-Directed Musical Activities in Blacktown's South Sudanese Community

Samantha Dieckmann

This chapter presents findings from an ethnographic grounded theory case study of self-directed musical activities in the South Sudanese community in Blacktown, New South Wales, Australia (Dieckmann, 2016). These activities were observed in 2011 and coincided with South Sudan attaining independence. The chapter opens with a brief overview of South Sudanese displacement, migration to Australia, and the complexity of South Sudanese tribalism. The findings examine the ways in which musical activities are used both to negotiate tribal and national identities and to mediate experiences of transnationalism in the context of resettlement. In so doing, the chapter highlights the tensions and intersections between tribalism, in which members most strongly identify with tribal kinship groups bounded by ethnicity, culture and/ or language, and national affiliations, in which one's sense of belonging is founded on allegiance to the same nation-state. The chapter concludes with reflections on the implications these musical mechanisms have for music education involving displaced persons, forced migrants, and former refugees.

South Sudan and Its Australian Diaspora

The South Sudanese communities that have resettled in Australia represent a significant proportion of the country's diaspora outside of Africa. Of the non-African countries that could vote in the 2011 South Sudan Independence referendum, Australia had the highest participation rate (SSRC & SSRB, 2011). In 2011, Blacktown had the highest concentration of South Sudanese migrants (Blacktown City Council, 2011a, 2011b). This chapter provides insight into how long-distance nationalism is experienced in displacement, "whereby people live in one country and are politically involved in another" (Eriksen, 2010, p. 188). For the South Sudanese diaspora, engaging in long-distance nationalism in 2011 was fraught with complexities because their home country's nation-building project was still in its infancy.

Issues related to post-independence stability are ongoing, and displacement continues to be relevant for this diasporic community. In December 2013, President Salva Kiir Mayardit, the leader of the youngest country in the world, the Republic of South Sudan, engaged in a political dispute with the former Vice President Riek Machar. The conflict spiraled into widespread violence with ethnic overtones that has resulted in serious breaches of humanitarian law on an immense scale (Lyman, Temin, & Stigant, 2014; UNMISS, 2014). Reports show that, as of December 31, 2017, South Sudan is the third major country of origin of refugees and also the country of origin of the largest-increasing refugee population[1] in the world (IDMC, 2018; UNHCR, 2018). On September 12, 2018—a few months following the publication of these reports—President Kiir and opposition leader Machar signed a peace agreement, apparently bringing an end to the civil war. Unfortunately, recent news indicates that incidents of political violence still lead to continued displacement (UN News, 2019).

Tribalism

Despite the North-versus-South discourse that dominates tales of South Sudanese independence and the preceding Sudanese civil war, "It was southerners killing southerners that took the largest number of lives" (Natsios, 2012, p. 79). This internal dissension continues to leave a legacy in South Sudan and contributed to the outbreak of civil war. Although tribalism has long been cited as a primary reason why South Sudan cannot exist as a successful sovereign state (see, for example, Khashan & Nehme, 1996), divisions form along ethnic or tribal lines are strongly determined by degrees of political access and representation. Pinaud (2014) argues that where "old ethnic enmities sometimes resurface," they are triggered by widespread corruption and the formation of a dominant class through "various strategies of resource capture and kinship networks" (p. 192).

Because independence removed a "unity of purpose" (Jok, 2012, p. 59), Deng (2012) has suggested that a cohesive South Sudanese national identity would necessitate inclusivity and the recognition of marginalized groups. While no consensus exists concerning the exact number of tribes in South Sudan (Frahm, 2012), the following passage gives an idea of their heterogeneity.

> There are 597 tribes and sub-tribes, which speak 133 languages and even more dialects, though many of these ethnic groups consist of no more than a few thousand people each. For example, a number of the largest

tribes, such as the Dinka of the South—with twenty-five subtribes, the largest ethnic group in Sudan—speak so many distinctive dialects that many are incomprehensible to each other. Rivalries and tensions among the Dinka subtribes remain a historical reality in southern Sudan...and thus it is something of an oxymoron to write about "tribal identity." (Natsios, 2012, p. 10)

There seem to be discrepancies between the concept of tribal identity in South Sudan and groupings such as the Dinka, who are labelled not as tribes but as *supra-tribal confederations*, because of the remarkable diversity within these larger groupings (Anwar, 1986). It has been argued that supra-tribal alliances were constructed by colonial powers, and that kinship and locality inspire more feelings of loyalty and belonging (Eriksen, 2010). Tribal classification, however, is granted legitimacy by both governments and intergovernmental and non-governmental organizations. Categorizations of tribal groupings have been published in Australia by umbrella South Sudanese organizations such as the South Sudanese Community Association in Victoria, Inc. (SSCAV). The SSCAV website explains that "South Sudan is a very diverse country with over 64 ethnic tribes. We represent multiculturalism in its finest and from this diversity come some complexities and challenges" (2017, n.p.). The map appearing on the website of the South Sudanese Embassy in the United States reflects the country's original division into 28 states, presenting "a very simplified portrait of the ethnic groups which would likely hold administrative control in the proposed states" but also "obscures the diversity of ethnic groups at the county, payam and boma levels" (2016, n.p.).[2] Irrespective of the origins of South Sudan's supra-tribal confederations, the various categorizations of tribal networks and the disputes over the soundness of tribal identification, tribalism continues to be discussed as politically relevant in conversations about South Sudanese nationalism, identity, and unity (Frahm, 2012).

Blacktown's South Sudanese Community as a Case Study

Participants in this study of the South Sudanese community living in Blacktown included ten interviewees[3] (5 female, 5 male) who ranged from 18 to 41 in age, and who were affiliated with varying ethnic tribes and language groups (including Dinka Bor, Dinka Agar, Aweil Panaruu, Madi and Lotugo). In addition to semi-structured interviews with the ten interviewees, I conducted observations of ongoing community music programs and music-making practices. I took part by singing, dancing, and playing keyboard in various ensembles.

Although data were collected throughout 2011, most of the South Sudanese Australian community from which this study's participants were drawn migrated to Australia before 2006, well before the country's independence. Musical expressions of tribal and national identity therefore highlight the ways in which the participants' relationship with the newly sovereign state were encountered transnationally and mediated by forced displacement.

These musical expressions involve a combination of singing and dance as central modes of performance. As with many other cultures across Africa, here, "music and dance are conceived as interwoven…evidenced by the use of one word…for music and dance" (Onwuekwe, 2009). In Dinka, a language spoken by many participants, the word *dheeng* signifies not only all singing and dancing (excepting prayerful or specific religious practices), but also other demonstrations of aesthetic value and dignity, pride, and respect (e.g. competitive sports) (Deng, 1973, 2006). All of the musical activities discussed in this chapter would fall under the concept of *dheeng*. Because these findings examine participants' musical lives prior to the South Sudanese civil war, I do not explore the ways the community's use of music intersects with the country's current political situation. This chapter contextualizes the continued evolution in the community's musical life. By examining how tribal differences were interrogated, negotiated, and expressed through music at an acutely political moment in South Sudan's recent history, these findings demonstrate how, in the words of Emmanuel Kondok, chair of the NSW Community of South Sudanese and Other Marginalised Areas group,

> The Southern Sudanese are working closely, the ethnic or tribal groups, to not have that difference [that divides those in South Sudan]…In a few cases, there are issues. But the slogan we use is that we are all South Sudanese, regardless of the differences back home, we are all united here. (Munro, 2018, n.p.)

Tribalism and Music in Blacktown's South Sudanese Community

Findings from qualitative observations and interviews are presented in relation to three forms of musical engagement through which participants' tribal and national identities were negotiated: the maintenance of (sub-tribal) music traditions; inter-tribal cultural exchanges through music and dance, and; the re-contextualization of music traditions in nationalist contexts.

Maintaining Music Traditions in Displacement

Tribal allegiances were most intense in relation to sub-tribes and ethnic sub-groupings determined by the indigenous locality. At *Dancing in Harmony*, a ticketed concert celebrating local African music and dance held at a major performance venue in western Sydney, most of the South Sudanese performing groups represented specific sub-tribes. Their performed tribal traditions were not shared by the entire supra-tribal confederation, such as the Dinka or Nuer, but were specific to sub-tribes including the Twic Mayardit or Dinka Bor communities. Prior to performances, leaders of each ensemble addressed the audience, sometimes in Arabic or Dinka (translated into English by an emcee), to explain the meaning behind the next song and dance. This explanation was aimed at those in the audience, including other South Sudanese, that were not members of the performing group's tribe.

In accounting for the distinctiveness of tribal traditions, Nyadeng distinguishes between the cultural traditions of her sub-tribe and that of other Dinka and South Sudanese. "No. We are the same [South] Sudanese, we are the same Dinka. But everybody here have culture, different culture" (Nyadeng, interview, June 6, 2012).

The parallel between Nyadeng's remark, "We are the same [South] Sudanese," and Emmanuel Kondok's comment that "We are all South Sudanese," demonstrates the resonance between community leaders' and individual community members' perspectives of nationalist identities. At the same time, Nyadeng indicated that community events were largely organized along these sub-tribal lines. She declared that within Sydney's South Sudanese community, her family was the only one from the Ngok Panaruu tribe. Panaruu is a sub-tribe within the larger Ngok tribe, itself a subset of the supra-tribal Dinka confederation. Living in Sydney meant that Nyadeng and her family had no local access to relevant tribal leaders, tribal associations, and tribal community events in which she could practice her cultural traditions. In contrast to her indifference towards her children's attendance at South Sudanese weddings and general South Sudanese events, such as a concert by popular musician John Kudusay, Nyadeng insisted her children attend Ngok events and learn the songs and dances of their tribal heritage. In January 2012, Nyadeng took her entire family to a Ngok community event, a financial and practical endeavor because it was held in Melbourne, where the majority of Australia's Panaruu community apparently resides. Although she had many South Sudanese friends in Sydney, in 2013, Nyadeng moved to Melbourne in order to stay close to extended family and friends who shared her Ngok Panaruu heritage.

Nyadeng was shown videos of traditional Panaruu music on YouTube. Three clips (Mathiang, 2011; Ngor Mayol, 2008, 2010) were played for her and her Bor friend Aluel, to whom the recorded music traditions were unfamiliar. Having never seen the videos, Nyadeng's enthusiasm for explaining its meanings was matched by her engagement with the music as a listener.[4] This was especially the case because she was viewing and listening to its performance in its traditional village setting, albeit across spatio-temporal borders. Nyadeng requested a copy of these videos for her private use and, in one particularly surprising and wonderful moment, spotted her father, a village elder, in the crowd of dancers.

YouTube proved an excellent resource for viewing the traditional songs and dances of various South Sudanese tribes, as users from around the world post videos of performances from the homeland and across the diaspora. In this way, the Internet addresses experiences of displacement and tribal isolation such as that experienced by Nyadeng; it strengthens transnational ties not only to traditional culture, but also to individual people and places of home. Through the broadcasting of traditional songs, South Sudanese YouTube channels are arguably utilized in the same way as the cassette tapes studied by Impey (2013), as "securing clan networks and anchoring cultural identities across cultures and continents...embody[ing] memories of locality and belonging" (p. 11).

Inter-Tribal Exchanges through Music and Dance

Tribal community associations organized events for Australian residents from their sub-tribe. Invitations were communicated by word of mouth, and interstate attendance, such as Nyadeng's family's attendance at the Ngok Panaruu event, was not uncommon. Despite the tribal partitioning inherent in this approach to organizing the South Sudanese community, life in Australia offers many opportunities for intertribal exchanges. Kuol explained that in South Sudan itself, music and dance traditions are exclusive to particular sub-tribes, inaccessible to others due to the geographical distance between villages:

> When I live my hometown, I did not know about the other people. And other people did not know about me...sometime in our country of origin people are divided by communities. So, each tribe is stick to itself... Which really minimize their chances of them interacting with each other, because whenever they have their own activity that they want to do, they just do it by themself, no invitation for the other community. So, I think changing life and getting to other places that are new, especially the refugee camp, offer you the opportunities to learn, learn new things, culture and people. (Kuol, interview, December 1, 2012)

Through natural intercultural exchanges between sub-tribes in refugee camps and resettlement societies, these traditions became available to all South

Sudanese regardless of their ethnicities, tribal affiliations, and prior familiarity—or lack thereof—with the practices. However, even in the sharing of such traditions some distinctions remain. Participants made it clear that on many occasions, while others were welcome to participate, music and dance cultures were still perceived as belonging exclusively to the original sub-tribes.

> [W]hen you see this different group of people dancing like Panaruu, you try to copy what they are doing exactly. So, if you try to copy, you learn from your work. But still there may be some, you know there may be some that this particular person is not from that particular community because of the way that you do dance...You may be, yeah people from within their community can tell that "This guy is not from, is not doing it correctly, maybe because he's not from our community." (Kuol, interview, December 1, 2012)

The phrase "our community" asserts an exclusivity that values tribal allegiance over nationalistic patriotism. The clear association between the accuracy of a performance and the right to claim identification with its owners conforms to the ways in which, in South Sudan itself, identity formation and community solidarity have developed within ethno-regional boundaries (see Komey, 2010). Since pre-colonial times, the distribution of resources and political contestation has taken place through groupings based on ethnicity and region. As a result, deep ideological significance is attached to the socially and spatially constructed territories and identities framed as tribal. With this in mind, and in line with the following observation by Smith (1998), the particularity of tribal traditions poses significant challenges to South Sudanese nationalism.

> The problems faced by many new states in Africa and Asia also suggest that the absence of pre-existing state-wide traditions, myths, symbols and memories greatly hampers the process of national integration, and that inventing national traditions does not, and cannot, by itself enable elites to forge a national community out of ethnically heterogeneous populations. Where such attempts are being made, they generally proceed on the basis of memories, myths, symbols and traditions of the dominant *ethnie* in the new state...that is, on the basis of the pre-existing culture of the dominant ethnic community which resonates with the majority of the population. (p. 130)

In South Sudan, building national traditions on those of a dominant ethnic community would be particularly contentious. Because finding a tribal-based tradition that "resonates with the majority of the population" is inconceivable, it is necessary to embrace and celebrate South Sudan's cultural diversity as part of the national identity (Deng, 2012; Frahm, 2012; Jok, 2011, 2012). Jok's suggestion (2011, 2012) that such an appreciation could be facilitated through the establishment of cultural centers and a National Museum of Heritage that could provide platforms for the recognition of all of South Sudan's cultures and traditions, resonates with the projects implemented by UNESCO Juba's culture program, such as the National Archives, the Traveling Exhibition, and the National Theatre (UNESCO, 2014).

Re-Contextualizing Music Traditions in Displacement

Inter-tribal cultural exchanges remained primarily within the realm of appreciation. Such appreciation, however, could lead to the tribal traditions taking on broader and, at times, patriotic meanings through processes of re-contextualization. In New South Wales, this type of re-contextualization was observed in practice at a number of community events, including the 2011 independence referendum. The meanings of several sub-tribal traditional songs and dances had not been known to other South Sudanese sub-tribes and were transformed by their use to expressions of freedom and independence for South Sudan generally. This emphasis on national sentiment was reinforced by the bearing of national flags. A video broadcast online demonstrated how a sub-tribal cultural artifact could be appropriated as a signifier of nationalistic sentiment. The host's commentary revealed his unfamiliarity with the traditional song and dance being recorded, but the host nevertheless considered it reflective of the patriotic joy experienced on the day of the referendum.

> Wow, wow, wow, as you can see from Sydney, the happiness is coming here. What you hear is the sound of freedom, the sound of happiness. Happiness is sound with drum, and singing and jumping. This is from South Sudan and a one of the tribe is showing that, how they so happy with the, how they're so happy, with the dance. Wow, wow, wow!

There were several other instances in which tribal traditions were adapted to express nationalist themes. At *Dancing in Harmony*, the leader of the Bor women singers and dancers introduced the group's performance with reference to what she assumed was the collective experience of South Sudanese independence. The emcee translated her introduction:

> She express how they perform the group based on the, after the independence and they basically saying they expressing how they feel through the, after the independence. Their happiness, their joy and the experience

that we all went through it, before the independence. So, they're really happy today and glad to express and share this experience with you guys today.

Nyadeng echoed these sentiments when she explained the meaning of the Ngok Panaruu tradition featured in Ngor Mayol (2008). She called this tradition *loth*.[5]

> Wow!...It's *loth*...Because the last year before she get the peace, we are get the separate from Arab,[6] everybody he dancing because he's happy...We are come to Southern Sudan...everybody is happy. (Nyadeng, interview, June 8, 2012)

Although these instances do not constitute the national operationalization of traditions as described by Smith (1998) and Neuberger (2006), in which integration is cultivated through the nationalization of particular ethnic groups' traditions, a nationalist function to the performances of tribal traditions remains in these instances. At *Dancing in Harmony* and the referendum event, many South Sudanese ethnic groups and tribes (of varying degrees of dominance in South Sudan and in the Australian diaspora), enacted their music and dance traditions. The performances reflected the polyethnic population of the emerging nation and embodied a supra-ethnic nationalist ideology that "stresses shared civil rights rather than shared cultural roots" (Eriksen, 2010, p. 144). This approach to nationalism encompasses aspects of Smith's (2010) state-nation, in which the aim of polyethnic states is national unification rather than national homogenization. At the Sydney referendum, tribal traditions were de-contextualized as national by virtue of their inclusion in a supra-ethnic South Sudanese event that centered on civil rights, freedom, and independence.

Music, Tribalism and National Identity in Resettlement Contexts
Although the notion of tribal identity is somewhat inconsistent with the complex and multi-layered organization of South Sudanese society (Natsios, 2012), it was relevant to the experiences of many of this study's participants. Several sub-tribes made a conscious effort to maintain their singing and dancing traditions. Events at which these performances took place were organized under the auspices of tribal community organizations. Although inter-tribal exchanges were made possible due to the conditions of Australia's South Sudanese diaspora, specific tribal ownership over such traditions remained intact at the time of this study in 2011. Evidence appeared of tribal musical traditions used to promote South Sudanese nationalism. Through re-contextualization

at national events, otherwise exclusive tribal traditions represented shared national sentiments about South Sudanese freedom, independence, and joy.

Music Education and Displacement

These findings problematize the boundaries drawn around displaced communities in the same resettlement contexts that have migrated in similar sets of circumstances. Concepts such as enclosed identity categories—for example, refugees from South Sudan—have implications for the ways in which music education functions within displaced communities. Similar categorical considerations arise in terms of music education's conventional divisions between music and dance. In some cultures, the two are integrally linked and may even (as in the case of *dheeng*) be incorporated into broader cultural concepts related to, for example, quality of character.

In community music, calls for cultural democracy highlight how music workshops can provide "a system of support and respect for the many cultures and communities...while attempting to give voice to those who have historically been excluded from the public domain" (Higgins, 2012, p. 168). In light of the political complexities highlighted here, the public domain to which Higgins refers should not be limited to Australia, but also to the participants' countries of origin. This is not to say that all music with political dispositions must be avoided, but rather, that music students should not feel as though a dominant culture other than their family's country of origin is being imposed upon them through music. Indeed, it cannot be assumed that students have any specific expertise, knowledge or interest in musical traditions or styles from their family's country of origin. For refugees and former refugees, in particular, transitory migrant patterns mean that even new arrivals may never have spent time in the nation with which they affiliate themselves. Because of this, incorporating music from a particular country in classrooms or workshops may be problematic for students who already struggle with relating to older generations or what might be seen as "more traditional" musical genres. In attempting to celebrate their culture in the classroom or on the commemorative stage teachers may discursively "Other" students because of visible difference or migrant status (see also Dieckmann, 2016; Karlsen, 2013; Saether, 2008).

Other implications relate to the nature of interventionist music programs used in displaced communities. Calls have increased to support community-led services and development programs for refugees and asylum-seekers (see for example, Asylum Seeker Resource Centre, n.d.). It is important, however, to recognize that in many resettlement contexts, communities fleeing from protracted conflicts achieve their own mechanisms for overcoming differences that might have previously divided them. Self-directed musical activities have played a role in negotiating the tensions between tribal and trans-national identifications for Blacktown's South Sudanese community. Rather than instituting programs to be implemented by external bodies, there is both the scope and a compelling rationale for music education practitioners, scholars, and funding bodies to support displaced communities' own efforts.

Notes

1 The author notes the representational problematics in assigning labels such as *refugees* and *refugee populations* to describe particular groups and the potential for homogenization. These statistics have been provided to contextualize the widespread, ongoing effects of conflict and insecurity in the participants' diasporic community.

2 In January 2017, South Sudan president Salva Kiir created four additional states; there are now 32 states in the country (Sudan Tribune, 2017). Payam, county, and states are the administrative divisions in South Sudan, in order of increasing size. These sub-national entities are used for the purposes of, for example, population projections (National Bureau of Statistics, 2015).

3 In line with this study's ethics procedures, interviewees are referred to by pseudonyms.

4 Nyadeng described the first clip as a "happy" song about a wedding, and the second and third clips as joyful traditional celebratory songs and dances performed in the context of South Sudanese independence.

5 Nyadeng's rudimentary literacy level necessitated that this spelling be approximated phonetically. According to a video source, *loth* refers to a Dinka big bell (Alithdit Alith, 2010).

6 The narrative of the Sudanese civil war, and South Sudan's ultimate separation from the (now) Republic of Sudan, sometimes leads to reductionist dichotomies among, for example, North-South, Muslim-Christian, and Arab-African identities (see Deng, 2012).

References

Alithdit Alith. (2010, August 1). South Sudan: The Dinka Big bell (Loth) [Video file]. Retrieved from https://www.youtube.com/watch?v=DxRQoBxISsM

Anwar, M. (1986). Sphinx on the Sudd: Southern Sudan behind and beyond the 6 April 1985 coup. *Haliyyat, 43*, 41–47.

Asylum Seeker Resource Centre. (n.d.). *Community engagement.* Retrieved from https://www.asrc.org.au/communityengagement/

Blacktown City Council. (2011a). *Blacktown City ancestry.* Retrieved from http://profile.id.com.au/blacktown/ancestry?BMID=30

Blacktown City Council. (2011b). *Blacktown City birthplace.* Retrieved from http://profile.id.com.au/blacktown/birthplace?BMID=50

Deng, F. M. (1973). *The Dinka and their songs.* Oxford: Clarendon Press.

Deng, F. M. (2006). *Talking it out: Stories in negotiating human relations.* New York, NY: Columbia University Press.

Deng, F. M. (2012). The paradox of Southern independence: Some personal reflections. In The Heinrich Böll Foundation & T. Weis (Eds.), *Sudan after separation: New approaches to a new region* (Democracy Series, 28, pp. 11–20). Berlin: Heinrich-Böll Stiftung.

Dieckmann, S. (2016). *Exploring the acculturation: The musical lives of South Sudanese Australians, Filipino Australians and White Australians in Blacktown* (Unpublished doctoral dissertation). University of Sydney, Sydney. Retrieved from https://ses.library.usyd.edu.au/handle/2123/14956

Embassy of the Republic of South Sudan in Washington DC. (2011). *Languages: Tribes.* Embassy of the Republic of South Sudan in Washington DC. Retrieved from http://www.southsudanembassydc.org/map.asp

Eriksen, T. H. (2010). *Ethnicity and nationalism: Anthropological perspectives* (3rd ed.). London: Pluto Press.

Frahm, O. (2012). Defining the nation: National identity in South Sudanese media discourse. *Africa Spectrum, 47*(1), 21–49.

Higgins, L. (2012). *Community music: In theory and in practice.* New York, NY: Oxford University Press.

Impey, A. (2013). Keeping in touch via cassette: Tracing Dinka songs from cattle camp to transnational audio-letter. *Journal of African Cultural Studies, 25*(2), 197–210.

Internal Displacement Monitoring Centre (IDMC). (2018, May). *Global report on internal displacement.* Retrieved from http://www.internal-displacement.org/global-report/grid2018/downloads/2018-GRID.pdf

Jok, J. M. (2011, October). *Diversity, unity and nation building in South Sudan* (Special Report No. 287). Washington, DC: United States Institute of Peace.

Jok, J. M. (2012). South Sudan: Building a diverse nation. In Heinrich Böll Foundation & T. Weis (Eds.), *Sudan after separation: New approaches to a new region* (58–67). Berlin: Heinrich-Böll Stiftung.

Karlsen, S. (2013). Immigrant students and the "homeland music": Meanings, negotiations and implications. *Research Studies in Music Education, 35*(2), 161–177.

Khashan, H., & Nehme, M. (1996). The making of stalled national movements: Evidence from Southern Sudan and Northern Iraq. *Nationalism and Ethnic Politics, 2*(1), 111–140. doi:10.1080/13537119608428461

Komey, G. K. (2010). Ethnic identity politics and boundary making in claiming communal land: The Nuba mountains after the CPA. In E. Grawert (Ed.), *After the comprehensive peace agreement in Sudan* (pp. 110–129). Oxford: James Currey.

Lyman, P. N., Temin, J., & Stigant, S. (2014, January). *Crisis and opportunity in South Sudan* (Peace Brief No. 164). Washington, DC: United States Institute of Peace. Retrieved from https://www.usip.org/sites/default/files/PB164-Crisis_and_Opportunity_in_South_Sudan.pdf

Munro, K. (2018, April 4). Who are Australia's South Sudanese? *SBS News.* Retrieved from https://www.sbs.com.au/news/who-are-australia-s-south-sudanese

National Bureau of Statistics. (2015, April). *Population projects for South Sudan by payam: From 2015–2020.* Retrieved from http://www.ssnbss.org/sites/default/files/2016-08/population_projections_for_south_sudan_by_payam_2015_2020.pdf

Natsios, A. S. (2012). *Sudan, South Sudan and Darfur: What everyone needs to know.* New York, NY: Oxford University Press.

Neuberger, B. (2006). African nationalism. In G. Delanty & K. Kumar (Eds.), *The Sage handbook of nations and nationalism* (pp. 513–526). London: Sage.

Onwuekwe, A. I. (2009). The socio-cultural implications of African music and dance. *Creative Artist: A Journal of Theatre and Media Studies, 3*(1), 171–185.

Pinaud, C. (2014). South Sudan: Civil war, predation and the making of a military aristocracy. *African Affairs, 113*(451), 192–211. doi:10.1093/afraf/adu019

Saether, E. (2008). When minorities are the majority: Voices from a teacher/researcher project in a multicultural school in Sweden. *Research Studies in Music Education, 30*(1), 25–42.

South Sudanese Community Association in Victoria Incorporated. (2017). *About us.* Retrieved from http://sscav.com.au/about/

Smith, A. D. (1998). *Nationalism and modernism.* New York, NY: Routledge.

Smith, A. D. (2010). *Nationalism: Theory, ideology, history* (2nd ed.). Cambridge: Polity Press.

Southern Sudan Referendum Commission & Southern Sudan Referendum Bureau. (2011). *Referendum results 2011.* Retrieved from http://southernsudan2011.com/results/state/359/index.html

South Sudanese Community Association in Victoria, Inc. (2017). *About us.* Retrieved from http://sscav.com.au/about/

Sudan Tribune. (2017, January 15). South Sudanese president creates for more states. *Sudan Tribune.* Retrieved from http://www.sudantribune.com/spip.php?article61403

United Nations Educational, Scientific and Cultural Organization (UNESCO). (2014, June 19). Communities of South Sudan build their National Museum. *UNESCO Media Services*. Retrieved from http://www.unesco.org/new/en/media-services/single-view/news/ and http://www.unesco.org/new/en/media-services/single-view/news/communities_of_south_sudan_build_their_national_museum//

United Nations High Commissioner for Refugees. (2018). *Global trends: Forced displacement in 2017*. Retrieved from https://www.unhcr.org/uk/statistics/unhcrstats/5b27be547/unhcr-global-trends-2017.html

United Nations Mission in the Republic of South Sudan. (2014, May 8). *Conflict in South Sudan: A human rights report*. Retrieved from https://reliefweb.int/report/south-sudan/conflict-south-sudan-human-rights-report

United Nations News. (2019, February 12). *Thousands flee fresh violence in South Sudan, many "suffering from trauma."* Retrieved from https://news.un.org/en/story/2019/02/1032541

CHAPTER 23

Waves of Freedom through Singing

Mathilde Vittu and Michele Cantoni

This chapter aims to present a music pedagogy project, its approach, and the challenges it faces in the context of the Occupied Palestinian Territory in the West Bank. Initially, we welcome our readers to Palestine with a reminder of the current geopolitical situation there. We then guide them through the project's pedagogical, social, human, and musical guidelines. As a third step, we complete our journey by focusing on the trajectory of the thoroughly thought-through repertoire, one shaped around the project's context and challenges (see Figure 23.1).

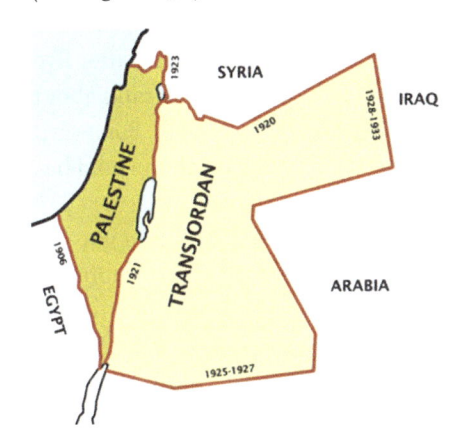

FIGURE 23.1
1930s British Mandate Palestine (Wikimedia Commons), https://commons.wikimedia.org/wiki/File:BritishMandatePalestine1930s.png

Welcome to Palestine[1]

For several millennia, the land and the people of Palestine have endured a continuous series of successive occupations. Egyptian, Assyrian, Persian, Roman, Arab, Ottoman, and British rule were followed by Zionist colonial domination with the establishment of the State of Israel on parts of Palestine in 1948 (what Palestinians call the *Nakba*, or catastrophe). Israel then occupied the rest of Palestine in 1967 (what Palestinians refer to as *Naksa*, or setback), a situation that persists to this day.

What is specific to the Zionist colonial enterprise is that Israel was created, to a very large extent, by *displacement* and *replacement* of the indigenous

© KONINKLIJKE BRILL NV, LEIDEN, 2020 | DOI: 10.1163/9789004430464_023

population by settler populations. This was achieved by massive Jewish migration to Palestine as well as by means of extreme violence and a well-planned and well-documented policy of ethnic cleansing that resulted in approximately 80% of the Palestinian population becoming Nakba refugees in neighboring countries (Lebanon, Egypt, Jordan, and Syria).[2] Those refugees were never allowed to return to their lands, and now, 70 years later, are estimated to number over five million.[3]

Palestinians who were able to remain in what became Israel in 1948, frequently internally displaced, were subjected to Israeli military rule that lasted until November 1966.[4] Less than a year later, in June 1967, Israel completed the occupation of Palestine and placed under military rule the Palestinian population of the newly conquered West Bank and Gaza Strip, which includes roughly one third of the 1948 refugees. Soon after 1967, a relentless Jewish colonization of the West Bank and Gaza begun.[5]

The 1993 Oslo Accords, signed between Israel and the Palestine Liberation Organization, have allowed for the creation of an interim Palestinian Government, the Palestinian Authority. The accords were supposed to lead, after five years of Palestinian self-government in the West Bank and Gaza, to talks about permanent status on the issues of borders, refugees, and Jerusalem. For a variety of reasons, those goals were never met, and the loss of Palestinian land has continued the worrying pattern that began in 1948 (see Figure 23.2).

It must be noted that the Palestinian Authority was, and still is, a government under foreign military occupation. It therefore, inevitably, is required to

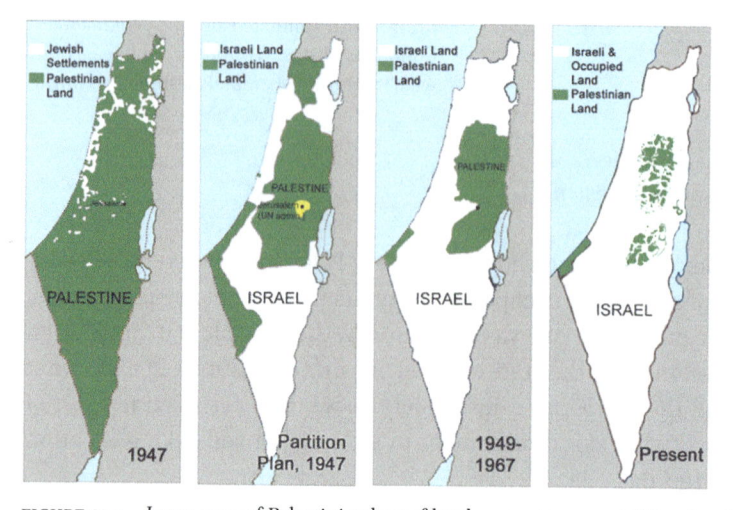

FIGURE 23.2   Large map of Palestinian loss of land—1947 to present (Mapsland)

closely collaborate with the occupier and, as a result, it has no effective autonomy of government, although it has a considerable load of responsibilities.[6]

Today, West Bank Palestinians are subjected to humiliating Israeli controls that comprises walls, check-points, and a complex system of permits they have to apply for if they want to exit the West Bank (to go abroad, or even to go to Jerusalem). They are often denied those permits, without any explanation and with a high degree of randomness. Furthermore, since Israel has complete control over Palestinian land, resources, and borders, any person wishing to enter or exit any portion of Palestine can only do so with the approval of the Israeli authorities. In many cases, Israel denies Palestinians the right to leave the country if one of their close relatives is in jail.

Foreigners wishing to go to Palestine (whether to visit, to volunteer or to work) may encounter all sorts of difficulties at Israeli border controls, from being interrogated for hours to being denied entry to the country (and banned from entering for five or ten years), again without explanation (the vague term used is "security reasons"). Over the last few years, several of our foreign colleagues teaching in Palestinian music schools were forced to stop working there because they were sent back by the Israeli authorities on arrival at Tel Aviv airport or at land border crossings, with devastating consequences for them, for their students in Palestine, and for the institutions who employed them.

The dispossession and displacement suffered by Palestinians since the *Nakba*, the post-Oslo territorial fragmentation of Palestine and its increasing subjugation by Israel,[7] have led to understanding the Palestinian people's condition as a combination of dispossession, displacement, statelessness, isolation, separation, fragmentation, subjugation, segregation, imprisonment, and apartheid.

For us, who have worked for many years within Palestine's cultural sphere, one of the most striking features of Palestine's civil society is its tireless creative effort to associate itself with beauty, joy, life, humanity, human rights, justice, and freedom. Music projects in Palestine have the potential to both expose the injustice and give visibility to the positive spirit that keeps Palestinian society alive.

Guidelines of the *Amwaj* Project

Amwaj is the Arabic word for "waves." Our waves are musical waves, the waves that bring music, the waves of a sea that Palestinian children from the West Bank have never seen. The Amwaj Choir[8] is a choir-based intensive educational program for children, established in Hebron and Bethlehem in 2015. Today, the Amwaj Choir numbers 60 children—30 from Hebron (new city and old city) and 30 from the Bethlehem governorate (towns, villages and refugee camps). Thirty-five girls and 25 boys, aged 7 to 17 are offered eight hours weekly of varied activities such as choral singing, voice training, foreign languages, music theory and history, conducting, introduction to piano and percussion, theater, and more. The children attend Amwaj after school and benefit from a musical and artistic program strongly linked to their country.

The project's approach is one of providing collective experience through choral activities (tuition and public performances), while promoting children's rights and equal opportunities, without discrimination based on social class, gender, religion, or political affiliation. Its multicultural and inclusive approach allows the project to create links and bonds, across multiple sections of Palestinian communities and beyond. Arbitrary Israeli-imposed restrictions on the freedom of movement in Palestine are obstacles that are more difficult to confront. The impossibility to predict whether travel (at any specific moment) is possible often creates an understandable choice not to travel. The project aims to encourage and facilitate both movement and discovery within Palestine, although with the necessary caution (and not underestimating actual risks or difficulties).

Utilizing singing as a form of creative expression, the project builds on the potential of culture as an avenue for socio-economic development, to foster social cohesion, and to mitigate the adverse effects of the territorial fragmentation of Palestine. Young generations are increasingly facing forms of inequality in accessing resources and life opportunities, and it is crucial to provide innovative opportunities for them in creativity and learning.

Since the acceptance by local communities of music activities, or unfamiliar repertoire might not always be obvious, the Amwaj Choir adopts the strategy of organizing concerts and public presentations in each community, in which the young singers showcase their creative skills and potential by singing in various languages and by always including songs linked to Palestine's traditions. Amwaj promotes cultural and social cohesion between Palestinian communities. It targets, attracts, and actively involves multiple audiences. Its public events, combined with its educational and audience-building actions, not only lead to audience growth but also contribute to creating a new generation of musicians.

The activities of the project give music and cultural events an increasingly prominent position within society and also help the formal integration of musical and cultural resources into other sectors of Palestinian society. Through partnerships with educational and community-based institutions, those activities stimulate cultural awareness, curiosity, respect and involvement, thus seeking to generate a sense of cultural identity and belonging. Furthermore, through prestigious international partnerships, Amwaj reinforces existing efforts abroad aimed at offering a cultural perspective of Palestine and of its society, a necessary condition to confront current political adversities and frequent misconceptions.

The Trajectory of a Thoroughly Considered Repertoire

Amwaj takes great care in its choice of repertoire. It must meet specific pedagogical criteria, but also allow for a reflection about the musician's role and activities within the Palestinian territories and beyond.

Paying Homage to the Palestinian Land

The choir aims to create encounters between Palestinians from rural areas, towns, or refugee camps, whether or not their families were displaced, which applies to two thirds of the children of Amwaj. Within this framework, during the first year (2015–2016), we chose several traditional and folkloric songs, including them in concerts such as "Hebron waves reaching Jerusalem" and "Palestine at the Heart of the world." Those same songs were included two years later to accompany the Dabke (traditional Palestinian dance) group of the Shoruq center (Daheisheh refugee camp) with the Nawa Arabic Music Ensemble: Promoting various aspects of Palestinian folklore through an encounter of music, singing, and dance in a show entitled "Palestine's vibrant heritage."

Subsequently, in 2016–2017, we included music written to honor Al-Quds (Jerusalem) by composers from Palestine, the wider Arab world or foreign countries, on texts by Palestinian poets. In the following phase, 2017–2018, we commissioned works from Palestinian composers.

In January 2018, Amwaj premiered *Aswat fil Hara* (sounds in the neighborhood), a children's opera by Dina Shilleh, a young Palestinian composer, based in Ramallah, whose family is originally from Lid (close to today's Tel Aviv airport). For the libretto, the composer worked alongside the young poet Maya Abu-Alhayyat. The staging was entrusted to dancer and choreographer Samar Haddad King. The three artists gave life to a new work that depicts life under military occupation and the children's desire to play, sing, eat, and drink. The work embraces fully the message of longing for a normal life, one of the main aspirations within Palestinian society. The opera was performed again in France, in June 2018, at the Institut du Monde Arabe in Paris, in the opening concert of Amwaj's first international tour.

During the same tour, in Lyon, the choir premiered a work by a French-Lebanese composer of Palestinian origin. Naji Hakim, born in 1955, grew up in Lebanon, where his family had landed after their expulsion from Haifa. As an adult, he moved to France, where he currently lives without having ever visited his ancestral land. Through music, he connects to that land as did Palestinian poet Mahmoud Darwish, who followed a similar path. In the work *Tibaaq* (counterpoint), Darwish pays homage to Edward Said, writing that "free travel between cultures" is a matter of exile and of plural identity. This identity concerns the other:

> I am two in one. I am from there. I am from here. I am not there and I am not here. I have two names, which meet and part, and I have two languages. I forget which of them I dream in. I have English for writing, obedient in words. I have also a language in which heaven speaks to Jerusalem. (Darwish, 2009, pp. 89–90)

Naji Hakim's composition mixes Arabic and French languages, and is accompanied by an Arabic traditional ensemble and an organ. This world premiere saw the Amwaj Choir perform alongside the French choir Les Petits Chanteurs de Lyon.

An Opening towards the Arab World, an Opening towards the Whole World

Through music, the children meet the Arab world and sing, in their own language, traditional repertoire originating from neighboring countries (Syria, Lebanon, and Egypt) as well as from North African ones. They become aware of their belonging to the Arab world and of the richness of cultures it encompasses.

To transcend borders, ever since the first year of Amwaj, the children have sung traditional and classical repertoire from countries throughout the world. Today, they sing in over 30 different languages. Through singing, they discover those languages, they become closer to other cultures and they sharpen their curiosity in front of the "other." To them, music becomes a means to communicate with the whole world.

Through thematic concerts, such as "Waves of Freedom," "Freedom, Dream and Anti-Racism," and "Spiritual music from all traditions," Palestinian children are encouraged to discover the realities of other peoples and to gain a wider perspective on their own daily situation.

Intercultural Dialogues

To fine-tune the encounter with other cultures, the choir regularly hosts artists from throughout the world. It has established ambitious intercultural projects after singing in Palestine with other international choirs. In 2016, Amwaj performed with the Choir of London and the Oslo Philharmonic Choir, both in Arabic and in the respective languages of those two choirs. In 2017, it benefited from workshops with the vocal ensembles Common Ground Voices and VOICES 21C. It is, however, Amwaj's intercultural exchange with France that is the most active and vibrant one to date. Since its beginnings, the choir has received numerous French educators. In 2017 and 2018, some of the children participated in a French language song competition in Bethlehem. Beyond those more individual approaches, a full-fledged exchange between children's choirs was consolidated in 2017.

In June–July 2017, the Lyon cathedral choir Les Petits Chanteurs de Lyon visited the Amwaj Choir school in Palestine. The 30 French children, aged 10–14 and of Christian upbringing, had a one-week joint residency with the 60 Palestinian children, aged 7–17 and of mostly Muslim background. The pedagogical and musical program advanced the idea of *métissage*, intended as a composition, each component of which maintains its integrity (Laplantine & Nouss, 2001). Gregorian chant was interwoven with Muslim, Arab Andalusian, or Syriac chant, and the French music of Berlioz, Delibes, or Ravel was in dialogue with Palestinian traditional music. At the end, the voices of the 90 children superimposed melodies inspired by different languages and musical cultures. During that project, the children were able to know the other and to merge into a single choir with a unique sound. This first exchange strengthened the relation between Les Petits Chanteurs de Lyon and the Amwaj Choir. In April 2018, it was the turn of 15 members of the youth choir from Lyon (aged 14–17) to have a joint residency in Palestine at the Amwaj Choir school.

In 2018, at the time of their French tour, it was the 60 Palestinian children's turn to visit their French colleagues. That tour's success led to an invitation for the choir to return to France five months later for a concert at UNESCO headquarters in Paris honoring the UN's International Day of Solidarity with the Palestinian People. The new tour was a further opportunity for cultural discovery and exchanges,[9] with Amwaj performing at the Paris Conservatoire and elsewhere in partnership with Les Petits Chanteurs de Lyon. Further phases of the exchange between Les Petits Chanteurs de Lyon and Amwaj aim to build the 120 French and Palestinian children as a homogeneous ensemble, ensuring that the French and Arabic literary and musical languages mix and interweave.

The trajectory of the Amwaj repertoire transcends the displacement experienced by most of the children's families. It allows for a broader, global perspective that could partially relieve the distress generated by that forceful displacement. In France, the children met other children, French, immigrants, or refugees. They were confronted by another reality that led them to an intimate reflection on their own reality. Despite the Israeli-imposed closures on Palestinians, when in Palestine, the children manage to mentally escape, daily, through music and singing. At the time of their first international experiences, supported by numerous cultural actors, they were also able to physically escape, for a few weeks, through the music-making activities.

Notes

1   There is no universally accepted definition of the terms *Palestine* and *Palestinian*. It is therefore necessary, for sake of clarity, to specify case by case how they are utilized. We wish to underline the fact that the definitions adopted in this chapter relate more to geographical and cultural realities in the region's modern history than to current, highly controversial, political or religious claims. We will adopt the use of the terms *Palestine* and *Palestinian* as defined in the Oxford online dictionary: "The name Palestine was used as the official political title for the land west of the Jordan mandated to Britain in 1920." *Palestinians* are "member[s] of the native Arab population of the region of Palestine (including the modern state of Israel)." The Collins online dictionary defines *Palestinian* as "A native or inhabitant of the former British mandate, or their descendants, especially such Arabs now living in the Palestinian Administered Territories, Jordan, Lebanon, or Israel, or as refugees from Israeli-occupied territory."

2   See, for example, *The Ethnic Cleansing of Palestine* (Oneworld, 2006) by Israeli historian Ilan Pappé.

3   For official data about Palestinian refugees, see the information provided by the United Nations Relief and Works Agency, https://www.unrwa.org/who-we-are

4   July 2017 factsheet of the independent human rights organization Adalah: 1948–1966: The Israeli government imposed military rule on [the Palestinian citizens of Israel], severely limiting their freedom of movement, livelihoods, and expression. Simultaneously, Israel passed numerous laws to transfer Palestinian land to state ownership or control; overall, Israel took 73% of Palestinian land. https://www.adalah.org/uploads/uploads/Palestinian_Citizens_of%20Israel_Adalah_July_2017.pdf (31/05/18).

5   Today, Jewish settlements (or colonies) in the West Bank and East Jerusalem count over 750,000 settlers (the Palestinian population there numbers around 3 million).

6 With the Oslo Accords, the Palestinian Authority was given responsibilities for guaranteeing the welfare of the Palestinian population in the West Bank and Gaza in health and education, for example, responsibilities which, according to international law, pertain to the occupying power.

7 It should also be noted that the Palestinian people, since 1948, were forcefully divided into several, disconnected, categories: Palestinians of the West Bank and Gaza, Palestinians of Jerusalem, Palestinian citizens of Israel, Palestinian refugees (neighboring countries, West Bank, Gaza) and Diaspora Palestinians (living outside the region). Relations between them are severely affected by the lack of freedom of movement within Palestine as well as the isolation of Palestine from the outside world (Israeli control of all borders). For further in-depth geopolitical analysis, see El-Ghadban (2005).

8 For further information on the Amwaj Choir, see amwajchoir.org

9 Having no choice but to travel via Jordan to reach France from Palestine, always because of Israeli restrictions, Amwaj decided to transform that imposed route into an opportunity for new musical encounters. As a result, the choir ended its tour with a concert in Amman, alongside the local Nai Children's Choir and Jordanian-Palestinian soprano Dima Bawab.

References

Darwish, M. (2009). Counterpoint (for Edward W. Said) (M. Shaheen, Trans.). In *Almond blossoms and beyond*. Northampton, MA: Interlink Books.

El-Ghadban, Y. (2005). La musique d'une nation sans pays: le cas de la Palestine. In J. Nattiez (Ed.), *Musiques. Une encyclopédie pour le XXIᵉ siècle: Musiques et cultures* (Vol. 3, pp. 823–852). Paris, France: Actes Sud.

Laplantine, F., & Nouss, A. (2001). *Dictionnaire des métissage*. Paris, France: Pauvert.

Pappé, I. (2006). *The ethnic cleansing of Palestine*. London: Oneworld.

CHAPTER 24

Singing for Life in South Madagascar

Arsène Kapikian

Recognized as one of the poorest countries in the world, Madagascar has undergone numerous crises since its independence in 1960, the causes of which are varied and complex. The 18 ethnic groups that predominantly occupy the island make up a scattered, mostly rural population, and people suffer the consequences of an extremely centralized government led by a small group of the politico-economic elite. These elites are comprised of powerful families that monopolize the wealth and profits of a country whose resources are not in short supply. In this paradoxical setting, widespread cultural diversity in conjunction with a rich yet fragile ecosystem and the deprivation of a population left to its own devices by the country's leaders have resulted in large numbers of inhabitants leaving their birthplaces to seek subsistence and survival in northern Madagascar.

In addition to the political issues faced by Madagascans, climate change contributes to the harsh realities of life. Agricultural practices employed by native communities as well as environmental instability, for example, serve as antecedents to mass migration whereby floods, droughts, deforestation, unsustainable farming practices, cattle theft, and shortages of potable water are chief concerns.

The Christian population, divided into Protestants and Catholics, is a product of repeated waves of English and French missionary operations throughout the 19th century. With evangelization came increased popularity of choral singing throughout the island. Choral singing and its religious connections form an integral part of the Madagascan cultural landscape. In these spiritual and cultural contexts, animist and Christian, it is important to note the extent to which music plays a key role in the perpetuation of cultural links that are often destroyed in the course of forced mass migration, especially in the South of the nation. I sought to find out where music might be situated within this complex story of politically and environmentally induced migrations. To answer this question, along with my music educator colleague, Emmanuel Fontana, I committed to a long residency in the southwestern city of Toliara. We wanted to make a documentary about the Malagasy Gospel Choir. "A Choir that Saves Lives"[1] (see Figure 24.1) was the result of our work. While following the choir, I gained insight into the production and transmission of music, and

FIGURE 24.1   Poster for the documentary "A Choir That Saves Lives" featuring Florence and
Harris, soloist singers of Malagasy Gospel Choir.
POSTER DESIGN: ARSÈNE KAPIKIAN

how it plays an important role in psychosocial survival, and the preservation of identity for the communities that make up this society (see Figure 24.2). In this complex, and seemingly tragic environment, which breeds insecurity, crime, and exodus, music appears to provide a powerful way to recount stories and for community support.

Malagasy Gospel Choir is a program of the non-governmental organization (NGO) Bel Avenir, part of the Coconut Water Network.[2] This NGO provides education and healthcare to children who live in situations of extreme poverty in South Madagascar. As part of the Documenting 21C film project, the Malagasy Gospel Choir's music director decided to share a concert at the Toliara prison. When the prisoners witnessed the performance, they were amazed and decided to give a concert in return as a way to express appreciation. While filming, I saw firsthand how music enabled these individuals to rebuild a link with the wider society and to reclaim their dignity (see Figure 24.3).

FIGURE 24.2   Malagasy Gospel Choir performing in Toliara Prison. Arsène Kapikian (camera)
and Emmanuel Fontana (sound engineer, seated).
PHOTOGRAPH: CRISTINA NAVAROL

FIGURE 24.3   Three prisoners singing "Azafady" in Toliara prison. Frame from the
documentary "A Choir That Saves Lives."
PHOTOGRAPH: ARSÈNE KAPIKIAN

The prisoners' thank-you concert was a demonstration of the singers' profound bond with music, through which their humanity manifested itself. The
prison population, neglected and ignored by society, according to several
inmates we spoke to, has nothing but this medium to help them feel as if they
fully exist, and to connect themselves to the outside world from which they
have been isolated.

After watching the Malagasy Gospel Choir's concert at the Toliara prison,
the Documenting 21C film crew was able to return regularly to watch the

prisoners rehearse. Madio Helène Volanzary was responsible for forming the thank-you concert prison choir which included male, female, and juvenile prisoners from different sections of the prison who would most likely never see each other again. During one of these practice sessions, we offered three prisoners, whose performance at the thank-you concert had particularly moved us, the opportunity to record a composition together. In this song, a number of regrets are expressed by the composers to their parents. They lament the errors they have committed, particularly that of not having listened to their advice.

Azafady (I Apologize)[3]

Toy zahay baba	*Here we are Papa*
toy zahay Neny	*Here we are Mama*
Voadona Tokoa	*Truly tested*
Mahatsiaro manegny zahay	*We apologize*
Ka mifona	*We offer excuses*
Atao ho naharaty	*We reacted badly*
Fagnanara nareo	*To your advice*
Tsy narahanay	*We didn't listen to you*
Mahatsiro manegny zahay	*We apologize*
Kamifona	*We offer excuses*
Zao ny valiny tsy fagnaraha	*This is the result of not following you*
Ny anatry ny Ray amandreny	*A parent's advice*
Zanako ô ô ô	*Oh oh oh, my child*
Fa nareo baba	*But you Papa*
Fa nareo Neny	*But you Mama*
Solony zagnahary	*You are the creator*
Tsy azo valeavalea	*You must be respected*
Fa mampisy havoa	*Or we will be cursed*
Azafady baba	*Sorry Papa*
Azafady Neny	*Sorry Mama*
Tsipazo nareo rano	*Bless us*
Mahatsiro manegny zahay	*We apologize*
Kamifona	*We offer excuses*
Zaho tsy voro hitroka atoly	*I am not a bad parent*
Hagnary anaky. Mandehana bakao	*Who would harm my child? Come here*
Ho tsipaziko rano ho afaka havoa	*I will bless you, to free you from damnation*
Zanakô ô ô ô	*Oh oh oh my child*

During the recording, we could also hear voices coming through the walls, from the women's section, where the prisoners were singing the South African song *Shosholoza*, which they had learned during their first rehearsal with Volanzary.

The prisoners' emotional singing expressed the depth of the suffering they felt at being trapped in prison. Some of them had fled misery and perhaps made bad choices, been led astray, or been the victims of misfortune; the destiny of these displaced individuals is to end up in a prison where they are deprived of fundamental human rights. They may never escape. However, as the director of the prison told me and the film crew in an interview: "Singing in prison is a means of escaping without breaking the law." The mission of our organization, Documenting 21C, is to use our documentary to carry prisoners' voices over the walls of the prison, and off the island of Madagascar, to let the world listen.

Music-making at the Toliara Penitentiary Centre has allowed prisoners to experience a temporary sense of escape. From our documentary experience in Toliara, we saw how music, through various practices and methods of transmission, can contribute to the positive transformation of local communities. We witnessed how practicing and playing music can have a profound impact on incarcerated people. Music at Toliara is more than a mere pastime, and it is more than a means of entertainment reserved for the elite classes. Music is a means by which prisoners transcend the walls that confine them.

Notes

1 The documentary can be viewed here, http://documenting21c.com/#teaser_choeur_sauve
2 For further information on this organization, see https://coconutwaternetwork.org
3 Felix Page translated the whole contribution from French to English, including *Azafady*. This song was previously translated from Madagascan to French by Nantie Razafinjohany from Bel Avenir NGO.

CHAPTER 25

"'Cause I'm Gonna Make This Place Your Home": The Jerusalem Youth Chorus

Micah Hendler

Introduction

The city of Jerusalem, contested for millennia, is home to the three Abrahamic faiths and two different nations,[1] Israelis and Palestinians. Yet it has been the site of tremendous displacement, as each group has sought to claim Jerusalem through physical, cultural, political, and structural violence. How is it possible to create a shared home for all in such a context?

The Jerusalem Youth Chorus[2] is a choral and dialogue program for Israeli and Palestinian young people from East and West Jerusalem. Through the co-creation of music and the sharing of stories, we empower youth in Jerusalem with the responsibility to speak and sing their truths, as they become leaders in their communities, and inspire singers and listeners around the world to work for peace, justice, inclusion, and equality. Founded in 2012, the chorus has met through wars and cycles of violence, home demolitions, visa denials, and pressure from singers' communities on both sides to stop singing. When we meet, we sing together and also speak to one another about our internal and external realities, thus expanding empathy and worldviews and activating our singers as agents of change (de Quadros, 2019).

All of our singers have been affected by dynamics surrounding displacement, whether through family stories, national narratives, or direct experience of physical or cultural displacement as is particularly the case with our Palestinian singers. Yet our community has been able to maintain a home for all our singers in the face of conflict and a predominantly zero-sum understanding of Jerusalem that perpetuates this displacement. How is it possible to create, protect, and grow this alternative shared space in Jerusalem and generate a feeling of inclusive community instead of existential conflict in this context? More broadly what role do we, as artists, have in the creation and facilitation of such communities in other contexts of conflict and displacement?

In this chapter, I tell a story of a defining moment for the chorus. I lay out elements of social-psychological theory pertaining to reducing prejudices and changing attitudes in intergroup encounters. I explore how music can be used as a tool within that context and describe how these ideas are put into practice in the Jerusalem Youth Chorus. I detail various on-the-ground constraints that influence the chorus's structure and its relationship to power, politics, gender, language, education, or musical background. I lay out our chorus model, combining the community-building power of music with the transformative power of dialogue and the shared goal and platform of performance, and I discuss how this has worked in practice since 2012. I conclude by opening a question of how our model might be adapted to other areas of conflict and displacement in Jerusalem and around the world.

July 2–3, 2014

On July 2, 2014, Mohammed Abu Khdeir, a Palestinian teenager from the East Jerusalem neighborhood of Shuafat, was kidnapped and burned alive by Israelis in the Jerusalem Forest. The previous day, three Israeli teenagers, Eyal Yifrach, Gilad Shaar, and Naftali Fraenkel, had been buried in a nationally televised funeral, having been kidnapped by Palestinians at a bus/hitchhiking stop in the West Bank and murdered. On July 3, the Jerusalem Youth Chorus, many of whose Palestinian and Israeli singers knew or had personal connections to the slain teenagers and all of whom could identify with their stories, was scheduled for a rehearsal to prepare for its first international tour the following month.

What does a director of a chorus for Palestinian and Israeli teens from Jerusalem do on such a day? After the murders of these four teens, violence erupted in Jerusalem; rioting and vigilante attacks were executed in both directions. Does one cancel the rehearsal or hold it *davka* then? (*Davka* is a unique Yiddish-Hebrew term that means simultaneously despite the given circumstances and yet more so because of those same circumstances.) What is safe, emotionally and physically? What is appropriate? What message does the chorus send if we cancel and what message do we send if rehearsal is held? Will teenagers from only one side show up? Will anyone attend? And how can we possibly provide a space that can contain and help process the fear, anger, and pain that they will bring with them and hurl at one another as the only people from the other side they know?

We met for a musical rehearsal and dialogue session, after I had called our Palestinian and Israeli singers to make sure they were OK and told them that, if they felt unsafe getting to rehearsal for any reason, they did not need to come, a sharp departure from the rigorous and strict attendance policy. About half of our 30 singers did attend that rehearsal that day, a balanced representation of Israelis and Palestinians. This alone was remarkable in a context in which most Israeli-Palestinian groups—even those meeting for years—had decided to cancel their meetings and wait for better times to see each other again.

A half hour into the rehearsal, Leen, one of our youngest singers and a Palestinian girl from Shuafat, walked in. Leen lived around the block from Mohammed Abu Khdeir. Her neighborhood had erupted in violence between its Palestinian residents and Israeli soldiers after news of his murder. Indeed, Shuafat had been closed down entirely; soldiers and police prevented people from entering or leaving. When Leen walked into our rehearsal, many of the singers, Palestinian and Israeli alike, rushed over to give her a hug and make sure she was OK. She joined us in our vocal warm-ups, and we continued as normally as we could given everyone's emotional state. Later, I took her aside to ask how she was doing and how she physically managed to get to the rehearsal. Her response:

> I woke up this morning to gunshots and tear gas. I was sitting in my living room going crazy because of all the violence and I needed to get out. So, I left my house, and walked down the street out of Shuafat. The soldiers tried to stop me, but I ran away. Now I'm here, and this is exactly where I want to be.

The Jerusalem Youth Chorus: Two Sides Come Together

Jerusalem is a place of endlessly fascinating complexity, shared attachment, and intertwined existence, yet it is also where exclusive narratives are built more easily than inclusive ones, and extremism and war come far more easily than sharing and compromise. In the last hundred years, Jerusalem has become increasingly contested and has changed hands numerous times. As a result of war and displacement, Jerusalem is split socially, culturally, economically, politically, linguistically, musically, religiously, and psychologically between the worlds of East Jerusalem, primarily Palestinian in population and culture, and West Jerusalem, primarily Israeli in population and culture. Although no physical border exists between East and West Jerusalem, Israeli and Palestinian Jerusalemites usually do not have personal relationships at eye-level across this divide and both communities generally feel that the city fundamentally belongs to them more than to the others.[3]

Even music has been mobilized in service of these one-sided narratives. For example, two of the most iconic songs about Jerusalem, the Jewish-Israeli "Jerusalem of Gold" and the pan-Arab "The Flower of Cities" either completely ignore or call for the destruction of the other side and its claim to the city

(Hendler, 2011). Moreover, music and sound more broadly are often used to demarcate exclusive cultural, religious, or national ownership of space in Jerusalem (Nusseibeh & Hendler, 2016). Music can nevertheless be harnessed to build alternative and inclusive social structures. Especially in combination with verbal dialogue, it can provide a frame for transformation on personal, interpersonal, intergroup, and societal levels. The act of singing with others has been used for millennia as a tool to build community. Manifested in tribal chants and national anthems, group singing has the power to give emotional, experiential weight to the definition of "who we are."[4] This process can work powerfully even across boundaries such as identity or conflict and can help interpersonal relationships to grow naturally within these new, inclusive boundaries (Hendler, 2011).

When I began to build the Jerusalem Youth Chorus, I situated our work theoretically at the intersection of Contact Theory, Realistic Conflict Theory, and Social Identity Theory—three different ways of thinking about how to structure an encounter between individuals from conflicting groups. Each of these theories has its imperfections, but together lend insights on the dynamics that occur within contexts such as ours and have helped us think more clearly about how we structure our work.

The contact hypothesis assumes that one's prejudices are fundamentally a product of one's individual psychology and that the right kind of contact with a member of the stereotyped group can change these misperceptions (Doubilet, as cited in Kuriansky, 2007). Experiments such as the famous Robbers Cave Experiment[5] have bolstered Realistic Conflict Theory, which holds that the external incentives for competition or cooperation in any given situation determine attitudes towards one another (Forbes, 1997). In contrast, Social Identity Theory emphasizes the importance of one's position *within* a social group in relation to fundamental psychological needs such as legitimacy, status, and pride as the primary determining factor for human interaction.[6] In my experience, each of these elements, and many others, play a significant role in our behavior in groups, and all must be carefully considered when structuring an encounter between individuals from groups in conflict.

A critical concept in these frameworks is to understand the distinction, developed by Social Identity Theory, between interpersonal interaction and intergroup interaction.[7] In this dichotomy, interpersonal interaction occurs when people from different groups meet primarily as individual human beings, first and foremost representing themselves regardless of origin. In contrast, intergroup interaction occurs when members of these groups consider and relate to one another primarily in terms of their group identification and as representatives of their communities (Hewstone & Brown, 1986). According to this concept, if those who come from a different group do not have an opportunity to engage with one another as representatives of their respective communities, there will likely be little change in the attitudes or behavior toward the other group as a whole, beyond the few individuals who participate in the encounter itself (Brown & Turner, 1981, as cited in Hewstone & Brown, 1986).

In more than a decade of experience with different types of encounter models for Israeli and Palestinian youth, I have found that a mixed model of interpersonal and intergroup interaction in the pursuit of a superordinate goal to be the most effective in creating transformative change for the group. This kind of model provides spaces both for the kinds of interpersonal change advocated for by Realistic Contact Theory, and the more challenging and yet necessary intergroup dynamics highlighted by Social Identity Theory. Moreover, in a group with a shared goal, the effects of Realistic Conflict Theory can also be harnessed well for maximum impact.

What does this mean in practice? What does interpersonal interaction look like? What does intergroup interaction look like? How do we identify attainable, yet meaningful, overarching goals for individuals coming from groups who view their relationship in zero-sum terms? Most important, how do we, as artists and musicians, create and facilitate the spaces necessary for each of these critical processes to take place?

In Jerusalem, a profound asymmetry exists between East and West in terms of power and resources in almost every sphere in which Israelis have great control over Palestinians. Palestinian, Israeli, and international chorus staff and singers must acknowledge, interrogate, and challenge this asymmetrical power dynamic between Israelis and Palestinians and work instead towards an alternative social structure that deliberately focuses on equality. Outside the chorus, discrimination and intolerance reign. Therefore, in the chorus we must cultivate the ability to respect differences. Most important, our alternative reality must be able to hold up against a constant barrage from the outside and the fact that our singers frequently travel between both.

The political landscape in Jerusalem has become increasingly desperate and cynical in its mentality, another challenge to maintaining a hopeful, empathetic, and collaborative culture in the chorus. Increases in violent public racism in Israel ostracizes the Left and erodes democratic values, all of which make it more difficult for Israeli youth to participate without resistance from their friends, families, and society. In Palestine, the concept of normalization plays a role in determining what is acceptable in society, given the Israeli occupation of the West Bank, Gaza, and East Jerusalem.[8] This concept holds that one cannot have normal relations between occupier and occupied, and that such relationships that exist merely normalize the Occupation and make it more difficult to fight (PACBI, 2011). It is important to be aware of social dynamics, and we endeavor to make the relationships formed within the chorus and their performances engines of change rather than acceptance of the status quo. The discourse on normalization and anti-normalization in Palestine, however, often indiscriminately accuses any program bringing Palestinians together with Israelis as being against Palestinian national interests. This poses an additional challenge for the chorus, particularly for the Palestinian singers, who face a great deal of resistance for their participation. Moreover, the chorus was for many years part of the Jerusalem International YMCA, a non-political organization, which has restricted the chorus from making political statements.[9] So, how can we still make meaningful change in our outside political realities, in a way that is inclusive and yet pushes the conversation forward? This is another major challenge we face in carving out the tiny patch of common ground that the Jerusalem Youth Chorus inhabits.

Aside from the political, other elements of life in Jerusalem are important to consider when constructing a shared space such as ours. Gender plays a critical role in the dynamics of the group. Because we are a mixed-gender ensemble, neither ultra-religious Jews nor ultra-religious Muslims attend. Both Israeli and Palestinian societies fear interreligious dating, and this fear also influences who parents allow to enter the group as well as the norms of the group itself.

Language also plays a significant role in our group. In the beginning, we faced a decision to choose either a common language requirement, such as English, or to be open to people of all linguistic backgrounds. We chose the inclusive option, and therefore we translate everything into three languages— English, Arabic, and Hebrew—as needed. This has social implications and creates additional challenges for group cohesion and power dynamics, but it also has musical implications, as those who are not English speakers often come to the group without a Western musical background. This situation provides both a challenge and an opportunity. It is much more difficult to develop a shared musical vocabulary, but that also means the resulting musical vocabulary we do develop, which includes shared elements and space and allows for each member's individual background to shine, is much richer. This provides an interesting, unexpected, tangible example of the beauty in diversity; because we decided to include all language constellations and abilities, the result is a unique and powerful musical ensemble sound.

"As We Create a Home for All of Our Singers..."

Creating a home for all in the chorus begins with the musical community-building processes discussed above. Singing together provides a collaborative mode of interaction for our members that serves as a foundation for the group. The reason that people join the chorus is to sing, and that commonality provides an excellent starting point for our work.

Just to sing together in a place like Jerusalem is not simple. *What* we sing and *how* we sing can be loci of conflict if not treated properly. We try to be constantly aware of the political and cultural implications of our music. For example, except in rare cases, we do not sing about peace. One can sing about peace without serious intention or thought, and many people and choruses do. Rather than singing about a discredited concept made empty in many ways, we sing about the tangible, active building blocks that could lead to peace: sharing a sense of home, seeing things from a different perspective, overcoming loss, or sharing a belief in the religion of love. We also program songs from each national tradition and often make an effort to show shared themes in their messages. Sometimes we forge links between traditions by creating fusions between songs on similar themes from different cultures. We do not sing national anthems or songs that serve as such, as we must be sensitive to what we are asking our singers to embody and we should consider the challenges they could face.

Culturally, we create a broad repertoire, so that all our members feel represented in the music we sing. We incorporate improvisation into our work, both because the Arabic musical tradition is highly improvisatory and because it is the easiest way to create space for individual singers to express themselves and their identities. Some of our music is Western in orientation and some Arabic; much is a mix of both. The repertoire process is challenging given that the choral practice we have adopted originated in European musical cultures and given that my own background is as a Western musician (with knowledge of and love for Middle Eastern music, but not expertise in it). We aspire, however, to equalize the playing field between Arabic and West in our music in several ways. We teach not only how to sing in harmony but also how to sing quarter tones. Both Western and Arab scales and modes are included in our warm-ups. While our choral vocal parts still favor Western musical concepts, our solo opportunities favor Arab ones. Finally, we try to push the boundaries of inclusiveness in choral music by teaching not only how to read music but also how to improvise without notation.

People come to sing, but stay because the chorus becomes their home. This begins in the music and spills into the interpersonal realm as our singers become close friends. They travel internationally together and work in high-stakes concert situations often followed by spontaneous dance parties. They socialize on weekends and text each other frequently. They return to the chorus—even in times of struggle—because it is a place for them to be celebrated for who they are. The value for them as individual humans often takes precedence over the political resistance they might receive.

We inculcate the values of inclusiveness, equality, acceptance of difference, seeing the beauty in diversity, not only implicitly through our musical process but explicitly in our dialogue. For us, dialogue is a place to conceptualize values (in the contexts of the individual, the chorus, and society) and to process the conflict in terms of this value language. This amounts to a critically important intergroup component of our chorus, and every weekly four-hour rehearsal includes an hour-and-a-half dialogue block in the middle to engage in this difficult but meaningful work.

Dialogue in the Jerusalem Youth Chorus is a year-long process whose content is ultimately provided by the singers sharing their life experiences and perspectives with one another. Professional facilitators lead these discussions and guide the group through stages of group development, values, tools, and content areas. The process begins by setting up ground rules for communication and proceeds to a discussion of a given value, such as equality. By interrogating the facets of this value and its interactions with other important values, a discursive framework is built in the group about topics related to equality. When the facilitators guide the group to topics of the conflict that touch on equality, the group can draw on a shared foundational vocabulary of value language to discuss them, rather than simply remain at the surface level of conflicting headlines. In this way, our singers emerge from dialogue with a broader perspective on these difficult issues and have internalized many of the core values of the group.

Dialogue serves many functions in the chorus, both protective and proactive. Dialogue protects the chorus by providing a conflict management space to handle issues that arise (whether related to the conflict or to the chorus). Moreover, the conceptualization of values that takes place through dialogue influences their actions when it comes to group solidarity and cohesion. For example, when the chorus was planning a tour to London, at the last minute, visas for all of our Palestinian ID holders were denied. When we told the singers this, and that we would not travel without everyone, no one protested, despite months of preparation and excitement, and the fact that the majority of the chorus had been granted visas. Everyone simply understood that this was the fair and right thing to do if we truly were a chorus based on the values we taught in dialogue. This sounds idealistic, but it really happened, and not often in communities of any kind is the powerful majority willing to give up something it really wants in order to accommodate the powerless minority. Those are the values we discuss and debate in dialogue, and those values that keep the chorus together.

Dialogue is, of course, also a proactive educational tool. A process of individual self-discovery through encounter with the other that challenges narratives of self and society, ultimately leads to new understandings of what is shared, what is not shared, and what might be possible were Jerusalem itself to look like our chorus.

In particular, dialogue helps us deal with the context of displacement in which we operate. Many of our singers' families have been displaced, whether to or from Israel/Palestine or from one part of Israel/Palestine to another. A particular complexity is that the displacement in the Israeli and Palestinian experiences are intertwined and causally related; many Jewish refugees were resettled at the cost of creating Palestinian refugees. Unpacking this tangled history of displacement and the narratives associated with it is one additional challenge we tackle in our dialogue process—we even devoted an entire five-day retreat to exploring collective trauma, healing, and expression in the context of two seminal tragedies that both heavily involved displacement: *Shoah* (the Hebrew word for the Holocaust) and *Nakba* (the Arabic word for "catastrophe" describing the Palestinian experience of the establishment of the State of Israel in 1948).

Moreover, this pattern of displacement continues today in Jerusalem, and many of our Palestinian singers experience it first hand, through home demolitions, settler encroachment, and the cultural displacement of Palestinian history and identity in Jerusalem. Dialogue is an important space for them in particular to share these stories and experiences with their Israeli counterparts in whose society this erasure is predominantly ignored or celebrated. Through this exposure, we hope to build solidarity between our singers, not only in a chorus context, but in a broader sociopolitical one as well, as they work together to raise their voices for a Jerusalem that can be a home for all.

"We Seek to Show What Jerusalem Could Be"

The experience of singing in the chorus has profoundly impacted our singers, one which many of them share by bringing friends to rehearsals and auditions, inviting family to our concerts, and actively posting on social media about the chorus and their friendships. We track and are consistently inspired by the many stories they tell of challenging friends, parents, or teachers regarding their prejudices, or of helping others see things from a new perspective.

As an ensemble, the chorus has a powerful ability to present a different reality for Jerusalem. It is of critical importance, particularly regarding the normalization paradigm discussed earlier, that we very consciously reject attempts to use the chorus to simply show "that everything is fine" or that "everybody gets along." Rather, we create cross-cultural, multinational spaces for our audiences to experience for themselves what Jerusalem *could* be—more inclusive, more equal, more just, and more cohesive—if everybody had the chance to meet and interact as equals and create something beautiful together. Our performances seek to inspire hope in our listeners, who come from many backgrounds, that it is still possible to create such a reality (even if just in microcosm), and our songs often inspire action by supporting the chorus or getting involved in peace-building work more broadly (see Figure 25.1).

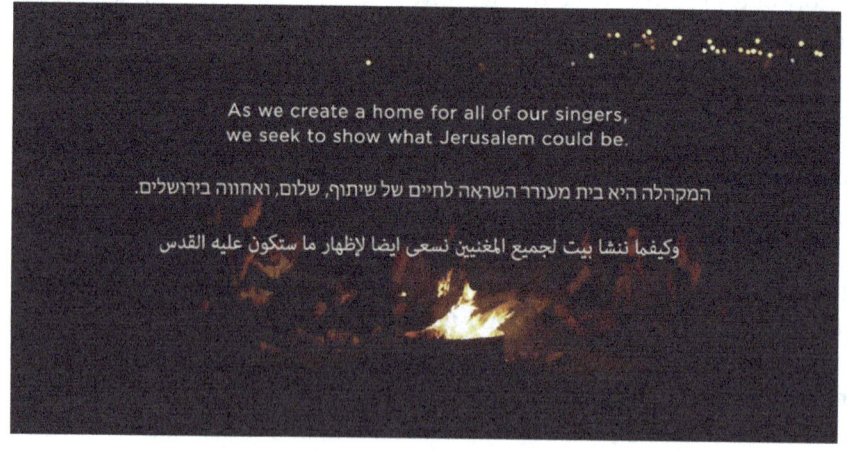

FIGURE 25.1   "As we create a home for all of our singers, we seek to show what Jerusalem could be."[10]

Our impact is not limited to Jerusalem; we tour frequently and thus have the opportunity to make our voices heard in the global conversation about the Middle East. Finally, we have reached millions of people through multimedia, providing a model for people anywhere to engage with their communities and with those who are different.

New Directions

Over the years we have experimented with integrating our musical and dialogue processes. By default, those tracks have run in parallel, but occasionally we have accepted the challenge of integrating them and produced profound results. In 2015, we embarked upon a collaborative composition pilot under the guidance of music educator Shoshana Gottesman in which the entire group of 30 singers composed an original song through a dialogue-based process that made space for the various individual voices and also gave voice to their collective experience of singing in the chorus. The following year, we incorporated group free improvisation in order to musically process the intense site visits to conflict and displacement-related spaces. Finally, our 2017–2018 season was the first in which we integrated the entire arc of the year's program between music and dialogue. We chose repertoire to reflect our dialogue themes and used songs as a springboard for dialogue. Both with our high schoolers and our alumni (who are continuing to work together even in a new stage of their lives), we continue to use the dialogue process to generate original musical content for our ensembles. In this way, we are building a new paradigm for youth choruses not only to include dialogue as a reflective and educational space in their programs, but also to harness it as a co-creative space that produces new music.

I argue that the most promising new direction for our work is its capacity for adaptation to other contexts. Singing in groups is a global human activity, as are conflict and displacement, unfortunately. Therefore, our model of musical community-building, dialogue-based transformation, and performance as a common goal and message platform might be able to contribute in similar and different ways elsewhere, whether in the Middle East or other regions of conflict and displacement.

The Jerusalem Youth Chorus model may also be adaptable to other musical and non-musical interactive structures. For example, bands, orchestras or other instrumental ensembles with a dialogue component could also address divides and educate in a similar fashion. Non-musical processes could be merged with dialogue processes according to a similar concept of discursive co-creation—whether through other art forms, such as drama, or even through contexts that foster non-artistic cooperation, such as sports teams. Throughout these contexts, however, it is critical that dialogue remain a core component of the experience; otherwise the group will produce little change on an intergroup level.

Another question is, to what extent these processes can be replicated at different age levels? There is something special about working with adolescents; for example, there might be a greater likelihood of open-mindedness and critical thinking. But our process may well be adapted to different stages of development. Among adults, dialogue grounded in a common goal may prove effective, and there are many organizations adopting similar processes, such as Convergence.[11] With this in mind, one of our goals is to inspire and foster the creation of many more such programs and build connections and alliances among them—to contribute to a movement of global bridge-building.

By sharing my journey with the Jerusalem Youth Chorus, I have sought to address the critical role that we as music educators can play in areas of conflict and displacement. With great sensitivity, flexibility, openness, creativity, and passion, it is possible to harness music's power to accomplish what many imagine as nearly impossible. Obviously, each community has its own needs, special dynamics, challenges, and opportunities, but the fundamental model of the Jerusalem Youth Chorus, that of combining musical community-building with encounter dialogue in the context of a performing ensemble, has great potential as an intervention in many other contexts. So much need exists in our world to address conflict and injustice, displacement, and division. Let us meet it with a movement of musicians who desire to bring more harmony and justice into the world, at every level of human interaction, and truly make this place a home for all.

 VIDEO 25.1   Home by Phillip Phillips performed by Sam Tsui and the YMCA Jerusalem Youth Chorus.
The video accompanying this chapter is freely available online at https://doi.org/10.6084/m9.figshare.12446051

Notes

1   I argue that Palestine is a nation, regardless of official statehood, consistent with United Nations General Assembly resolution 67/19 recognizing Palestinian sovereignty.

2   For further information about the Jerusalem Youth Chorus, see www.jerusalemyouthchorus.org

3   The situation between Israelis and Palestinians in Jerusalem is exceedingly complex, and my statements here represent my personal observations. Israelis and Palestinians live in segregated worlds, but this binary is only one binary that exists. For example, there is also a great segregation between secular Jewish Israelis and

ultra-orthodox Jewish Israelis. What is critical to note in contextualizing our work is that cultural norms in Jerusalem are generally suspicious of, at least, or violently opposed to, at worst, positive interaction with the other, beyond immediate mutual economic interest, and view conflicts between the parties as irreconcilable and fundamental to one another's core identities and existence as peoples

4 Note, however, that this process can both unite "us" but also distinguish us from or pit us against "them." Therefore, it is critical to note the ends to which the process is marshaled.

5 In the Robbers Cave Experiment, boys at a summer camp developed ethnocentric behavior based on random division into two competing groups. When they needed to cooperate on a superordinate goal, however, these behaviors and accompanying attitudes dissolved.

6 Experiments show that even in randomly generated groups A and B, people in one group would rather have more money relative to people in the other group (and the resulting feeling of pride and a higher status) than allow everyone to obtain an equal, larger amount of money (Forbes, 1997).

7 Many critiques of social identity theory are forwarded, but the concept of interpersonal vs. intergroup interaction has proven helpful in my understanding the dynamics that I experienced in the context of intergroup encounters that both do and do not explicitly discuss group differences.

8 Israel annexed East Jerusalem in 1967, but Palestinians still view it as under Occupation along with the West Bank and Gaza, and many of the same social, cultural, and political dynamics apply in all three areas.

9 As of 2019, we are in the process of reexamining our political statements, mindful of the complexity and implications for a group such as ours.

10 See https://www.youtube.com/watch?v=xMkqMTK1_Oo&feature=youtu.be

11 Convergence occurs when an organization works with policymakers across American divides to find common ground and move discussions forward on major issues of national concern. For further information on convergence, see https://www.convergencepolicy.org

References

de Quadros, A. (2019). *Focus: Choral music in global perspective*. New York, NY: Routledge.

Forbes, H. D. (1997). *Ethnic conflict: Commerce, culture, and the contact hypothesis*. New Haven, CT: Yale University Press.

Hendler, M. (2011). *Music for peace in Jerusalem* (Undergraduate senior thesis). Retrieved from https://traubman.igc.org/hendlerpaper.pdf

Hewstone, M., & Brown, R., (Eds.). (1986). *Contact and conflict in intergroup encounters.* Oxford: Basil Blackwell.

Kuriansky, J. (Ed.). (2007). *Beyond bullets and bombs: Grassroots peacebuilding between Israelis and Palestinians.* Westport, CT: Praeger.

Nusseibeh, S., & Hendler, M. (2016). *Sound and self – A space to call "Home".* Keynote Presentation, The East-West Philosophers Conference. Honolulu, Hawaii. Retrieved from https://youtu.be/YY_ViGEyn-w

Palestinian Campaign for the Artistic and Cultural Boycott of Israel (PACBI). (2011). *Israel's exceptionalism: Normalizing the abnormal.* Retrieved from http://www.pacbi.org/etemplate.php?id=1749

CHAPTER 26

Relocation, Research, and Reconciliation in Unama'ki

Marcia Ostashewski and Shaylene Johnson

This is sacred, this work that's being done here,
that we're all doing here together,
it's sacred.

> GRAHAM MARSHALL (Membertou Band Council Member and Research
> Project Participant, personal communication, June 18, 2018)

∴

This chapter provides an account of, and highlights some key aspects of understanding that have been gained through collaborative and participatory arts research in Unama'ki. Unama'ki is the L'nu,[1] or Mi'kmaq word for Cape Breton Island, Nova Scotia, Canada. Unama'ki is part of the ancestral and unceded territory of the Mi'kmaw people. This territory is covered by the Treaties of Peace and Friendship (INAC, 2015) that Mi'kmaq and Wolastoqiyik (Maliseet) people first signed with the British Crown in 1725. These treaties did not deal with surrender of lands and resources. Rather, they recognized Mi'kmaq and Wolastoqiyik title and established rules for what was to be an ongoing relationship between nations. Yet, in 1916, after having already been restricted to reserve lands, the members of the Kun'tewiktuk Mi'kmaq community were forced by the Dominion of Canada to move from their homes on the Kings Road Reserve near the city of Sydney. They were relocated to the current Membertou First Nation site.

The grand arc of the story of the people of Membertou is one of resilience and prosperity in the face of extraordinary challenges on individual as well as broader community and nationwide levels. Theirs is not a story of people who belong nowhere—it is a story of a people who know where they belong but have been disenfranchised of their land and resources. Nonetheless, these people continually worked to reclaim their place, their histories, practices and identities, as have their descendants. This chapter is the story of a group of these descendants who, nearly a century after the relocation to Membertou, are taking action through music and other creative research processes to discover and uplift the memory of their ancestors, to honor them and the legacy that they created for the generations that came afterward.

In this chapter, we describe the research-creation[2] project titled, *Songs and Stories of Migration and Encounter* (hereafter *Songs and Stories*). More specifically, we address the phase of the project that attends to a history of the Kun'tewiktuk Mi'kmaq reserve community, an indigenous community on Cape Breton Island off the coast of Nova Scotia, Canada. *Kun'tewiktuk*, the theatrical production, the outcome of this phase of the project, focuses on one instance of displacement of indigenous peoples that was a direct result of settler colonialism, and some ways in which that event continues to reverberate in the community that experienced it. This work is also understood by the project participants as an example of a broader reconciliation model, with an eye to the activities and recommendations of the Truth and Reconciliation Commission of Canada (TRC). Through the process of investigating, conceiving and performing *Kun'tewiktuk*, Mi'kmaq youth and Elders critically engaged with and creatively (re)articulated their community's history from the perspectives of their own community members.

Songs and Stories of Migration and Encounter: The Collaborative Team and Process

The larger research project, of which the work discussed in this chapter is a part, is titled *Songs and Stories of Migration and Encounter*. This project investigates experiences, narratives and understandings of migration and encounter in Cape Breton, through critical, creative research processes. *Songs and Stories* is one of several recent collaborative, community-engaged research-creation projects supported by the Centre for Sound Communities (CSC) at Cape Breton University (CBU), collectively facilitated by its Director, Marcia Ostashewski, and community members of different ages and walks of life who come together to address a concrete problem or critical issue. The lead community-based researcher for the current phase of the project, in Membertou First Nation, is culture bearer and youth worker Shaylene Johnson. Johnson invited a number of Elders and other traditional knowledge holders to join her in supporting our research process, including Shirley Christmas, Nelson Paul, Peter J. Paul, Peter Christmas, and Shaylene's father, Clifford Paul. Toward the end of our workshop process, as we readied ourselves for a public performance, culture bearers Jeff Ward and Graham Marshall also joined the group, the latter of whom is a member of the Membertou Band Council. About a dozen Membertou youth aged 7–16, primarily teenagers, also participated at different stages.

Our collaborative working group drew on both indigenous and settler ways of knowing, skills, capacities and other resources, and each member contributes according to their abilities and interests. All of the Membertou-based research team members identify as L'nu or Mi'kmaq. Neither Ostashewski, nor the other university-based research team members Sheila Christie and Todd Hiscock, identify as indigenous. Two visiting postdoctoral researchers also brought expertise in theater and socially-engaged art to the project, Heather Fitzsimmons Frey and Marnie Badham. Our team also included two student research assistants - Kalo Nicholas, a Mi'kmaq woman from Eskasoni Reserve on Cape Breton, and Michelle MacQueen, originally of Cape Breton. Finally, our team was joined just ahead of performance by both indigenous and settler community members, who played the roles of additional characters.

The larger *Songs and Stories* project from which the *Kun'tewiktuk* theatrical production component has evolved has included the launch and/or delivery of multiple project phases to date. The basic model for the project involves an initial period during which the Elders and other culture bearers are asked to share their knowledge and experiences related to a given topic with the youth. This is followed by a period of collaborative creation—the collective writing of a song, or play, for example—that expresses the youth's understandings of the topic at hand, including aspects of the issue that are significant in their own lives. This work includes technology-enhanced interactions that support training, learning, knowledge exchange, and other research-creation activities such as archival research, ethnographic interviews, music, theatre, and filmmaking.

Kun'tewiktuk: The Community, the Play, the Performance

This chapter focuses on the third phase of *Songs and Stories* that addresses the relocation of the Kun'tewiktuk reserve community. Although the decision to remove the Mi'kmaq people of Kun'tewiktuk was made in 1916, not until 1928 were all of the community members actually removed from Kings Road Reserve. This occurred after a suitable place for their new reserve could be purchased by the Department of Indian Affairs and construction could begin on new homes (Membertou Communications, 2016). Such a brief overview does no justice to the hardworking, industrious families of people of Kun'tewiktuk who were maligned and treated harshly in the process. Maria Campbell referred to a commemoration ceremony held at Batoche, the site of an historical battle between Métis people and Canadian authorities, saying "There's a plaque, but the people still have no land" (Robinson & Martin, 2016, p. 1). This sentiment was echoed in the words of Elders Nelson Paul, Peter J. Paul and Peter Christmas at Membertou who, in early 2018 workshop sessions, noted a plaque at the edge of Kings Road marking where the reserve had been—but not telling the real stories of the people who lived there. The travesty of their treatment has not yet been properly acknowledged.

With this sense of injustice and a desire to learn more about the realities of the lives of the Kun'tewiktuk community members, and to honor them, Shaylene Johnson requested a workshop in order to explore and to share knowledge about the Kings Road Reserve community's relocation to the Membertou site. The workshop process was emergent in nature. For example, originally the idea had been to write a song about Kun'tewiktuk and the resilience of the community. It soon became clear, however, that the group as a whole felt a theatrical production would be a more suitable medium through which to tell a more complex story—and that songs would be vital components of the story (see Figure 26.1).

FIGURE 26.1   During any given workshop session, some members of the group might be creating material objects for the production, as they are here working on papier-mâché "heads" for the puppets, while others are discussing the action of the play. Elders Room, Membertou Heritage Park, June 2018.
PHOTOGRAPH: MARCIA OSTASHEWSKI

The Making of Songs and Stories for the Stage

In the process of learning about Kun'tewiktuk, Elders told stories of how Mi'kmaq people came from disparate parts of the island to camp there. They brought with them crafts such as baskets and wooden clothesline poles they had made. For this reason, the working group decided to integrate the process of making baskets into the play. In our process, Elders also recounted evocative stories about various people who lived at Kun'tewiktuk after it became an official settlement for Mi'kmaq people—mothers and gardeners, steel plant workers, stonemasons, horse-traders, firefighters—their mishaps and joyous moments too. These people were the ancestors of the members of our working group—the stories were a window into life at Kun'tewiktuk and into family histories. Thus, aspects of life stories of Kun'tewiktuk community were spoken aloud, in the voices of those who lived them, during parts of the play. The courthouse trial through which the decision was finally made to relocate the Kun'tewiktuk reserve also arose as a critical component of the story of Kun'tewiktuk. Interwoven through the entire play was music, singing, drumming, *ji'qmaqn*,[3] and fiddling, all of which the Elders and youth indicated are a vital part of Mi'kmaw traditions and long histories of experience in Cape Breton (see Figure 26.2).

FIGURE 26.2   The final scene of the performance, in which baskets are offered to the audience and to future generations. Actors visible from left to right: Noah Matthews-Cremo, Graham Marshall Jr., Jeff Ward, Shirley Christmas, Shayla Paul, Gabby Doucette, Nelson Paul, Donald Wells, Janine Christmas, Shaylene Johnson. Membertou Convention Centre, June 21, 2018.
PHOTOGRAPH: MARCIA OSTASHEWSKI

In *Songs and Stories*, Elders serve as storytellers, as knowledge holders and culture bearers (Ostashewski et al., 2018). This is in keeping with indigenous knowledge and traditions; "engaging with Elders has been recognized as an essential means of accessing Indigenous knowledge and histories as oral histories" (with reference to Miller, 2011, as cited in Ostashewski et al., 2018, p. 10). Through the process of the project, youth began to share the responsibility of retaining the oral histories of their community. Now as carriers of those narratives young participants take on the responsibilities of witnessing, listening, and they share responsibility for the consequences of their knowledge; they could choose how (and if) their song would reflect Elders' stories, contemporary globalized media cultures, or something else entirely (Ostashewski et al., 2018, p. 11).

Grandmother and Elder Shirley's final words to the audience of *Kun'tewiktuk* asked them to take up the work that the *Songs and Stories* group started for the community, the work of remembering and of passing on the histories that we had learned through our research. Now, as we reflect, we look back to the beginning that started with a prayer, then, sharing knowledge, we made a commitment and created. Now that we have gifted you with this basket and knowledge, we must remember to continue this process and pass on the knowledge to future generations (paraphrased from the unpublished working script).

Kun'tewiktuk was gifted to the audience, to the broader community, as a presentation. It was also a request to the community to help to carry this heavy knowledge, so that it would no longer be only the young people of the working group but the wider community continuing to do the work of remembering and creating together, for the benefit of future generations. In this way, the audience, too, became a part of our process (see Figure 26.3).

FIGURE 26.3
Center stage during the play, showing Shirley Christmas as the grandmother, with Graham Marshall Jr. and Shayla Paul as her grandchildren listening at her feet. The three puppets of the lawyer, judge, and plaintiff, with their young Mi'kmaq puppet-masters and voice actors behind. Membertou Convention Centre, June 21, 2018.
PHOTOGRAPH: CAPE BRETON POST

Music Carries a Message: Songs and Stories as Sacred

An in-depth analysis of the play, as a whole, is beyond the scope of the current publication. A discussion of the music involved in the *Kun'tewiktuk* production, however, provides further insight into significances of our team's creative research process. This discussion illustrates how the histories and experiences of Kun'tewiktuk community members and others were embodied in performance through music.

From the first moments that our group began to articulate a vision for the stage performance that would eventually take shape as *Kun'tewiktuk*, it was clear that music needed to be a part of what was presented. It was wholeheartedly agreed that traditional songs and drumming, and the *ji'qmaqn*, a Mi'kmaq percussive instrument, should be used. It was likewise strongly agreed that some fiddle music should be part of the production, to show both historical culture and newer cultural elements. "Indians loved fiddle music as they transitioned to new times," said Nelson Paul (personal communication) and it was agreed that an "upbeat, dance-y" tune should be played because it was indicative of much of the fiddle music enjoyed in indigenous communities.

There was much concern in our workshops about choosing the right songs. For example, a strong theme of "welcoming" was taking shape in the work. A number of people quickly remarked that a well-known traditional song performed as a welcome might be appropriate to sing. Nelson Paul cautioned, however, that the song was originally from another First Nation and was intended as a song of friendship between two nations. A traditional Mi'kmaq gathering song was chosen instead, and local singer Karina Matthews was asked to perform it. She chose two additional songs, including a friendship song taught to her by her grandmother. Although Karina grew up in another Mi'kmaq community, her grandmother had grown up in Membertou (Karina Matthews, personal communication). Her third song was "the Kitpu song" or eagle song. Nelson Paul's comments about this song resonated with the recognition of eagles in many North American indigenous cultures: "the eagle should always be honored, as it carries messages between us and the Creator" (Nelson Paul, personal communication). He noted that the eagle song that Matthews sang was sung once a year in Potlotek (Chapel Island) by the *Putu's*, the holder of the Wampum belts and related knowledge of treaties, sometimes referred to as the War Chief (Nelson Paul, personal communication) (see Figure 26.4).

Traditional knowledge-holder Graham Marshall observed that our work in *Songs and Stories* is sacred, as quoted at the outset of the chapter. He explained:

FIGURE 26.4   Shawnee Paul and Karina Matthews, the two musicians who performed in
               Kun'tewiktuk. Membertou Convention Centre, June 21, 2018.
               PHOTOGRAPH: CAPE BRETON POST

> Mik'maq peoples' history has always been told by a fire or even during a
> feast. When we mix that with modern production, with mics and lights
> and real production technique, we are bringing two worlds together and
> the stories that happened over a century ago get brought back to life.
> Therefore, personally, the theme and event become sacred. (Marshall
> Graham, personal communication)

Marshall observes that traditional means of creating and sharing continue
through our research-creation methods, which use current technologies and
resources. The relationship with traditional indigenous ways of knowing,
being, and doing, and the ceremony and the sacred are maintained.

Enrolling Practice-Based Ethnomusicology Research in Reconciliation

Like many of the *Canada 150*-funded projects, *Songs and Stories* anticipated
that young people would use the opportunity to critically engage with the
issues at hand. The project was conceived of shortly after the release of the
report of Canada's TRC that addressed the country's legacy of Indian residential
schools. The importance of building relationships through arts-based inquiry
in this context was highlighted, including intergenerational relationships. The
empowering nature of creative process through embodied practice was also

emphasized, as was the importance of understanding our research practice with indigenous partners through indigenous paradigms of knowledge.

The significance of foregrounding indigenous theories and methods, and the importance of relationships in this process, are not new ideas to scholars who work in this area (Chilisa, 2012; Denzin, Lincoln, & Smith, 2008; Kovach, 2009; Smith, 2012). In initial publications about earlier phases of *Songs and Stories*, our team cited scholarship on indigenous theories and methods that are particularly meaningful in our local Mi'kmaq context. Shaylene Johnson noted the relevance of "Two-Eyed Seeing" (Bartlett et al., 2012), a paradigm first articulated in publications created collaboratively by Mi'kmaq Elders and a Cape Breton University scholar. Two-eyed seeing means "learning to see from one eye with the strengths of indigenous knowledges and ways of knowing, and from the other eye with the strengths of Western knowledges and ways of knowing" (Bartlett et al., 2012, p. 355). In our workshop process, music served as "a shared experience and as a metaphor for integrating encounters between Mi'kmaq and non-indigenous peoples, alongside engaging with traditional indigenous and non-indigenous ways of knowing, knowledges and research methods" (Ostashewski & Fitzsimmons Frey, 2018, p. 11). As is noted in other publications on this research (Ostashewski et al., 2018), Johnson described Cape Breton music as holding a Mi'kmaq instrument in one hand and an instrument of a similar organological structure of a settler culture (say, percussion instruments) in the other hand (Ostashewski et al., 2018, p. 12).

Membertou Elders and other culture bearers also pointed out that the work being done through the project was a prime example of the TRC in action (Ostashewski et al., 2018). The song creation and performance processes that were integral aspects of the research took place several months after the TRC hearings and other meetings had been completed. What did it mean that our collaborators felt so strongly that our process was the TRC in action? Shaylene Johnson explains.

> TRC in action means to tell the truth about the effects that residential school has on our people...Our people endured all types of abuse which had a trickle effect on everyone: alcoholism, sexual abuse, trauma, lateral violence, inability to love. We [in *Songs and Stories*] had to ask people to search their long-term memories, through all this pain to come out with stories of endurance and triumph even given all of the after-effects of residential schools. Talking about history will always be a touchy subject. And it requires extra finesse in asking questions in a good way so that it remains respectful to the youth and respectful to the Elder because everyone carries trauma and pain.

Performance artist and scholar Peter Morin (2016) has written about aesthetic action related to the memories and the TRC specifically, "to remember is an act that resonates in your bones" (p. 85). To remember is one act, but we live with our memories, we interact with others: "'the body is a resonant chamber'—a place where experiences echo, sinking deep into the bones before reverberating back out into the world" (Robinson & Martin, paraphrasing Morin, 2016, p. 11). Morin's statement reminds us how deeply felt personal experiences can be, and the ways in which personal experiences and the ways in which they become part of us, reverberate in the lives of those around us through our own ways of being and actions. Our *Songs and Stories* process allowed us to do the work for caring and respecting one another—the difficult experiences of ancestors who lived at Kun'tewiktuk, and of the people around the table who gathered together each week. The performance of the play was also a unique embodiment of the histories and experiences of Kun'tewiktuk stories.

Morin has also drawn attention to the encounters and engagements between indigenous people and settlers in the process of the TRC—similarly, our research team involves indigenous people and settlers, dealing with a terrible instance of our shared pasts resulting from a colonial encounter. Of the TRC, Morin wrote: "The difficult task is finding actions to activate this space where indigenous knowledge meets settler ways of being. They are bodies of knowledge that mingle and impact each other. And often their meeting requires yet another meeting" (Morin, 2016, p. 71). As we read Morin's words, we thought perhaps this is part of why the process, ideally designed as six weeks, actually required nearly six months. Our difficult task was to find ways to activate a space where indigenous knowledge meets settler ways of being—and to find ways to move forward in our task together in a good way (see Figure 26.5).

The significance of the TRC in *Songs and Stories* is evident well beyond method—a process of unearthing the past into the light. The way in which the research was conducted, through creative process, through songs and stories, comes to the fore. "Ceremony and song are widespread in indigenous public culture," writes Dueck (2016), who described in detail the ways in which song was "enrolled" in the public intervention that was enacted in the TRC proceedings (p. 269).

The multimodal practice-based research of *Songs and Stories* is valuable both in terms of process and outcomes. *Songs and Stories* activities were initiated as research. We deliberately sought to create new knowledge about local experiences of migration and encounter, particularly of Membertou First Nation, through an emergent critical, creative process. Our team enrolled theatrical production and performance, including music as a means of co-creating and sharing new knowledge. And, as Shaylene Johnson commented during

Feasting and friendship in Membertou on National Indigenous Peoples Day

Cape Breton Post • Published: Jun 22 at 12:06 a.m.

FIGURE 26.5   The journalist told Ostashewski that the image of the youngest of the group's participants, Skyla Paul, as puppet-master was so compelling, that he wanted to be sure to feature it in his story the next day.
PHOTOGRAPH: CAPE BRETON POST

those fall workshops, the kinds of knowledge accessed and the quality of relations that characterize our research could only have come to pass through a creative process given the significant role of song in the traditional culture and lives of our Mi'kmaq collaborators.

Here, I return to the request for contributions to this book, where we were called to actions that affirm, support, uplift, and honor the people who experience displacement, disruption, trauma. As contributing authors, scholars and researchers, we are charged, to attend to ways that we might "create opportunities for scholars, practitioners, and silenced voices to share theories and stories of progressive and transgressive music pedagogies that challenge the ways music educators and learners think about and practice their arts relative to displacement."

These authors' instincts resonate remarkably with Canada's TRC, which brought indigenous people and settlers together to begin to work to redress a legacy of the past, of the trauma experienced by indigenous people as a result of Canada's residential schools system. The TRC created opportunities for the silenced voices of the survivors to tell their stories, for their voices to be heard and their experiences affirmed—for indigenous people and settlers to both publicly uplift and to honor those who endured those experiences, and to articulate ways (in the TRC's *Calls to Action*, see TRC 2015) to productively challenge previously accepted knowledge, including historical events and relations. Although on a much smaller scale, this same instinct was taken up by the Membertou working group of *Songs and Stories* in our work toward the *Kun'tewiktuk* production. A group of researchers, indigenous and settler, from different walks of life came together to begin to redress a legacy of a past local trauma related to the displacement and relocation of the Kun'tewiktuk Mi'kmaq community, by creating opportunities for silenced voices to speak their truth from the depths of archives and memories, by hearing and reading and affirming these events and experiences, and by publicly uplifting and honoring those who endured those experiences.

Songs and Stories was envisioned with the directives of Canada's TRC and its recommendations in mind, particularly with respect to young people, culture, and education. Inspired by the courage and strength of the survivors who carried out the difficult work of the TRC, the researchers of *Songs and Stories* are working to rewrite histories and relations in ways that affirm, uplift, and honor those who endured the difficult events of displacement and relocation in the past.

A powerful moment occurred in early June 2018 as we were beginning to envision how the play might look on stage. At a key time, Clifford Paul, a revered local storyteller and culture-bearer, now in his 50s, raised his voice. He saw that some of the youth were starting to get nervous and shy. "Just remember kids! Because of all this Reconciliation stuff—you take center stage now! We worked the sidelines. We grew up on the sidelines. The center stage is yours!"

Acknowledgements

The Songs and Stories team acknowledges with gratitude the strength and courage of the Elders, culture bearers and other community members who have supported us in our learning process—for guiding us and inspiring a reconfiguration of relationships in our communities and in our scholarship, among both peoples and practices. *Wela'lioq.*

While the authorship of this chapter is ascribed to Ostashewski and Johnson primarily, other researchers provided considerable content and have been consulted continually throughout the writing process. Their own words are used throughout. Although several *Songs and Stories* publications are currently in press or in process, all team members contributed to each in different ways. The writing of this chapter involved Ostashewski working most closely with Shaylene Johnson, Graham Marshall, as well as Elders Nelson Paul and Shirley Christmas.

Notes

1 L'nu is the word that Mi'kmaq people use, in their own language, to refer to themselves. Mi'kmaw is based on a more recent term first used by Europeans to refer to people of this nation. Recent public discourse includes a call to use L'nu rather than Mi'kmaw, but the overwhelming sentiment in informal discussions with research participants, including Elders and other culture bearers, suggests that since L'nu is not yet a widely familiar term, it may be more suitable here to use the terms Mi'kmaw (to refer to the people as a whole) and Mi'kmaq (to refer to individuals, or the language).

2 The Social Sciences and Humanities Research Council of Canada (SSHRC) defines research-creation as an integrative approach that combines creative and academic research practices. See SSHRC 2016 for more information.

3 A traditional Mi'kmaq idiophone. "*Ji'kmaqn* (Mi'kmaq) a shaker or rattle made by splitting an ash strip into thin layers along about half its length; played by hitting the split segment against the hand" (Diamond, 2008, p. 157).

References

Bartlett, C., Marshall, M., & Marshall, A. (2012). Two-eyed seeing and other lessons learned within a co-learning journey of bringing together indigenous and mainstream knowledges and ways of knowing. *Journal of Environmental Studies and Sciences, 2*(4), 331–340.

Cape Breton Post. (2018). Feasting and friendship in Membertou on National Indigenous Peoples Day. *Cape Breton Post.* Retrieved from http://www.capebretonpost.com/news/local/feasting-and-friendship-in-membertou-on-national-indigenous-peoples-day-220606/

Chilisa, B. (2012). *Indigenous research methodologies.* Los Angeles, CA: Sage.

Denzin, N. K., Lincoln, Y. S., & Smith, L. T. (Eds.). (2008). *Handbook of critical and indigenous methodologies.* Los Angeles, CA: Sage.

Department of Canadian Heritage. (2017). Canada 150 Fund. *Government of Canada.* Retrieved from https://www.canada.ca/en/canadian-heritage/services/funding/canada-150-fund.html

Diamond, B. (2008). *Native American music in Eastern North America*. New York, NY: Oxford University Press.

Dueck, B. (2016). Song, participation, and intimacy at truth and reconciliation gatherings. In D. Robinson & K. Martin (Eds.), *Arts of engagement: Taking aesthetic action in and beyond the Truth and Reconciliation Commission of Canada* (pp. 267–282). Waterloo: Wilfrid Laurier University Press.

Indigenous and Northern Affairs Canada (INAC). (2015). *Peace and friendship treaties*. Retrieved from http://www.aadnc-aandc.gc.ca/eng/1100100028589/1100100028591

Kovach, M. (2009). *Indigenous methodologies: Characteristics, conversations, contexts*. Toronto: University of Toronto Press.

Library and Archives Canada. (1915, September 20–25). *Transcript of evidence and proceedings of the exchequer court hearing*. RG10 vol. 7762, file 27061, Microfilm reel C-12051.

Membertou Communications. (2016). *Kings Road Reserve 100 years later, the Journey on...: The story of Membertou's reconciliation*. Retrieved from http://www.membertou.ca/sites/default/files/KingsRoad_8Page%20Spread_final.pdf

Miller, B. G. (2011). *Oral history on trial: Recognizing Aboriginal narratives in the courts, 67–86*. Vancouver: University of British Columbia Press.

Morin, P. (2016). This is what happens when we perform the memory of the land. In D. Robinson & K. Martin (Eds.), *Arts of engagement: Taking aesthetic action in and beyond the Truth and Reconciliation Commission of Canada* (pp. 67–92). Waterloo: Wilfrid Laurier University Press.

Ostashewski, M., Fitzsimmons Frey, H., & Johnson, S. (2018). Youth-engaged art-based research in Cape Breton: Transcending nations, boundaries, and identities. *Jeunesse, 10*(2), 100–125.

Robinson, D., & Martin, K. (Eds.). (2016). *Arts of engagement: Taking aesthetic action in and beyond the Truth and Reconciliation Commission of Canada*. Waterloo: Wilfrid Laurier University Press.

Social Sciences and Humanities Research Council of Canada (SSHRC). (2016). *Definitions of terms*. Retrieved from http://www.sshrc-crsh.gc.ca/funding-financement/programs-programmes/definitions-eng.aspx#a22

Smith, L. T. (2012). *Decolonizing methodologies: Research and indigenous peoples* (2nd ed.). London: Zed Books.

Tang, J. (2017). Respect indigenous people who don't want to celebrate Canada 150: Trudeau. *The Globe and Mail*. Retrieved from https://www.theglobeandmail.com/news/national/indigenous-demonstrators-erect-teepee-on-parliament-hill-to-protest-canada-day/article35497784/

Truth and Reconciliation Commission of Canada (TRC). (2015). *Truth and Reconciliation Commission of Canada: Calls to action*. Retrieved from http://www.trc.ca/websites/trcinstitution/File/2015/Findings/Calls_to_Action_English2.pdf

CHAPTER 27

Taking back Cape Town: Music Education in the Townships

Henriette Weber

The horrors of Apartheid in South Africa have been well documented, particularly concerning the Group Areas Act of 1950. Cherryl Walker (2005), writing about the South African land question, noted that 87% of the land was appropriated by Whites with only 13% for the Black majority. Moreover, the White minority was allocated the best lands with access to the best services and facilities. The unequal distribution of lands and resources was a means of enforcing White supremacy over Coloured and Black people who were forced by law to accept subjugation. An evaluation of the impact of legislation such as the Group Areas Act on music education, however, is still in its infancy (see Walker, 2019). This chapter aims to shed some light on the consequences of this act on music education and the challenges faced in addressing past inequalities. As a young democracy of 25 years, South Africa still grapples with the inequalities left by Apartheid and part of its systemic oppresssion—involuntary displacement.

I was born in 1966 into what the Apartheid government classified as a Coloured (mixed race) family in Cape Town, the third generation of the Weber family to be exposed to the brutal Apartheid laws and the Group Areas Act. Aside from dictating the areas in which Coloured people were allowed to live and work, failure to comply with these laws resulted in harsh punishment. In 1956, my family was forced to relocate from an affluent White area to a newly formed township. Similarly, my mother's parents relocated from an area demarcated for Whites only. Even within this cruel and oppressive system my grandparents were allowed to choose an area in which to settle where my parents and their siblings were able to sustain themselves. Many other families, however, were literally dumped into township communities without any choice. The flats, as these Western Cape townships became known, were a wasteland, a place reserved for the victims of forced removals.

My Music Education Experience

Both my parents' families were musical, but music ran strongest in my father's family.[1] I attended a primary school that offered group music teaching only, and I received my first piano lessons from family members and nuns at a nearby convent. I attended the only Coloured high school that offered music, speech, drama, and dance as part of the curriculum. During the transition from primary to high school my awareness of Apartheid laws of separation was heightened as young people were being brutally murdered by police throughout the country during the youth uprisings of 1976. These protests escalated throughout my high school career with mass action and class boycotts that were disruptive to our educational goals.

After high school, I spent a year at the University of Cape Town (UCT). It was 1984, about 20 years after the forced removals dictated by the Group Areas Act. UCT had just rid itself of the permit system for non-White students, one in which access became less restrictive for non-White students. Easing the permit rules was a political tactic that may have forwarded the cause of integration within higher education; yet, it did little to quell Black and Coloured people's feelings of being marginalized by the colonial education system. Non-White students had to constantly prove themselves and work harder to negate the inferior basic education system that had been formulated for them during the mid-20th century. For music education, Walker (2019) noted that "[p]rioritizing the cultural output of the European art music tradition (and its derivatives in South Africa) over all others implie[d] a hierarchical value of expressive culture" (p. 145). Rather than contradict the system, we worked hard to conform to international standards of Western classical music. In other words, it was important for us to don the White culture in order to be respected.

Studying in the White area of Rondebosch (UCT's neighborhood), I was one of a few Coloured students who were allowed to study at the South African College of Music at UCT without applying for a permit. I shared lecture halls and practice rooms with the privileged White students who had matriculated from the best schools. Upon reflecting on my education at UCT, I believed that my passion and vision were to serve talented musicians in the financially marginalized communities of the Western Cape. Instinctively I knew that UCT, with its historical roots grounded in a colonial model of higher education, would not understand the journey I wished to pursue. Therefore, I decided, after one year of study to leave UCT, because that institution definitely was not for me within the context of the South African political climate.[2]

In 1986, I was accepted as a music student at the University of the Western Cape (UWC), which had been established in 1960 following a parliamentary decision to establish separate universities without autonomy. UWC came into being on an inferior, open space of land and initially was known as a bush college. In comparison to an all-White university such as UCT, the planners "hoped that, hidden from view, it would offer no [intellectual] views of its own" (Lalu, 2012, p. 37). As a technikon, a training college where "Eurocentric ideologies were largely propagated" (Walker, 2019, p. 151), UWC, was earmarked to serve exclusively the academic needs of the Coloured and eventually Black students. The assembly of so many oppressed persons in one common place naturally set the grounds for organization and activism. By 1975, the government appointed UWC's first Coloured rector, an act that moved the institution to change gradually from a site of inequality, inferiority, compliance, and mediocrity to one that formally rejected the political ideology on which it was first established. UWC, in the 1980s, had become known as "an intellectual home of the democratic Left" (Martin, 2012, p. 27).

As a student in the UWC Music Department, I was encouraged to develop my music skills—teaching and performing—by a supportive faculty. In the 1980s, UWC was already a community-focused university and understood the need for community engagement as relevant and integral to music education. "In thinking about the idea of the struggle around the concept of community, UWC was…a space for contesting and elaborating a concept of community. This bound the university in a unified project" (Lalu & Murray, 2012, p. 21). As students, we were reaching out to communities near the university where no outreach had previously occurred. While outreach does not sound like activism, it represented a kind of resistance in which we pushed minority government-imposed geographical and educational boundaries to take music into remote areas of the Western Cape to teach and perform. This foundational work in township-based music teaching inspired me to serve youth from marginalized communities. Today, UWC's music department graduates lead the public-school sector in communities that had been established under the Group Areas Act, providing music education in townships.

My Teaching Life

Having grown up in the Anglican Church, a denomination that opposed segregation, I chose to teach students from financially marginalized communities in the Western Cape. In my early career, I taught at four township schools as an instrumental music teacher, providing education in recorders, marimba, brass, and guitar, as well as music theory and history. I was the first Coloured educator employed as a full-time instrumental music teacher at a Black school. In each of the schools, a colonial system of music education was implemented, particularly that of Trinity College of Music (London), and students' achievement was measured by external examiners brought to South Africa from the United Kingdom. While the students were schooled in Western musics, learning skills and attaining some successes in Eurocentric performance mediums (e.g., church music, jazz, and Broadway musicals), the practice of external examination by a former colonial government only served to reinforce the subordinate position of local musical practices and advance the dominance of Western art music from the global north. University music departments staffed by White, Black, and Coloured people still teach Western art music as the central focus of their programs. Walker (2019) surmized that "music departments appear to still be continuing their segregation era obligation as institutions that promote the state-sponsored ideological values that helped fuel apartheid, most notably the superiority of European culture" (p. 154).

Music educators who were forced to teach mainstream subjects during the school day began to develop music projects in the townships. The Department of Cultural Affairs became active in funding community-based music projects such as Christmas bands, Church Lads' and Church Girls' Brigades, and cultural groups like the Minstrels and Cape Malay Choirs. Professional companies such as the Cape Philharmonic Orchestra created outreach and education initiatives in order to address the lack of music education within schools.

The geography of residence, especially for the poor and marginalized, remains unchanged at the time of the publication of this volume. Students who suffer the latent effects of forced displacement find themselves living in communities that still offer little or no arts education in their schools. In order to participate in music programs, these students must commute, relocate, or join a community music project suited to their needs. Community-based music projects continue to serve as the primary form of music education.

Higher education has done little to advance the cause of music education. University students are only trained in life skills, and no formalized music education curriculum for teacher training is provided.[3] There has been some forward movement to include music teacher education within university settings. For instance, I am part of a research project called Performing Arts Research Project 2020–2022, requested by the Department of Higher Education and Training and funded by the National Research Foundation. The committee is designing curriculum that will be introduced at University of the Witwatersrand and UWC. The program starts with music, dance, and drama as degree electives for interested students. The ultimate goal is to bring formal arts education into mainstream curriculum in schools. This effort is the first step in creating a new model for music education nationally.

Negotiating Space, Making Place

Before 1994, the dawn of a democratic nation, Black and Coloured South Africans could not envisage living and working in the 'Whites Only' areas from which they were banned. One of the most difficult aspects of the experience of Blacks and Coloureds in South Africa was the feeling that we did not belong in places that, under Apartheid, had been foreclosed to us. To illustrate this lack of comfort with our still-new freedom, I share a situation from my teaching experience in the Cape Town region.

From 2000 to 2006 I served as the Western Cape director of the Field Band Foundation, a non-profit organization that uses "the joyful and transformative power of marching bands to prepare self-confident and healthy young people to participate constructively in society."[4] Armed with two sets of instruments stored in a truck and trailer, we transported our cargo to communities as far away as Stellenbosch, about 50 kilometers from Cape Town, where activities took place after school and on Saturdays. Band members found it difficult to cross the geographical borders between poor townships and the affluent cities. They also retained the same sense of uneasiness when they entered certain buildings once reserved for Whites. On one occasion, my students were invited to participate in workshops and rehearsals at Artscape Theatre Centre in Cape Town's central business district. During Apartheid, Artscape was called the Nico Malan Opera House; Coloured and Blacks were not allowed to attend performances. Ten years into democracy, the students still felt as though they did not belong in this space. Their feelings of not belonging had little to do with Artscape as a place, but rather with their personal experiences of conforming to the dominant narrative. In order to counter that narrative, the instructors encouraged regular attendance, which gave us time to develop artistry and more importantly, a sense of belonging. We wanted the students to know that they mattered, that their talents were important, and that exclusion was not their reality and should never be accepted as normal.

After serving with the Field Band Foundation, as well as eight years as an education coordinator and outreach manager at the Cape Philharmonic, I returned to the University of the Western Cape to head its Centre for the Performing Arts (CPA) and amid the educational restructuring, the CPA needed to find relevance in the changing music education environment, particularly that of community music. The extracurricular programs in music aimed to address the imbalances caused by Apartheid, its resultant displacement situation, and the failing education system in the new democracy. The programs provided a means to level the playing field for financially marginalized communities by providing access to higher education and encouraging students to develop their talents. As of 2019, the university music program places senior music students into township-situated internships to teach music under the supervision of UWC CPA staff. In 2017 and 2019, the community engagement projects expanded to include a music education program for special needs students at Athlone School for the Blind.

Conclusion

In his estimation, Walker (2019) considered that, "it must be recognized that coloniality will continue to exist so long as a still-powerful minority continues to exploit previously disadvantaged South Africans" (p. 149). But many Black and Coloured South Africans aspire to be defined by something other than the Apartheid regime, the Group Areas Act, displacement, and inhumane practices associated with forced dislocation, but Apartheid still affects us. Involuntary displacement was more than losing homes; it was losing the ability to work when unjust practices dictated future employment; it was being located in townships on inferior land that dictated status and sociality; it was being identified as lesser than humans (or as animals that herd together) in a certain demarcated area; and it was losing identity and being branded by skin color.

Separation and segregation are responsible for having devalued the human spirit and created a lack of self-belief in young people living in financially marginalized communities, grappling with their identity, and feeling helpless and unworthy. As of this writing, each step of our journey in community-based music education helps to rectify the imbalances of the past. Music education in the township communities may be rekindled with care, compassion, understanding, and most importantly, create opportunities for a new reality.

Notes

1 *The Weber Family of Genadendal: Their Contribution to Religion, Education, Art, Music, and Science* (Williams, 2013, p. 3), follows the Weber family from their first arrival around 1765 until 2013.

2 Incidentally, the land upon which the University of Cape Town was "'donated' by colonial tycoon Cecil John Rhodes" (Walker, 2019, p. 152) was recently reclaimed during student movements called #RhodesMustFall and #FeesMustFall. The movement was successful in its efforts to have Rhodes's statue removed from the campus grounds.

3 There are eight learning areas in basic education; one of the eight is called Life Skills. Music, art, and dance are included within the life skills cluster.

4 Teacher training colleges closed down one by one from 1998; hence, no future music educators are being trained. Teachers who graduated as music educators prior to the close down were absorbed into mainstream education. Others, like myself, moved into arts administration. For further information on Field Band Foundation, see https://fieldband.org.za

References

Lalu, P. (2012). Campus: A discourse on the grounds of an apartheid university. In P. Lalu & N. Murray (Eds.), *Becoming UWC: Reflections, pathways and unmaking apartheid's legacy* (pp. 32–57). Bellville: Centre for Humanities Research, UWC.

Lalu, P., & Murray, N. (2012). *Becoming UWC: Reflections, pathways and unmaking apartheid's legacy*. Bellville: Centre for Humanities Research, UWC.

Martin, J. (2012). An open space. In P. Lalu & N. Murray (Eds.), *Becoming UWC: Reflections, pathways and unmaking apartheid's legacy* (pp. 22–31). Bellville: Centre for Humanities Research, UWC.

Walker, C. (2005). The limits to land reform: Rethinking 'the land question.' *Journal of Southern African Studies, 31*(4), 805–824.

Walker, G. R. (2019). Music research in a South African higher education institution. *Action, Criticism, and Theory for Music Education, 18*(3), 144–171. https://doi.ofg/10.22176/act18.3.144

CHAPTER 28

...Wandered to Find a Rhythm

Derrick Washington

Story 1: Find a Rhythm

I been doing a lot of studying and just trying to make sense out of being trapped within an institution unable to see my family, move about freely, interact with the opposite sex and having absolutely no privacy relating to everything I do. The instant thought that comes to mind are parallels between slavery of earlier times and how incarceration mirrors a great deal of its practices. It must have been extremely tough for an enslaved person to give birth to a child and the child be shipped away to a distant plantation never to be seen or heard from again. How can the human mind piece together such an unnatural practice of separation? Incarceration separates mothers from sons and fathers from daughters leaving families in tatters. Prior to my incarceration, I was expecting to give birth to a son for which my child's mother was already five months pregnant. I knew at the time she was really dependent on me being around given that this was her first child and she was only 18 years old. I was 19 years old and at the time we were living together and very excited about the new life we were preparing to bring into this world.

On February 7 of 2005, I was taken by authorities and placed in a cage after being accused of taking the life of another. There was no evidence assuring such claims were accurate other than another individual who was charged with a crime unless he provided a statement giving names of persons who could have done it. Myself along with two others were thrown in the pool of suspects following this government facilitator's statement. This accusation gave authorities reason to indict me for murder and separate me away from everything I knew. From that point, the meaning of life and my understanding of the world I live in would never be the same.

The beginning years of my incarceration really shook the foundation of every relationship I had prior to coming in. My child's mother was broken and could barely understand the weight of the situation. I was told by her mother that she falls to sleep in my Tupac T-shirt every night to feel closer to me. I tried to do all I could to comfort her regarding the situation but expensive 30-minute phone calls and life-draining trips to rural parts of the state to visit me in distant prison camps for merely one hour became grueling within itself. I was also

© KONINKLIJKE BRILL NV, LEIDEN, 2020 | DOI: 10.1163/9789004430464_028

going through my own mental hell trying to process what was being done to me and feeling completely powerless. The majority of my friends disappeared and most of my family was incarcerated also. The reality of life caused me to push the remaining people I did have in my life further away. I began being verbally abusive to my child's mother because of my own feelings of insecurity and loneliness—almost like I was trying to push her away even though I could see she was trying to do her best toward me. She was definitely doing time with me and making space in her life to accommodate the reality of our situation, at least until she was no longer able to bear the weight.

The Magic of Empowering Song

Being a student in the Empowering Song class was a revolutionizing experience for me to say the least. It allowed me to feel more humanized than I've ever felt while incarcerated within the state of [xxx].[1] One of the most distinctive memories I have while in the Empowering Song class was my first day, as it had been unique from the beginning. I would describe it as a brief transfer from a world of hell to a world of relief. In fact, I'll share some insight into how my day unfolded concerning my first introduction to Empowering Song.

As I lay on my steel bunk within the #307 cell of the I-I unit of [xxx], I glanced to my left to discover my watch read 5:02 AM. I knew the morning count would be in another hour and 28 minutes (6:30 AM). So I wanted to try to get some reading in and a quick exercise before the count. In prison, count time is one of the many dehumanizing daily functions incarcerated people experience—it's a process in which officers make those incarcerated stand up four times a day (morning, afternoon, evening, and night) shining a flashlight in the faces of the incarcerated to ensure body accountability. For those being observed and counted (inmate population) by prison guards, it officially marks the start of, in my opinion, another day trapped inside of a hell on earth. However, the institution in which I was incarcerated at the time, hosted a college Prison Education Program (PEP) where professors and sometimes students from universities came into the prison to teach classes. For the 1,400 incarcerated persons in [xxx], the PEP only allowed a small minority (85 persons) to participate in the college courses. However, those who were able to gain access to the program were required to pass a number of qualifying entrance exams and to undergo an interviewing process by [xxx] faculty. Fortunately, for me, I was able to be one of the lucky few to access [xxx] PEP and I knew today would be an interesting day because it would be the start of some new classes. One of them, a class I had not been so excited about was a music class titled "Empowering Song" that was scheduled to begin at 8:30 AM. The lack of excitement was mainly because I felt like for me to be learning about subject matters such as Beethoven, or developing skills to read and interpret music notes, would be of no assistance within the world I lived in—or served no purpose in my fight against what I realized to be 21st-century slavery through the practices of the [xxx] criminal punishment system and sanctioned through the 13th Amendment of the United States Constitution. I was in for a big surprise!

"10 more push-ups, you can do it, 9, 8, seeevennn..." I said as I counted aloud, hyping myself up to finish my morning exercise before the 6:30 AM count. I managed to complete my reading and exercise, reading a chapter from Paulo Freire's *Pedagogy of the Oppressed* and completing my goal of 300 pushups. I then endured the daily humiliation of the first standing count, passed up on the watered-down oatmeal and the breakfast cake that was provided for morning chow, and then headed to the program building to begin the first day of my music class. So far, the day had begun seemingly well. I was now inside the program building and made my way past the throngs of my incarcerated peers headed to their school program destinations as I began to approach the designated classroom assigned for the [xxx] courses in room 207. What followed after I entered room 207 that day would change my perception of music and how I interacted with people in general for the rest of my life.

Upon entering, I saw that the desks, tables and chairs that were normally sequenced in successive rows had been pushed up against the walls leaving an open, broad ballroom-like space exposed. I noticed two males and one woman graciously greeting students as we came in. One of the guys, a slim, brown-skinned figure who had a sort of South Asian Indian type of look, gave me a really kind handshake greeting in which the energy he conveyed was really comforting as if I had been a beloved family member or longtime friend. In prison, regardless of where you're at, upon the initial introductions of meeting new people, there is usually an emotional guard and/or wall put up to shield certain aspects of yourself. I say this because, this guy, whom I'd later learn to find out was our music professor André, created an atmosphere (along with his two teaching assistants Emily and Trey) that made me feel like I was no longer in prison and had been temporarily restored dignity and a sense of humanity. Once everyone had arrived, the students were told to form a circle and do these weird breathing exercises, I was initially skeptical and just felt like "OK, this is new." Then, André told us to join hands, I was immediately floored by his instruction—especially because it was Emily who stood to the left of me while on my right, stood a fellow inmate/student. I've been incarcerated up to this point for about 10 years and had never held anyone's hand beyond a handshake while in prison, certainly not a woman because in here (prison) if an "inmate" even looks at one of their woman correctional officers or administrators the wrong way, let alone touch a hand, the guards would likely first beat you to a pulp then bury you in solitary confinement until infinity. So, you can imagine my mental confusion—in addition, I also did not fancy the idea at all of holding another incarcerated person's hand because I felt like it gave off an appearance of being soft or weak within this hyper-masculine environment I've been so accustomed to living in my entire adult life. Nonetheless, I went through with it and I amazingly felt an extreme sense of serenity, love, warmth, and togetherness. This was indeed a novel experience. As we remained in the circle formation, hands locked in a chain-like link, we commenced singing. Trey and Emily initiated a mode of behavior that set a tone for others to feel free to express themselves openly—whether it be in the shape of a random shout, off-pitch serenade, or an individualized rhythmic movement. Up to this point, this was nothing what I was thinking this class would be like. The experience had been priceless as I had come to realize I was in the room with some guys I've known for years who I believed were hardened from long hard years of prison life and who were, in this instance, wearing smiles larger-than-life itself while moving about gracefully, unconcerned about their security or prospective thoughts and opinions that could arise from their present behavior. It was mind blowing! Following that period of open expression, we were then instructed to collectively set up the chairs in a circle formation and find a seat. At this point, I figured "well, I guess the fun part is over, time to do the traditional, rigorous music study now." I had been wrong again!

André ingeniously began introducing his own form of table topics to the student body. He began speaking about a relevant topic and then gave us an opportunity to be heard on the topic, letting the students take it in whatever direction we allowed while he still maintained order and masterfully prompted class engagement. The effects of our class discussions were truly empowering and proved to be invaluable as it allowed men an avenue to release things that many likely had been holding in for years but just had no place in the prison environment to express themselves and share their feelings. During this portion of the class, people's thoughts were respected, there was no criticism or judgment passed and ultimately, after listening to feedback from others who attended the Empowering Song class, proved to be one of the most fruitful, comforting and therapeutic components of the class among other things. For me, that first day was really fulfilling as the time seemed to just zoom past. Following our group discussion, André assigned for us to write a journal that aligned with a class theme he introduced to us at the start of the class that we'd turn in for next week's class. And just like that, the first day of my Empowering Song class came to an end. When the class ended and I began to exit from 207 after waving bye to André, Trey, and Emily—I literally felt like I was leaving the free world and returning back to prison with all of its strict rules, tense faces, racist guards and mind-bleeding stress. All throughout the day I found myself reflecting on the magical moments casted upon my consciousness in the form of the [xxx] PEP Empowering Song class. I was in shock by the degree of humanity that was shown to us throughout the class.

Fortunately, each class following the first class, the experience only grew greater as volunteers from across the Atlantic Ocean in Sweden, others from California, Harvard University faculty, students from Boston University, and all sorts of guests came to participate in our class. With these guests, we created plays, wrote poetry, performed in-class concerts and received a level of brother/sisterhood that was entirely non-existent outside of classroom 207. André's music class taught me how to find value not only in myself—but in every living creature, expanding my perception of what music is and the powers it has, allowing me to see music as a marginless art able to take the shape and form of many different things. Empowering Song also helped me discover more about me and tap into areas of me I had not known how to access, essentially strengthening my ability to effectively and harmoniously communicate with the human family at large.

I will carry Empowering Song with me throughout my entire life and will be forever grateful to André, Emily, Trey, and my fellow students who helped bring out a unifying power in me that I was not aware had existed within me.

Story 2: Wandered About

Beginning

I wandered about to find my rhythm. The world is large but yet my focuses remained limited. Limited not as a lack of ambition, but merely as a lack of exposure. My interests have been shaped by prosperity—as it had always been my intent to prosper in the limited activities I had become accustomed to doing. Initially, basketball, football, and neighborhood activities became the instant refuge from boredom. The neighborhood did not offer much to release all the built-up energy it harnessed from its youth population. We rode bikes and explored distant areas in neighborhoods we were unfamiliar with. One by one, many of us begun to realize our limited resources and the differences between our own communities and the communities we'd been riding our bikes through. The white kids had the Mongoose and BMX bikes while we rode the Huffys and other cheap make bicycles. We began to want better bikes and overall have money in our pockets to make better use of our time.

Fledgling

I wandered about to find my rhythm. "Cleveland Metroparks Zoo, you bet not lose dat job Brah!" I got my first job and was somewhat happy to be earning some honest pay. Most of my bike crew had already started selling drugs and living a lifestyle that would likely get them into trouble but it would definitely make their financial troubles disappear. I had to walk four miles or catch two different buses to get to work every day. My best friend L.D. sold crack, and used to give me a lift when I could catch up with him (because cell phones were not around at the time). I used to see him with big wads of money in his pocket and have about two to three pagers all for different uses. He drove a nice car and was always busy. Around the time, drugs started to infiltrate my household, almost as if it had crept through the back door. What it was doing to my family I wouldn't wish upon any family. Eventually, law enforcement raided my house and took my mother and her partner away. My mother was pure and innocent and was only guilty of being blindly in love with a weak person. Her capture and kidnap by law enforcement brought the worst out of me. How could someone so precious to me be taken from me by the people who are supposed to help and protect us? A part of me went to sleep (the better part) and I became all about survival.

Trapped

I wandered about to find my rhythm. "Damn, my phone just won't stop ringing." It was 2 AM and I'm back in the kitchen cooking up more crack to sell. I had moved to [xxx] because I had some close, but distant family in the state. I was planning to make a trip to Cleveland to drop my mother off a few hundred dollars because these maggot prison officials made a rule stopping people from sending prisoners money through the mail and it could only be given by dropping it off at the visit. I needed to at least make $3,000 tonight so I could head out on [xxx] West to make my trip. The night was still young believe it or not, most nights we (my friends and I) didn't go in until about 5 AM. Life was very demanding, I put the baking soda in the bottom of a freshly wiped down Smucker's jar and dumped the cocaine atop of it placing it into the pot. I dipped and stirred, dipped and stirred, until the powder and soda condensed into a solid rock form. It was now time for me to let it dry out and I'll be ready to go to work. Phone calls were a constant from family to females to friends. I had no reservations about my actions. I figured because someone turned my mother on drugs, I couldn't care less about somebody else's mother being turned out on drugs. The roller coaster of life has a way of speeding up in moments designed to coast. "Bang, bang" as I heard two shots ring out in the direction of my comrade Ray. Our crack spot had just been broken into and robbed. In the process of seeking out the culprits, Ray got hit two times. Before we knew it, we're involved in a volley for territory owned by the state. Sirens sound off, and I'm pulled over by state troopers and the next day I'm being arraigned for two gang associated homicides.

Awake

I wandered about; I began to find a rhythm. "Count time, stand for count." These people got me in a cut-out swatch of a forest in the middle of nowhere. I've just been thinking about life and what the hell was it that led me to this point. Either way, I guess I just have to make the most of it. Rotating between pushups and pull-ups I started to see the reward of having a fixed routine of daily exercise. I felt healthy and became purged of all the garbage I was feeding my mind with when I was free. I learned discipline is a recipe for accomplishment in whatever I apply the role of discipline to. I commenced to read and study my history to gain some sort of insight into the world and all of its happenings. I began to study the dictionary and subscribe new words to my regular vocabulary. I realized that the tools for survival were different in my new environment, I had to become mentally prepared to take on the demon of oppression that sustains the malignant cycle of hardship and pain to the common person. I came to understand myself through building and critically analyzing my circumstances. Now it's time to lock in my rhythm and work towards transitioning into my next stage!

Story 3: The Music of Our Emancipation Initiative

"Count motherfuckers! Wake up and stand for Count!" hollered the pudgy white prison guard whose potato shaped head mouthed every syllable before beginning his 7:15 AM "Major Standing Count." Throughout the day we have four major standing counts (7:15 AM, 11:15 AM., 4:15 PM and 10:00 PM) where guards activate a bright high beam light within the cells throughout the unit and commence to count body for body along the panopticon outline of the "N-I" unit at [xxx] maximum security prison in [xxx]. This is how the arms of the state (prison guards) account for their state sanctioned property (prisoners). Two days prior (November 30, 2018), the entire prison was placed on locked-down status. During that particular morning's major standing count, two separate articles of the state's chattel property (human beings) where found dead, one hanging from a bedsheet in his cell, while another had been discovered to be dead when a guard found him to be unresponsive during the count. The discordant tone of 21st-century slavery and hardship strung from Life Without Parole (LWOP) prison sentences, incarcerated persons' political exclusion, family separation, hateful prison guards, and abject conditions of confinement, have been the song of struggle for the 9,100 persons deeply enmeshed within the webs of [xxx] criminal punishment system. With the birth of our prisoners/people's movement in 2012, our Emancipation Initiative (EI) has been a baritone for prison abolition through the rhythm of participatory and legislative planning in which the monotone of our activism manufactures a fine musical element of resistance that ultimately aims to end LWOP, restore prisoner suffrage in [xxx] and in turn, revolutionize how criminal justice in [xxx] and all throughout America is viewed, interpreted and/or practiced (see Figure 28.1).

An alarm for action and renewed push for Emancipation from the new mode of slavery (in the form of incarceration) came from the cries for true justice and humanity percolating through steel gates, institutionally secure phone lines and agitative maximum-security visiting spaces where slaves of the state have been stamped and branded as numerical articles of chattel property. Hopelessness danced throughout the common area "Day Room" N-2 unit as one dejected soul shouted out "turn the fuckin high beams off, Bitch!" as officers kept the high beam lights on all night and day. Three weeks prior, a prejudiced prison guard had been "jigged" through the side of his neck with a makeshift prison knife resulting in a massive institutional lockdown when we were not allowed to leave our cells, take showers, call our loved ones, stretch our limbs and/or be free of the systemized oppression fostered from a revengeful administration. Broken glass lay in pools of overflowed toilet water throughout the unit. The constant banging and kicking of cell doors had been the music of our pain crystallized in our isolated capsule of environmental chaos. Trapped within this matrix of helplessness, the fact that I had no control over my physical environment fueled an invigorated motivation to begin my personal W.A.R. (Writing And Reading) report in an effort to consolidate incarcerated persons power and to have our voices heard. Following a rigorous, trained schedule in developing my W.A.R. report in combination with many sleepless nights of letter writing in tandem with day to day planning for organizing internally—our Emancipation Initiative (EI) was born.

What makes our EI special and unique is that our push for inclusion on behalf of the men and women buried within our state's living graveyards (prisons) is the resuscitating tune of music we invoke. Music is the art of arranging sounds in a way that yields an aesthetic response to all those who become recipients of these sounds. EI has been conceived from a single drumbeat thronged of incarcerated persons' families, friends, and loved ones left in suspense after the guards' assault and incarcerated persons had been caged for upwards of a month with no phone calls, showers and absence of officials' recognition of their humanity. This drumbeat initially was without rhythm, spurted out dissonantly in staccato-like flails and, was not at all synchronized but, symbolized the isolated voices of the 11,000 families and loved ones within the [xxx] Department of Corrections. Nonetheless, the drumbeat proved to be powerful and demanded an orchestra of external revolutionary voices to band together with internal voices and create a sweet melody of activism. Within the prisons, our common interests were for better conditions of confinement and to have our voices heard in relation to our humanity which is why as incarcerated persons we had to first identify our "instruments" of power. We learned that through writing letters and various other forms of outreach to advocacy groups, we in essence take the shape and become the musical sound of an instrument which draws attention to the inhumane treatment of incarcerated persons. From there, the merge between EI, the peoples/prisoners struggle movement and music began to assimilate in the sense that the prisoners' struggle had become the people's struggle. The merge had become embodied through free persons singing and participating in EI's participatory projects ranging from our "Legal Institution of Slavery in America" events to our "Donate Your Vote" effort in which we pair free persons with incarcerated persons to influence the political process.

Finally, EI's journey from its fledgling beginnings to meeting some of its triumphant climaxes has been astounding. Big shout out to [xxx] Prison Education Program (PEP) professor André de Quadros who was something like an educational father to me. André taught me the essence of music and showed me through his courses that music is accommodating and is able to take the shape and form of all things in existence, essentially revealing to me the music of life. I've come to discover the correlations between music and our people's struggle by way of our EI, is one in the same as music, as music is not absolute but yet permeates throughout every action, sound, and air wave. The initial challenge for most is only finding their rhythm—but once discovered, everything from that point will become rhythmic (productive) and in turn will be attractive, as it is the musical spirit that links all living things.

FIGURE 28.1   Emancipation Initiative.
ARTWORK: DERRICK WASHINGTON

Note

1 [xxx] represents blacked out words, censured ideas, and forced silences. In some cases, the [xxx] represents locations that should be left unnamed in order to protect people affiliated with such spaces.

Index